D0504660

bs

SEASONALITY IN TOURISM

ADVANCES IN TOURISM RESEARCH SERIES

Series Editor: Professor Stephen Page
University of Stirling, UK

Advances in Tourism Research is a new series of monographs and edited volumes which comprise state-of-the-art research findings, written and edited by leading researchers working in the wider field of tourism studies. The series has been designed to provide a cutting edge focus for researchers interested in tourism, particularly the management issues now facing decision-makers, policy analysts and the public sector. The audience is much wider than just academics and each book seeks to make a significant contribution to the literature in the field of study by not only reviewing the state of knowledge relating to each topic but also questioning some of the prevailing assumptions and research paradigms which currently exist in tourism research. The series also aims to provide a platform for further studies in each area by highlighting key research agendas which will stimulate further debate and interest in the expanding area of tourism research. The series is always willing to consider new ideas for innovative and scholarly books and inquiries can be made to the Series Editor.

Published:

ASHWORTH & TUNBRIDGE
The Tourist-Historic City: Retrospect and Prospect of Managing the Heritage City

RYAN & PAGE
Tourism Management: Towards the New Millennium

SONG & WITT
Tourism Demand Modelling and Forecasting: Modern Econometric Approaches

TEO, CHANG & HO
Interconnected Worlds: Tourism in Southeast Asia

Forthcoming titles include:

PAGE & WILKS
Managing Tourist Health and Safety

PAGE & LUMSDON
Progress in Tourism and Transport Research

Related Elsevier Journals – sample copies available on request
Annals of Tourism Research
Cornell Hotel and Restaurant Administration Quarterly
International Journal of Hospitality Management
International Journal of Intercultural Relations
Tourism Management
World Development

SEASONALITY IN TOURISM

EDITED BY

TOM BAUM

University of Strathclyde, Glasgow, UK

SVEND LUNDTORP

Research Centre of Bornholm, Nexø, Denmark

14 1155x

CHESTER COLLEGE

ACC No.	DEPT
01076625	

CLASS No.

338. 4791 BAU

LIBRARY

2001

Pergamon
An Imprint of Elsevier Science

Amsterdam – London – New York – Oxford – Paris – Shannon – Tokyo

ELSEVIER SCIENCE Ltd
The Boulevard, Langford Lane
Kidlington, Oxford OX5 1GB, UK

© 2001 Elsevier Science Ltd. All rights reserved.

This work is protected under copyright by Elsevier Science, and the following terms and conditions apply to its use:

Photocopying
Single photocopies of single chapters may be made for personal use as allowed by national copyright laws. Permission of the Publisher and payment of a fee is required for all other photocopying, including multiple or systematic copying, copying for advertising or promotional purposes, resale, and all forms of document delivery. Special rates are available for educational institutions that wish to make photocopies for non-profit educational classroom use.

Permissions may be sought directly from Elsevier Science Global Rights Department, PO Box 800, Oxford OX5 1DX, UK; phone: (+44) 1865 843830, fax: (+44) 1865 853333, e-mail: permissions@elsevier.co.uk. You may also contact Global Rights directly through Elsevier's home page (http://www.elsevier.com), by selecting 'Obtaining Permissions'.

In the USA, users may clear permissions and make payments through the Copyright Clearance Center, Inc., 222 Rosewood Drive, Danvers, MA 01923, USA; phone: (+1) (978) 7508400, fax: (+1) (978) 7504744, and in the UK through the Copyright Licensing Agency Rapid Clearance Service (CLARCS), 90 Tottenham Court Road, London W1P 0LP, UK; phone: (+44) 207 631 5555; fax: (+44) 207 631 5500. Other countries may have a local reprographic rights agency for payments.

Derivative Works
Tables of contents may be reproduced for internal circulation, but permission of Elsevier Science is required for external resale or distribution of such material.

Permission of the Publisher is required for all other derivative works, including compilations and translations.

Electronic Storage or Usage
Permission of the Publisher is required to store or use electronically any material contained in this work, including any chapter or part of a chapter.

Except as outlined above, no part of this work may be reproduced, stored in a retrieval system or transmitted in any form or by any means, electronic, mechanical, photocopying, recording or otherwise, without prior written permission of the Publisher.
Address permissions requests to: Elsevier Science Global Rights Department, at the mail, fax and e-mail addresses noted above.

Notice
No responsibility is assumed by the Publisher for any injury and/or damage to persons or property as a matter of products liability, negligence or otherwise, or from any use or operation of any methods, products, instructions or ideas contained in the material herein. Because of rapid advances in the medical sciences, in particular, independent verification of diagnoses and drug dosages should be made.

First edition 2001

Library of Congress Cataloging in Publication Data
A catalog record from the Library of Congress has been applied for.

British Library Cataloguing in Publication Data
A catalogue record from the British Library has been applied for.

ISBN 0-08-043674-9

∞ The paper used in this publication meets the requirements of ANSI/NISO Z39.48-1992 (Permanence of Paper).
Printed in The Netherlands.

Contents

Contributors

Robin R. D. Barden

Management Centre
University of Bradford
Bradford, UK

Tom Baum

The Scottish Hotel School
University of Strathclyde
Glasgow, UK

R. W. Butler

Professor of Tourism
University of Surrey
Guildford, UK

Jane Commons

Center for Tourism Research
Massey University
Albany, Aukland
New Zealand

James Deegan

School of Economics
University of Limerick
Limerick, Ireland

Thor Flognfeldt

Department of Tourism and Applied Social Sciences
Lillehammer College
Lillehammer, Norway

G. Hickey

Faculty of Physical Education and Recreation
University of Alberta
Edmonton, Alberta
Canada

T. D. Hinch

Faculty of Physical Education and Recreation
University of Alberta
Edmonton, Alberta
Canada

E. L. Jackson

Faculty of Physical Education and Recreation
University of Alberta
Edmonton, Alberta
Canada

Douglas Jeffrey   Department of Environmental Science
                           University of Bradford
                           Bradford, UK

Elizabeth Kennedy   Dublin Institute of Technology
                           Cathal Brugha Street
                           Dublin 1, Ireland

Mary Klemm   Management Centre
                           University of Bradford
                           Bradford, UK

Svend Lundtorp   Research Centre of Bornholm
                           Grannegade 21
                           Nexø, Denmark

Stephen Page   Department of Management
                           University of Stirling
                           Scotland, UK

Charlotte Rassing   Research Centre of Bornholm
                           Grannegade 21
                           Nexø, Denmark

Julian Rawel   Management Centre
                           University of Bradford
                           Bradford, UK

Nils Karl Sørensen   Danish Institute of Border Region Studies
                           Persillegade 6
                           Aabenraa, Denmark

Stephen Wanhill   Research Centre of Bornholm
                           Grannegade 21
                           Nexø, Denmark

Chapter 1

Seasonality in Tourism: An Introduction

Tom Baum and Svend Lundtorp

Seasonality in tourism demand is one of the most consistently vexing policy issues, particularly in peripheral, cold-climate environments. Tourism strategies from destinations such as Iceland, Prince Edward Island, Scotland and Norway place considerable emphasis both on extending the existing tourist season and on developing new markets for periods that are traditionally "down" in terms of tourist arrivals.

The impact of seasonal demand variation is one of the dominent policy and operational concerns of tourism interests in both the public and private sectors. There are few destinations where demand is not variable according to clearly defined seasonal patterns; indeed, Butler in his chapter in this book argues that seasonality is one of the main defining characteristics of global tourism.

Seasonality, as a concern, impacts on all aspects of supply-side behaviour in tourism, including marketing (packaging, distribution, pricing); the labour market (nature and quality of employment, skills availability, sustainability of employment); business finance (cashflow, pricing, attracting investment); stakeholder management (suppliers, intermediaries); and all aspects of operations.

Butler's comprehensive review of seasonality notes two basic origins of the phenomenon, "natural" and "institutional" although there is a significant level of interdependence between the two. Natural seasonality is the result of regular variation in climatic conditions — temperature, rainfall, snowfall and daylight. Natural seasonal variation increases according to distance from the equator and, indeed, the most acute impacts of seasonality are to be found in peripheral destinations in locations close to the polar extremes.

However, seasonality is also an issue in tropical regions such as the Caribbean and the Indian sub-continent where extremes of temperature, monsoon rainfall or humidity also reduce demand at certain times of the year.

Institutional seasonality, according to Butler, is the result of human decisions and is much more widespread and less predictable than natural seasonality. It is the outcome of a combination of religious, cultural, ethnic and social factors — periods of religious worship, holidays or pilgrimages as well as school or industrial holidays are good examples of institutional seasonal variation in demand for tourism services. Butler also notes the impact of fashion on seasonal tourism behaviour, influencing choice of sun destinations on the basis of prevailing fashion with regard to skin pigmentation, for example. Likewise, choice of particular sporting or leisure pursuits is subject to fashion and influences seasonal demand for activities such as hunting and snow skiing. Inertia or inflexibility

This chapter draws substantially on Baum, T., "Seasonality in tourism: understanding the challenges", *Tourism Economics* Vol. 5, No. 1 (March 1999), pp 5–8.
© 1999 IP Publishing Ltd. Reproduced by permission.

within wide institutional frameworks also creates seasonal inflexibility with respect to vacation patterns so that major shifts in seasonal behaviour are difficult to achieve, despite the best efforts of governments and marketing. School holidays are a good example of institutionalized inertia because their basis in most Northern European countries is an agricultural cycle which has relevance today to less that five percent of the populations of countries in question.

Seasonality is widely seen as a "problem" to be "tackled" at a policy, marketing and operational level. On the basis of an extensive review of the literature, Butler notes that tourism is generally seen as a problem that needs to be overcome. Flognfeldt, in this volume, develops the argument that, in certain circumstances, seasonality in demand presents opportunities to rural destinations, particularly where their economy balances tourism alongside other activities. The same author, in an earlier paper, (Flognfeldt, 1988), argues that, in considering employment in remote seasonal destinations, tourism jobs frequently complement other areas of traditional employment such as forestry, fishing or agriculture and, therefore, is not as problematic as normally portrayed. These wider social, cultural or ecological implications of seasonality are not widely addressed although these may lead to conclusions that periods of low demand can have direct "recuperation" benefits for both the natural and socio-cultural environment.

The rather more common perspective adopted is that seasonality presents business challenges to a destination and to individual operators. On the basis of this form of analysis, the downside of major variation in seasonal demand is seen as:

- short business operating season with major periods of closure or reduced level of operation;
- the consequent need to generate a full year's revenue within a short operating season while servicing fixed costs over a twelve month period;
- under utilisation of capital assets which are inflexible and, generally, do not have obvious alternative uses;
- the consequent problems of attracting inward investment in tourism;
- problems in maintaining the supply chain on the basis of a short operating season;
- problems in ensuring sustained support from transport providers such as airlines and shipping companies who are reluctant to maintain commitment to and invest in highly seasonal operations;
- short-term employment rather than sustainable long-term jobs creating high levels of either off-season unemployment or temporary outward migration (Baum, 1993); and
- problems of maintaining service and product quality standards in the absence of permanent, long-term employees.

Both the public and private sector in tourism invest significantly in seeking to overcome the perceived problems which seasonality in tourism presents. Within both sectors, marketing strategies which provide added value, product variation and pricing incentives have been long used in order to stimulate demand during shoulder and off-season periods. Such strategies have shown some significant successes, especially where entirely new markets have been addressed within the campaigns. The development of Florida and a number of Caribbean islands as summer destinations was based on attracting new European markets as well as creating value for money access to all year attractions such as those in the Orlando area. As a result, Florida's former dependence on a winter season for the North American market has been translated into a twelve month operation. Hawaii, likewise, has used effective strategies to spread demand throughout the year.

In northern, cold water destinations, the challenges of seasonality are rather more intractable. The focus, generally, is on season extension rather than on the creation of a twelve month business. Thus, Prince Edward Island in Canada has been able to develop an effective and attractive September product for its older markets, based on sport and culture, as a means of complementing traditional dependence on summer family vacations. Similar locations have invested heavily in strategies designed to achieve similar outcomes (Tourism Nova Scotia, 1997; Scottish Tourist Board, 1998). While generally optimistic about the potential to extend the season to some extent or to create high demand but short-term events and festivals off season (such as Edinburgh's Hogmanay), these inputs to policy come up with few new answers which address fundamental tourism demand patterns.

One of the problems in really understanding seasonality in tourism is a lack of in-depth and longitudinal research. One of the few studies to take this approach is the seminal work by Bar-On (1975) where the author examined data for sixteen countries over a seventeen year period. However, it is only through detailed empirical analysis of seasonal behaviour that a more comprehensive picture of tourism and its demand variation patterns can be created. Through such analysis, strategies may be developed which may make a more significant contribution to balancing tourism demand on a temporal basis for those communities which desire such change. The papers which follow in this collection are all contributions to the empirical analysis of seasonal tourism behaviour at a national or specific destination level. The papers mainly deal with cold water destinations — Denmark, England and Ireland, Canada and New Zealand — and thus are a contribution to a common literature. Kennedy and Deegan take a longitudinal look at seasonality in Irish tourism and is able to extract clear market changes over a period when the destination has experienced major growth in tourist arrivals as well as market and product changes. Jeffrey and Barden and Sørensen look at demand variations within the accommodation sector, using time series data for England and Denmark respectively. Such analysis is invaluable to marketing and decision making in tourism in general but few destinations have the quality and depth of time series data available to these authors. Lundtorp, Rassing and Wanhill analyse the off-season market in order to gain a better understanding of who it is that will travel outside of the main season, again pointing to possible new marketing strategies.

The collection of papers in this book is a contribution to research in a largely neglected area and can form part of a wider jig-saw of studies which, cumulatively, may assist destinations and private sector operators in cold water environments to make better use of the shoulder and off-season periods. The principle enshrined in what is an eclectic range of contributions relating to Scandinavia, the British Isles, France, Canada and New Zealand is one that Rose (1991; 1993) calls "Lesson Drawing". Rose articulated the concept of Lesson-Drawing in the context of public policy formulation. Although generally programme-focused, Lesson-Drawing seeks to establish the circumstances and extent to which effective experiences from one context can be transferred to that of others (Rose, 1991, p. 2) and thus provided a useful framework for the thematic approach adopted in a collection of studies about seasonality. Lesson-Drawing addresses the question "under what circumstances and to what extent can a programme that is effective in one place transfer to another?" (p. 2). In the context of public policy:

> *"Lesson-drawing can be sought by searching across time and/or across space; the choice depends upon a subjective definition of proximity, and epistemic communities linking experts together, functional interdependence between governments, and the authority of intergovernmental institutions. The process of lesson-drawing starts with scanning programmes in effect elsewhere, and ends with the prospective evaluation of what would happen if a programme already in effect elsewhere were transferred here in the future. Lesson-drawing is part of a contested political process; there is no assurance that a lesson drawn will be both desirable and practical."* (p. 2).

Lesson-Drawing is relatively new in its application within the context of tourism (Baum, 1999) but in relation to a policy-related theme such as seasonality, its application has considerable merit. This book provides the basis for academics and practitioners to draw their own lessons from the diverse experience of seasonality that is presented in its ten chapters.

References

Bar-On, R. (1975). *Seasonality in Tourism*. London: The Economist Intelligence Unit.

Baum, T. (1993). Human resource concerns in European tourism: strategic response and the EC. *International Journal of Hospitality Management, 12(1)*.

Baum, T. (1999). Themes and issues in comparative destination research: Cases from the North Atlantic. *Tourism Management, 20(3)*, 627–633.

Flognfeldt, T. (1988). The employment paradox of seasonal tourism, paper presented at Pre-Congress Meeting of the International Geographical Union, Christchurch, New Zealand.

Rose, R. (1991). *What is Lesson-Drawing?* Glasgow: Centre for the Study of Public Policy.

Rose, R. (1993). Lesson-drawing in public policy. A guide to learning across time and space, Chatham, NJ: Chatham House Publishers Inc.

Scottish Tourist Board/System Three, (1998). *Seasonality in Scotland. Final Report*. Edinburgh: STB/ System Three.

Tourism Nova Scotia/Nova Scotia Economic Development and Tourism (1997). *The Nova Scotia November to May Tourism Opportunities Study*, Halifax: Tourism Nova Scotia.

Chapter 2

Seasonality in Tourism: Issues and Implications

R. W. Butler

Introduction

Seasonality has long been recognized as one of the most distinctive features of tourism, and after the movement of people on a temporary basis, may be the most typical characteristic of tourism on a global basis. Seasonality, in the context of this chapter is defined as a *temporal imbalance in the phenomenon of tourism, which may be expressed in terms of dimensions of such elements as numbers of visitors, expenditure of visitors, traffic on highways and other forms of transportation, employment and admissions to attractions.* Seasonality has frequently been viewed as a major problem for the tourism industry, and has been held responsible for creating or exacerbating a number of difficulties faced by the industry, including problems in gaining access to capital, in obtaining and holding full-time staff, for low returns on investment causing subsequent high risk in operations, and for problems relating to peaking and overuse of facilities. Conversely, it has also been blamed for the under-utilization of these resources and facilities, often preventing tourism being accepted as a viable economic activity in many areas. It is not surprising, therefore, that considerable efforts have been made by both public and private sectors to attempt to reduce seasonality in destination areas through a variety of approaches.

In spite of the widespread concern over seasonality and its generally perceived negative effects upon tourism and destination areas, and the fact that it is a long established feature of the industry, there has been relatively little research devoted to this topic which has been published in the academic literature. It is clear that while there is often general agreement about the seasonality "problem", comparatively few detailed studies have been made of its nature or all of its effects. Problems still exist in identifying the basic causes of the phenomenon, the reasons for its persistence, and its measurement. Despite years of effort by the public sector involving policy formulation, concessions and financial aid, and the private sector through marketing and pricing in particular, seasonality continues to persist in many areas, suggesting that the causes have not been properly understood and thus have not been adequately addressed. One might, with some legitimacy, ask if indeed it is appropriate to continue to try to "solve" this "problem" given its apparent intractability. In addition, very little research has been done to explore any of the positive aspects of seasonality. There is a need to determine, for instance, if this phenomenon really is a problem for all parties involved in tourism or whether it can be regarded as having beneficial effects in some situations to some sectors of the industry and communities engaged in tourism.

This chapter is a revised and updated version of
R. W. Butler (1994) "Seasonality in tourism: issues and problems",
in Seaton *et al.*, *Tourism – The State of the Art,* (Chichester: Wiley) pp 332–339.
Reproduced by permission of John Wiley & Sons Limited.

Equally little research has addressed the problem of whether seasonality varies in nature and intensity on a spatial basis, either within or between destination areas, although there has been speculation that such is the case.

The discussion which follows represents a revision of an original paper that first appeared in 1994 (Butler, 1994). In this chapter some additional literature is included, and the discussion expanded in certain areas. The specific discussion of seasonality in tourism in Scotland which concluded the earlier paper has been omitted from this chapter as it has been the subject of other studies (Butler, 1998; System Three, 1998). The four basic issues reviewed in the original paper, all related to resolving or clarifying the problems raised above, remain the principal focus of this chapter. The first of these deals with the causes of seasonality, to provide a foundation for the rest of the discussion. The second relates to the perceptions and impacts of seasonality, and whether these are better viewed as costs or benefits to tourism. The third briefly examines approaches which have been taken to reduce the level of seasonality and the overall effectiveness of such measures. The fourth, and final point concerns assessing whether there is a spatial aspect to seasonality, and what form this might take.

Causes and Forms of Seasonality

It has been generally accepted that seasonality in tourism has two basic elements, one which may be called "natural", and one "institutionalised" (Bar-On, 1975:2; Hartmann, 1986). The first relates to regular temporal variations in natural phenomena, particularly those associated with climate and the true seasons of the year. Typical variables included are cycles or patterns of differences in temperature, rainfall and snowfall, sunlight, and daylight (see, for example, Barry & Perry, 1973 and Boucher, 1975). Seasonal variations are different from the daily fluctuations of the weather at a particular destination, and are regular and recurring. In general, seasonal differences increase with distance from the equator, and thus are more marked in high latitudes than in equatorial locations, and consequently have varying impacts upon human activity (Budyko, 1974; Mauss & Beuchat, 1979; Smith, 1973). As discussed in the conclusions, while the natural seasons have traditionally been regarded as permanent features, it is becoming clear that climate change is making these less certain and less predicable (Houghton *et al.*, 1995).

The second form of seasonality is that caused by human actions and policies, and normally refers to traditional and often legislated temporal variations in activities and inactivity. Institutional seasonality varies much more widely and with much less consistency of pattern than does its natural counterpart, although precise dates may be established for commencement and termination of such seasons, unlike the situation for the natural seasons. It is the result of religious, cultural, ethnic and social factors, in some cases representing links to natural phenomena, and in others nothing more than age-old whims or preferences (Osborn, 1992). One of the most common forms of institutionalised seasonality which affects tourism is the public holiday. These are found in almost all countries although the dates involved vary greatly around the world. They may be based on one of, or a combination of, religious holy days, days of pagan significance, celebration of specific events, and the occurrence of natural features, e.g., solstices. Although public holidays were mostly single days which had only minimal influence on tourism, over the years, particularly since the early nineteenth century, days have been expanded into weekends and breaks of longer duration, and assumed increasing relevance for tourism and long-distance travel.

The most significant elements of institutionalized seasonality are school and industrial holidays. The origin of a long summer school holiday stems from the necessity of students being available to assist with the summer harvest, and periods of from six to ten weeks traditionally have been allocated for this. Despite the fact that such needs no longer exist in most western countries, the summer school holiday continues to exist and to dominate holiday patterns and hence the tourist industry, in much of the world (Netherlands, 1991). This is for two main reasons. The tradition of a family taking a holiday together meant that if there children of school age, the summer holidays were the only time when holidays could be taken without the children being absent from school. The effect of this was compounded by the fact that for most developed countries, the summer months offered the best weather for the traditional holiday, whether this was by the beach, the lake or in the mountains. Thus families not only had to go then, it was the time of the year when most desired to go. The second reason for the importance of this factor is that the bulk of world tourism is still generated by western industrial countries which were the first to enshrine summer school holidays in legislation. This is one of the reasons that Hartmann (1986) suggests tourist seasonality may be thought of as a western concept.

In the same countries, as the Industrial Revolution progressed, along with social reform and related legislation, the idea of holidays with pay became accepted. In most countries such holidays became tied to the main summer season to allow families to holiday together. In some urban centres whole industrial sectors would close for a one-or two-week period, a pattern clearly illustrated in the industrial cities of Scotland by the "Fair Fortnights". In these periods virtually all industrial activity would cease within a particular community, accompanied by a mass migration to the closest seaside resorts, a pattern reflected in the visitation to the Clydeside resorts (Pattison, 1969).

It is clear, however, that there are other factors causing institutionalized seasonality in tourism apart from legislated holidays. One is social pressure or fashion. In many societies the privileged elite frequently divided their year into specific "seasons" during each of which it was considered socially necessary to participate in selected activities and visit certain locations. Examples include a season for taking waters at spas, a season for social-izing in appropriate capitals, a season for hunting and fishing on country estates, and in Europe, a winter season on the Côte d'Azur (Nash, 1979). While such seasons may have become institutionalized at one level of society, they do not normally feature in what is generally thought of as institutionalized seasonality. Rather, perhaps, they form a third category, perhaps most appropriately called "social" seasonality. While the process of the democratization of leisure, or mass following class has done much to reduce the signifi-cance of such seasons, other, perhaps smaller, but still significant seasons exist. The affluent and privileged still flock to specific recurring events such as regattas, racing meets and classical music festivals, although their length of stay is usually much shorter than in earlier times. The shooting season on grouse moors, while still about the same length, is rarely observed in full by families or households any more, and while the "Glorious

Twelfth" may still be celebrated fervently, a week or two on the moors is probably all that most can afford, in either time or money (Eden, 1979).

In the late twentieth century it may be appropriate to recognize a fourth form of seasonality in tourism, related to climatic factors, but also reflecting the changing patterns of recreational and tourist activity, and this is the sporting season. While shooting (of birds or deer) may be viewed as a sporting activity, it has traditionally been characterized as a social activity linked with privilege and affluence. In the last decade of the twentieth century the sporting attributes of some activities have tended to replace the social aspects in terms of importance to most participants and particularly spectators. It is clear that there has emerged the appearance of a distinct season associated with at least one set of sporting activities, specifically those related to snow, including skiing, snowboarding and snowmobiling. The combination of climatic and physical requirements, i.e., snow and hills, along with the necessary infrastructure for such activities has seen the appearance of distinct seasonal variations in tourism visitation in a significant number of mountain destination areas across the globe over the last century in particular. To a lesser degree seasonal variations in tourism associated with other popular sporting activities such as surfing and golf can also be identified in a number of specific destinations such as Hawaii and Australia for the former, and the southern United States for the latter.

There are reasonable grounds for suggesting that one can identity a fifth form of seasonality in tourism, which is related to inertia or tradition. There can be little doubt that many people take holidays at peak seasons because they have always done so and such habits tend to die hard. In some cases there may be good reasons for continuing a pattern even when it is no longer necessary, for example, after children have left school. The traditional holiday months are often the best for weather, specific activities and events may retain traditional dates (James, 1961), and transportation and other services may not be available or as frequent out of the traditional season (points which will be commented on in more detail below). The role of inertia and the persistence of established habits in patterns of consumption is not confined to tourism (Osborn, 1992). The numbers of people continuing such behaviour may be large, and failure to recognize the importance of this behaviour in maintaining seasonality may be a major cause of the apparent continued inability to change or reduce seasonality. Tourism researchers have a considerable amount to learn with respect to lifestyle patterns from researchers in consumption and other elements of human behaviour (Osborn, 1992).

It is the interaction between the forces determining the natural and institutionalised elements of the seasonality of tourism in both the generating and receiving areas as modified by actions of the public and private sector which creates the pattern of seasonality in tourism that occurs at a specific destination (see Figure 1 below).

Seasonality is rarely a simple phenomenon and takes a number of forms which display different patterns of visitation. Butler and Mao (1997) identified three basic patterns, single peak, two-peak and non-peak. Single peak seasonality occurs where the seasonal pattern of demand in a generating region matches the seasonal pattern of attractiveness of a destination, tending to produce extreme seasonality, for example, in some Mediterranean destinations where summer peak traffic may be more than ten times winter traffic. Two-peak seasonality occurs where there are two seasons, most commonly a major summer one

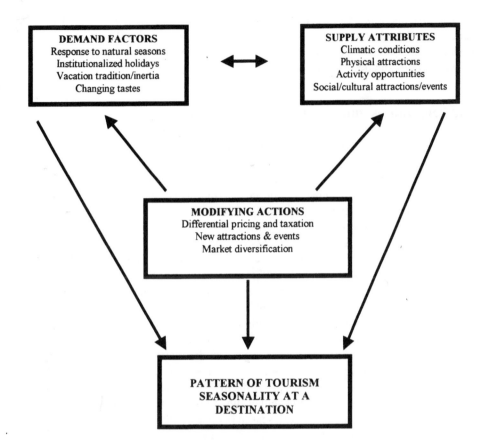

Figure 1: Influences on Patterns of Seasonality.

and a minor winter one, reflecting two seasons of attractiveness in the destination region, for example, in mountain regions, which attract both summer tourists and winter sports enthusiasts. An alternative situation producing the same pattern can occur where demand in generating regions produces two peaks. The Caribbean is an example of this, with a peak of winter demand from northern Caucasians and a summer peak in demand primarily from Caribbean émigrés living outside the region. Finally, non-peak patterns occur mostly in urban destinations such as Singapore and Hong Kong, where seasonality indices of peak to non peak visitation of less than 1 to 1.2 have been recorded (Butler & Mao, 1997). Even in these destinations, however, visitation is usually affected by seasonal variations in demand in the generating regions.

Finally it should be noted that the patterns of seasonality, while being resistant to modification, are dynamic. As discussed above, individual destinations change in seasonality as conditions, both natural and institutional change. Thus the overwhelmingly summer dominated seasonality displayed in tourism in the Central Highlands of Scotland for a century or so began to change with the establishment of winter sports in the Spey and Dee Valleys in the 1960s, and this area now displays a two-peak pattern of seasonality (Butler, 1973; Butler, 1998). As the attractiveness of the destination has changed, so too has the pattern of demand in the generating regions, indicating the relationship common throughout tourism between origins and destinations, and demand and supply.

The Perceptions and Impacts of Seasonality

The still rather limited literature on seasonality in tourism has several foci. These include: the relationship of seasonality to demand and visitation; particular regional and destination characteristics of seasonality; the effects of seasonality on employment and the financial well-being of tourism; its impacts upon destination areas; and policy implications and attempts to reduce the level of seasonality. Relatively little of the literature deals with concepts or theory (Hartmann, 1986; Phelps, 1988), or with definitions and causes of seasonality, and only a few specific works examine problems of measurement (Bar-On, 1975; Soesilo *et al.,* 1987; Sutcliffe & Sinclair, 1980; Wanhill, 1980) or of seasonal variations in types of visitors (Bonn *et al.,* 1992; Calantone & Johar, 1984).

Much of the literature which examines the economic aspects of seasonality does so from the point of view of the management of tourism supply and identifies seasonality of demand as a problem of considerable magnitude (Lim, 1988; McEniff, 1992; Witt *et al.,* 1991). It is seen as a major problem with respect to investment in tourism because of the frequent shortness of the business season in tourism destination areas (Jeffrey & Hubbard, 1986), with potential investors being deterred because of the compression of the operating period into a few months. This poses problems in securing return on capital, and in inefficiency in plant operation, which must either run at low levels of use for much of the year or run at over-capacity during the peak season (Cooper *et al.,* 1993).

Yacoumis (1980) summarizes a frequently expressed viewpoint when he describes seasonality in tourism as "an almost universal problem, varying only in the degree of its acuteness from one country to another", and his review of seasonality in tourism in Sri Lanka represents one of the few detailed discussions of this phenomenon in a specific location. By far the most exhaustive review of the issue is that by BarOn (1975) who examined the issue for 16 different countries using data covering a period of 17 years. Such a study is unique in the literature and most references to seasonality occur either as a brief discussion in books on tourism (e.g., Cooper *et al.,* 1993; Mathieson & Wall, 1982; Murphy, 1985; Pearce, 1989; Shaw & Williams, 1994; Witt *et al.,* 1991), or in articles which have other topics as their principal focus (e.g. Bonn *et al.,* 1992; Dieke, 1991; Hannigan, 1980; Kemper *et al.,* 1983; Ronkainen, 1983).

The overwhelming consensus of opinion in such writings is that seasonality is a problem, that it has a number of facets and implications as noted above, and that it is something to be overcome, or at least modified and reduced in effect. Ronkainen (1983) notes that "The encouragement of tourism outside the high season is one of the few recommendations [of a European conference] not having direct political connotation [and that] seasonality of tourism is plaguing most of the signatory countries". This is a viewpoint addressed at a national level by various organizations in different countries such as NEDC (undated) and Netherlands (1991).

The discussion of seasonality in specific destinations is often linked to the impacts and effects of seasonality in those locations (Belisle & Hoy, 1980; Dieke, 1991; Drakatos, 1987; Donatos & Zairis, 1991; Netherlands, 1991). In many cases the impacts discussed are primarily those dealing with either employment (Ball, 1989; Clarke, 1981; Krakover, 2000) or with under-utilization of physical plant (Jeffrey & Hubbard, 1988; Van der Werff, 1980). Only in a very few cases (Mathieson & Wall, 1982; Mitchell & Murphy, 1991; Murphy, 1985; Pearce, 1989) has there been discussion of the environmental effects of seasonality. In such cases the discussion is often generalised and notes the intensity of pressure on often fragile environments because of crowding and overuse during the peak season. Specific studies of the effects of seasonality of visitation on wildlife and habitat are rare (Muir & Chester, 1993).

It is generally only in the discussions on employment and to a lesser degree of environmental and social effects, that any mention is made of the fact that seasonality may not be totally negative for tourism destinations. Murphy (1985) notes that "seasonality is not necessarily bad for everyone", and goes on to add that, to some communities, the end of the tourist season is regarded as "the light at the end of the tunnel". In this vein he discusses the fact that individuals need release from stress and that some populations would not be capable of, or at least content to, experience the stress of catering for tourists throughout the year. This is an argument echoed by Mathieson and Wall (1982) in noting "locals view the approaching [tourist] season with mixed feelings and value the off season when only permanent residents are present". Similar findings were made by Brougham & Butler, (1981) in their study of the perceptions of residents of the Isle of Skye towards tourism. This aspect is discussed at more length by Lundtorp *et al.* (1998 and in this volume).

Discussions on the effects of seasonality upon employment in the tourism industry in destination areas present two viewpoints. The most frequently expressed opinion appears to be that the seasonal nature of tourism presents problems for employers, making it difficult to recruit full-time staff and to retain them (Krakover, 2000; Pearce, 1989; Stynes & Pigossi, 1983; Yacoumis, 1980). Associated with this is the argument that tourism related employment may create competition with other seasonal employers such as agriculture for what may be scarce labour in rural areas (Mathieson & Wall, 1982). An alternative viewpoint has been expressed, however. Mourdoukoutas (1988) argues that unemployment is not caused by seasonal employment, and that in the Greek islands a considerable number of employees choose seasonal tourism employment because it pays better than alternative work that is available, and also because it allows those who wish to pursue other activities during the off-season to do so. In a similar vein, Ball (1989) notes that rural seasonal employment in fields such as tourism may offer relief, albeit temporary, to urban unemployment, although such relief has declined considerably over the past 50 years.

Perhaps the most strongly argued case for seasonal tourism employment being a positive rather than a negative factor has been made by Flognfeldt (1988). He identified that employment in the tourism industry, particularly in remote and small communities, may complement traditional patterns of employment rather than compete with them. Shaw & Williams (1994) cite evidence from the Scilly Isles which supports this argument. Similar trends can also be seen in peripheral regions of many countries, where, for a variety of reasons, it has been necessary to import labour to meet seasonal demands from tourism and other economic activities (Baum, 1998). In Shetland, and elsewhere in insular Scotland, for example, employment plurality combining jobs in several fields, including tourism, oil-related activities and more traditional activities such as agriculture and fishing is not uncommon and often essential for economic viability (Nelson & Butler, 1993).

Undoubtedly, however, the overwhelming impression from the literature is that seasonality in tourism is a problem. It is equally true to say that this viewpoint primarily is one taken from an economic position, and reflects concerns with the difficulty of ensuring efficient utilisation of resources (Sutcliffe & Sinclair, 1980). To managers and owners of tourism enterprises, seasonality compounds the problems of trying to make a living in a dynamic industry vulnerable to changes in fashion and external forces (Snepenger *et al.*, 1990). From an environmental viewpoint there are advantages and disadvantages to seasonal fluctuations in demand and visitation. While areas may experience very heavy use during peak seasons, in the long run they may well be better off than having that same level of use spread more evenly throughout the year. It has been shown that environmental impacts of recreation and tourism have heavy initial loadings and that continued use has proportionally less effect for each additional unit of use (Mathieson & Wall, 1982). A lengthy rest period, particularly where much of that period is still within climatic limits for growth, may allow almost complete recovery, or at least a new level of stability, to be achieved. As noted in the conclusions, however, changes in the length of seasons due to global warming and other aspects of climatic change may well affect such situations in some areas in the future.

It is in human, and hence cultural and social, terms that the greatest benefits of a seasonal pattern of tourism, such as they are, may be identified. There is no doubt that tourism can disrupt traditional social patterns in a community, and have effects upon cultural activities (Mathieson & Wall, 1982; Murphy, 1985; Pearce, 1989). The off-season often represents the only time that the local population can operate in what to it is a "normal" manner, and engage in traditional social and cultural activities. While an off-season may be a relatively inefficient way of operating in economic terms, it may well be preferable to some communities, particularly those which have alternative sources of income, and do not rely entirely upon tourism for their economic survival and have learned to adapt accordingly (Lundtorp *et al.,* 1998 and this volume).

Policy Implications of Seasonality

As noted earlier, there have been very considerable efforts made by both the public and the private sectors to overcome or reduce the seasonal aspects of tourism. A significant proportion of Bar-On's (1975) comprehensive study of seasonal is devoted to discussing methods for improving the seasonal pattern of tourism. The literature reveals a limited number of approaches which have been used in attempts to overcome seasonality. These include: trying to lengthen the main season, establishing additional seasons, diversifying markets, using differential pricing and tax incentives on a temporal basis, encouraging the staggering of holidays, encouraging domestic tourism in off-seasons, and providing off-season attractions such as festivals and conferences (Bar-On, 1975; James, 1961; Lewis & Beggs, 1982; Manning & Powers, 1984; Smale & Butler, 1991; Somerville, 1987; Sutcliffe & Sinclair, 1980; Witt *et al.*, 1991).

Seasonality in tourism has proved a difficult phenomenon to overcome. Bar-On (1975) noted that "the changes which have occurred in the range of seasonality indicate that despite the importance of reducing the seasonal peaks and the efforts that have been applied, the seasonal range has in fact increased for many countries with the growth of tourism". His comments anticipated what has been implied in other studies (Netherlands, 1991), namely that when a country is experiencing rapid growth in tourism, that growth is often of such magnitude that it swamps any efforts to redirect visitation into quiet periods of the year. It is likely also, when countries are entering a period of rapid growth in tourism, often characterised by aggressive marketing, that little thought is given to trying to attract tourists at particular times of the year. Rather, the emphasis is simply upon attracting tourists.

This viewpoint is supported by Bar-On's comment (1975) that in the countries which he examined in the mid-1970s, "the expansion of tourism has been largely an expansion of the main season". Elsewhere it was noted (Netherlands, 1991) that northern European countries appeared to be the most successful at spreading tourism temporally, probably because they had older-established industries which had already experienced peaking problems in the 1950s and 1960s. In such countries tourism has ceased to grow at the rapid rate which characterised tourism in Mediterranean countries during the 1960s and 1970s. When tourism plant and facilities are not being rapidly expanded, and when tourism numbers are relatively stable or only increasing slowly, then attention is more likely to be focused on the off-season and methods to spread tourism throughout the year, as well as to increase overall numbers.

The stubbornness of tourism in remaining seasonal despite intensive efforts of industry and governments suggests that the problem is more complex than generally thought. It may also be that the reasons are somewhat simpler than may be expected. It was noted above that inertia and tradition may be causes of seasonality in some situations (Osborne, 1992). Most efforts to overcome a temporal imbalance in demand have not been aimed at these factors. Instead they have been concentrated upon the destination areas to make them more attractive in off-seasons rather than focusing on the consumer, and trying to change their attitudes and behaviour through approaches such as intensive marketing (Lewis & Beggs, 1983; Somerville, 1987; Spotts & Mahoney, 1993). Many efforts have been made to diversify the appeal and attractions of the destinations, for example by lowering prices, or adding value, on the assumption that if they are made more attractive in relatively unattractive seasons, then tourists will come at those times, Implicit in these efforts has to be the assumption that tourists coming in the off season would represent additional visitation to that which would otherwise have been experienced in the peak season, rather than substituting for this, otherwise there is no gain and possibly a loss. This assumption would appear not to be entirely correct in many cases, as in some situations tourists may well transfer holidays from high to low seasons, producing no net gain in visitation and reducing net gain at the destinations.

It would appear that the shift to off-season holidays that has occurred has taken place because of an increase in the taking of additional holidays, rather than because of a shift of the primary holiday. The Netherlands report notes that the main restriction on the timing of trips is the school holiday and that "Long holidays are more likely than other types of trip to be concentrated in the peak summer months" (1991). The author concludes that "Unless the number of long holidays decreases significantly, which ... seems unlikely, tourism congestion will continue to be a problem in the EEC" (1991).

It has to be borne in mind also that the provision of additional holidays will not necessarily reduce seasonality in any area, indeed, such a process may simply create seasonality in another location. There is no evidence to suggest that a person receiving an additional holiday is likely to spend it in the same location as he or she spent their primary holiday, but at a different season. Rather, the tendancy is to spend it at another location, perhaps at another season. Perhaps the best example of this is the increasing frequency of second holidays taken by North Americans, where the most common pattern is to take a primary (usually summer) holiday in temperate climes, and a secondary (usually winter) holiday in tropical climes, or at a winter sports resort. As a result of the development of this pattern there has been a marked seasonality in tourism in the Caribbean for many years (CTRC, 1980; WTO, 1999). The relative level of affluence of residents of industrialised countries, coupled with legislated free time and ease of transportation has meant that many tourists can overcome real seasonal (climatic) problems and pursue the sun or snow at whatever time of the year they prefer, often creating inverse seasonal peaking in destinations with different climates to that of their home region (Butler & Mao, 1997).

The long-term nature of the seasonality of tourism tends to suggest that it is caused by more than only the basic climatic and institutional factors, although there is no doubt that these are still major influences. The long summer school holiday remains the largest single impediment to reducing seasonal concentrations of tourists. However, even if this were removed or significantly changed, as has been proposed at various times in several countries, there would still be seasonal fluctuations in tourism. Some people would not wish to go at alternative times, some would find the off-season weather at some destinations to be unattractive, and a full range of services and attractions may not be available in destination areas. Finally, there may well be reaction in host communities against a lengthening of the season or the attraction of more visitors at non-traditional times. It has to be understood by policy makers and tourism developers that actions intended to reduce seasonality need the support of destination area communities if they are to be successful in all aspects.

Spatial Aspects of Seasonality

It is clear that although seasonality may be an almost universal characteristic of tourism, it varies considerably from location to location. Climatic seasonality is much less marked the closer a location is to the equator, but even in equatorial destinations seasonal fluctuations in tourism are often experienced because of seasonal factors (both climatic and institutionalized) in tourist origin areas, and this relationship is shown below in Figure 2.

It is also clear that the degree of seasonality varies within destination countries and perhaps even within regions. Murphy notes that large cities such as London have a less seasonal pattern of tourism than do tourist resorts in the same country (Murphy, 1985), a view supported by the World Tourism Organisation which indicated that "Tourist destinations supported by large urban centres, while having high points of activity, have more continuous operation throughout the year because they depend upon a more diversified demand" (WTO, 1984).

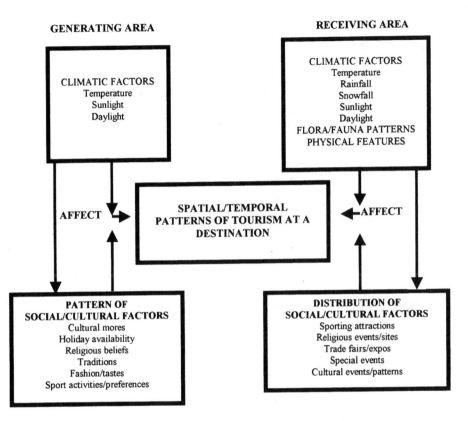

Figure 2: Factors Influencing Spatial Pattern of Seasonality at a Destination.

There are also indications that seasonality varies with the relative location of destinations within a country or major region. Snepenger *et al.* (1990) found that the seasonality of demand in Alaskan tourism was almost ten percent higher in the more remote interior than in coastal areas. In his study of Sri Lanka, Yacoumis (1980) suggested that it was necessary to analyse seasonality at three levels, national, regional, and sectoral, and went on to show considerable variations in a seasonality ratio on a spatial basis. Butler, in an early study of tourism in the Scottish Highlands and Islands also recorded significant variations in seasonality between central and more remote locations (1973).

This aspect of seasonality has not been explored to any degree in the literature. The World Tourism Organisation commented (1984) that "the most specialised destinations are usually the most seasonal" but this point was not pursued further, and there was no discussion of any possible spatial implications of that statement. Shaw & Williams (1994) made the point that *"temporal polarisation has the effect of reinforcing spatial polarisation* (their emphasis) which can have serious implications for the environment". If attempts to disperse tourism in time as well as space are to be successful, it is crucially important to determine if seasonality has a spatial dimension as well as the prerequisite temporal one.

It can be reasonably expected that remote or peripheral destinations are likely to experience seasonality in tourism to a greater degree than are more centrally located destinations for several reasons. In the first place, remoteness implies relative difficulty of access, which could involve longer time involved in travel. Given that most tourists have only limited vacation time available, and as travel consumes time, trips to such destinations can only be made when considerable time is available. Long trips tend to be made in the peak season much more than short trips (WTO, 1999). Remote locations generally receive relatively few visitors, and thus transportation and other services also tend to be limited, and may only operate at certain times of the year, when demand justifies their availability. Such a situation also encourages, if not mandates, visitation within limited periods. Finally, in some destinations, remote areas are climatically marginal, and visitation may be attractive, or even practical, only at specific and limited times of the year, e.g. polar regions (Hall & Johnstone, 1995).

Butler and Mao (1997) examined these assumptions in the context of seasonality of tourism in Ontario (Canada) and concluded, on the basis of seasonality as illustrated by accommodation occupancy figures, that seasonality was indeed more extreme in the more remote and peripheral parts of the province, and less marked in the more urban areas. The data used in that study covered only a five year period, and did not allow formal hypothesis testing but all urbanised areas scored lower than the provincial seasonality mean and all "remote" areas scored higher than the mean. In a preliminary study of seasonality in the Highlands of Scotland, measured using indices of regional hotel occupancy, airport traffic and visitation to selected properties, Butler (1998) identified similar trends in that the more remote locations tended to have higher indices of seasonality than locations closer to the central belt of Scotland, whatever indicators of seasonality were used.

In undertaking such research two problems emerge, one of obtaining data which demonstrates seasonality, and the second, related to this, of obtaining time series data to ensure any patterns are consistent over time, rather than possibly illustrating a single year's aberration. Given that tourism statistics often have been collected over time with great inconsistency and often inaccuracy, it is almost inevitable that most longitudinal data are incomplete and non-comparable. Few agencies collect data in the same format and manner over a period of decades; routes and highways change, railways close, air services develop and change, hotels and other accommodation units change in size, class and opening times; some information is confidential and thus unavailable, and some has simply not been retained.

In most cases the use of an index rather than absolute figures is required as it is not reasonable to compare actual numbers of tourists from month to month or year to year because of annual fluctuations in numbers. As well, there are real problems relating to motivations and purpose of travellers in comparing numbers of passengers on a ferry with numbers of entrants to an attraction or bed-night occupancy in an accommodation unit. There are some difficulties also in comparing the levels of seasonality from one location to another, unless the two locations are similar, particularly when traffic figures are used. Small absolute changes in seasonal tourist visitation can cause major changes in seasonality indices for communities in remote areas where total traffic volume and tourist numbers are very low. Areas which receive relatively large numbers of tourists in a highly seasonal pattern could still receive low seasonality indices if the volume of seasonal tourist traffic is masked by high levels of non-tourist traffic throughout the year. It is best to compare different locations only in terms of similar measures of tourist seasonality, where possible compensating for differences in local populations and non-tourist factors (Butler, 1998).

Conclusions

This discussion has focused on the topic of seasonality in tourism, and in particular on aspects of this phenomenon which previously have not been examined in detail. Seasonality is a subject which has been frequently discussed in the literature of tourism, but rarely analysed in detail. One result of this is that there has been little development of theory or concepts pertaining to the topic, and much of the discussion has not been based upon empirical research but more on assumption and supposition. There can be little doubt that seasonality represents a problem to maximizing the efficient operation of tourism facilities and infrastructure, and results in unnecessary excess capacity for most of the year in most destinations. On the other hand, very little research has been done to examine the advantages to destination areas of one or more off-seasons, which provide periods of recuperation and restoration, and allow residents and the environment to prepare for the next tourist season.

One point, which has not been addressed so far, has been the issue of the dynamics of seasonality. It was noted in the discussion of the causes of seasonality that the seasons have traditionally been regarded as relatively permanent and predictable. The appearance of the monsoon rains, or "The Wet" in tropical Australia are anticipated and their non-appearance would be catastrophic, and even a week or so delay from the norm can have severe negative effects on crop production and other activities. Adjustment to annual climatic events has been the norm for most civilisations and it is only recently that we have reluctantly accepted that climates and the seasons are now experiencing instability and a dynamic element and that they cannot be taken to be as permanent and predictable as we once believed (Houghton *et al.*, 1995; Watson *et al.*, 1995). Global climatic change, and in particular in this context, global warming and its effects, could significantly change a number of major aspects of tourism, including seasonality (Agnew & Viner, 2001; Wall & Badke, 1994). Some areas of the world will become appreciably warmer, with potentially extended "summer" seasons. Others, especially winter sports destinations, may face seasons significantly shorter in length because of reduced or less reliable snowfall, thus no longer being economically viable (Harrison *et al.*, 1999). The full ramifications of climatic change on seasonality in tourism cannot be discussed here, but it is a disturbing fact that even within the tourism literature in general, there has been an incredibly small number of publications on this vitally important topic. Climatic change has the potential to change the nature and extent of tourism from complete disappearance in some destinations such as low lying islands, to extending seasons and enlarging resources in other locations (Agnew & Viner, forthcoming; Pernetta, 1992). It may, perversely, go some way to achieving what governments and industry have generally failed to do so far, namely, significantly alter the pattern of seasonality in tourism in some destinations.

Very little has been documented or reported in the literature on the causes of seasonality, beyond the very general assumptions discussed earlier. The relationship between seasonality and visitor motivation has not been explored to any degree, and it is not known, for example, whether dissatisfaction with conditions in the origin region or the attractions of the destination play a greater role in shaping the seasonal patterns of tourism. It is not known with any certainty whether tourists travel in peak season because they want to, because they have to, or because they have been conditioned to. Considering the efforts and investments which have been made in attempting to reduce the level of seasonality in destinations across the world, it would seem appropriate for more attention to be given to research which might explain the phenomenon before continuing to attempt to modify what is essentially a poorly understood, if widely known, facet of tourism. The following chapters in this volume represent a considerable step in this direction.

References

Agnew, M. D., & Viner, D. (2001). Potential impacts of climate change on international tourism. *Tourism and Hospitality Research, 3(1)*, 37–60.

Ball, R. M. (1989). Some aspects of tourism, seasonality and local labour markets. *Area, 21(1)*, 33–45.

Bar-On, R. V. (1975). *Seasonality in Tourism.* London: Economist Intelligence Unit.

Barry, R. O., & Perry, A. H. (1973). *Synoptic Climatology-Methods and Applications.* London: Methuen.

Baum, T. (1998). Responding to seasonality in peripheral destinations (pp. 107–115). *Insights,* London: English Tourist Board.

Belisle, F., & Hoy, D. (1980). The perceived impact of tourism by residents: A case study in Santa Marta, Colombia. *Annals of Tourism Research, 7(1)*, 83–101.

Bonn, M. A., Furr, H. L., & Uysal, M. (1992). Seasonal variation of coastal resort visitors: Hilton Head Island. *Journal of Travel Research, 31(1)*, 50–56.

Boucher, K. (1975). *Global Climate.* London: English Universities Press.

Brougham, J. E., & Butler, R. W. (1981). A segmentation analysis of resident attitudes to the social impact of tourism. *Annals of Tourism Research, 13(4)*, 569–590.

Budyko, M. I. (1974). *Climate and Life.* New York: Academic Press.

Butler, R. W. (1973). Tourism in the Highlands and Islands. PhD thesis, University of Glasgow.

Butler, R. W. (1994). Seasonality in tourism: Issues and implications. In A. V. Seaton (ed.) *Tourism — A State of the Art* (pp. 332–339). Chichester: Wiley.

Butler, R. W. (1998). Seasonality in tourism: issues and implications. *Revue de Tourisme, 3*, 18–24.

Butler, R. W., & Mao, B. (1996). Seasonality in tourism: Problems and measurement. In P. E. Murphy (ed.) *Quality Management in Urban Tourism* (pp. 9–23). Chichester: John Wiley and Sons.

Calantone, R. J., & Johore, J. S. (1984). Seasonal segmentation of the tourism market using a benefit segmentation framework. *Journal of Travel Research, 23(1)*, 14–24.

Clarke, A. (1981). Coastal development in France: Tourism as a tool for regional development. *Annals of Tourism Research, 8(3)*, 447–461.

Cooper, C., Fletcher, J., Gilbert, D., & Wanhill, S. (1993). *Tourism: Principles and Practice.* London: Pitman.

CTRC (Caribbean Tourism Research Centre), (1980). *Caribbean Tourism Markets: Structures and Strategies.* Christ Church, Barbados: CTRC.

Dieke, P. (1991). Policies for tourism development in Kenya. *Annals of Tourism Research, 18(2)*, 269–294.

Donatos, G., & Zairis, P. (1991). Seasonality of foreign tourism in the Greek island of Crete. *Annals of Tourism Research, 18(3)*, 515–519.

Drakatos, C. G. (1987). Seasonal concentration of tourism in Greece. *Annals of Tourism Research, 14(4)*, 82–586.

Flognfeldt, T. (1988). The employment paradox of seasonal tourism. Paper presented at Pre-Congress meeting of International Geographical Union, Christchurch, New Zealand. 13–20 August.

Hall, C. M. (1991). *Introduction to Tourism in Australia.* Melbourne: Longman Cheshire.

Hall, C. M., & Johnstone, M. E. (1995). *Polar Tourism: Tourism in the Arctic and Antarctic Regions.* Chichester: John Wiley.

Hannigan, J. A. (1980). Reservations cancelled: Consumer complaints in the tourist industry. *Annals of Tourism Research, 7(3)*, 364–384.

Harrison, S. J., Winterbottom, S. J., & Sheppard, C. (1999). The potential effects of climate change on the Scottish tourist industry. *Tourism Management, 20(2)*, 203–211.

Hartmann, R. (1986). Tourism, seasonality and social change. *Leisure Studies, 5(1)*, 25–33.

Highlands and Islands Enterprise (1992). *Tourism–the Way Forward.* Inverness: Highlands and Islands Enterprise.

Houghton, J. T., Meira Filho, L. G., Callander, B. A., Harris, N., Kattenberg, A. *et al.* (1995). (eds) *Climate Change 1995: The Science of Climate Change.* Cambridge: Cambridge University Press.

James, E. O. (1961). *Seasonal Feasts and Festivals.* London: Thames and Hudson.

Jeffrey, D., & Hubbard, N. J. (1986). Weekly occupancy fluctuations in Yorkshire and Humberside hotels 1982–84: Patterns and prescriptions. *International Journal of Hospitality Management, 5(4)*, 177–187.

Jeffrey, D., & Hubbard, N. J. (1988). Temporal dimensions and regional patterns of hotel occupancy performance in England: A time series analysis of midweek and weekend occupancy rates in 266 hotels, in 1984 and 1985. *International Journal of Hospitality Management, 7(1)*, 63–80.

Johnson, R. L., & Suits, D. B. (1983). A statistical analysis of demand for visits to U.S. National Parks: Travel costs and seasonality. *Journal of Travel Research, 22(2)*, 21–24.

Jordan, J. W. (1980). The summer people and the natives: some effects of tourism in a Vermont vacation village. *Annals of Tourism Research, 7(1)*, 34–45.

Kemper, R., Roberts, J., & Goodwin, D. (1983). Tourism as a cultural domain: the case of Taos, New Mexico. *Annals of Tourism Research, 10(1)*, 149–172.

Krakover, S. (2000). Partitioning seasonal employment in the hospitality industry. *Tourism Management, 21(5)*, 461–471.

Lewis, R. C., & Beggs, T. J. (1982). The interface between national tourism and the hotel industry in promoting a destination area in off-season: The Bermuda case. *Journal of Travel Research, 20(4)*, 35–38.

Lim, C. (1998). Seasonality in international tourism to Australia. Paper presented to CAUTHE Conference, Gold Coast, Queensland, 11–14 February.

Lundtorp, S., Rassing, C. R., & Wanhill, S. (1998). Off-season is no season — with Bornholm as a case. Paper presented to Harnessing the High Latitudes Conference, University of Surrey, Guildford.

Manning, R. E., & Powers, L. (1984). Peak and off-peak use: Redistributing the outdoor recreation/tourism load. *Journal of Travel Research, 22(1)*, 25–31.

McEniff, J. (1992). *Seasonality of Tourism Demand in the European Community.* London: Economic Intelligence Unit.

Mathieson, A., & Wall, G. (1982). *Tourism: Economic, Physical and Social Impacts.* Harlow: Longman.

Mauss, M., & Beuchat, H. (1979). *Seasonal Variations of the Eskimo.* London: Routledge & Kegan Paul.

Mitchell, L. S., & Murphy, P. (1991). Geography and tourism. *Annals of Tourism Research, 18(1),* 57–60.

Mourdoukoutas, P. (1988). Seasonal employment, seasonal unemployment and unemployment compensation: the case for the tourist industry of the Greek Islands. *American Journal of Economics and Sociology, 47(3),* 314–329.

Muir, F., & Chester, G. (1993). Managing tourism to a seabird nesting island. *Tourism Management, 14(2),* 314–329.

Murphy, P. E. (1985). *Tourism: A Community Approach.* New York: Methuen.

National Economic Development Council, (undated). *Seasonality* Report of NEDC's Tourism and Leisure Industries Sector Group. London: N.E.D.C.

Nash, D. (1979). The rise and fall of an aristocratic culture, Nice: 1763–1936. *Annals of Tourism Research, 7(1),* 61–75.

Nelson, J. G., & Butler, R. W. (1993). Assessing, planning, and management of North Sea Oil development effects in the Shetland Islands. *Environmental Impact Assessment Review, 13,* 201–227.

Netherlands (1991). *Improving Seasonal Spread of Tourism.* Rotterdam: Netherlands Ministerie van Economische Zak,

O'Driscoll, T. J. (1985). Seasonality in the trans-Atlantic vacation market. *Annals of Tourism Research, 12(1),* 109–110.

Osborne, D. R. (1992). Seasonality and habit persistence in a life cycle model of consumption. In S. Hylleberg (ed.) *Modelling Seasonality* (pp. 193–208). Oxford: Oxford University Press.

Pattison, D. A. (1969). *Tourism in the Fifth of Clyde.* PhD thesis, University of Glasgow.

Pearce, D. G. (1989). *Tourist Development.* Harlow: Longman Scientific and Technical.

Pernetta J. C. (1992). Impacts of climate change and sea-level rise on small island states: National and international responses. *Global Environmental Change, 2 (1),* 19–31.

Phelps, A. (1988). Seasonality in tourism and recreation: the study of visitor patterns. A comment on Hartmann. *Leisure Studies, 7(1),* 33–39.

Ronkainen, I. (1983). The conference on security and co-operation in Europe: Its impact on tourism. *Annals of Tourism Research, 10(3),* 415–426.

Scottish Tourist Board (1992). *Development, Objectives and Functions.* Edinburgh: Scottish Tourist Board.

Shaw, G., & Williams, A. M. (1994). *Critical Issues in Tourism.* Oxford: Blackwell.

Smale, B. J. A., & Butler, R. W. (1991). Geographic perspectives on festivals in Ontario. *Journal of Applied Recreational Research, 16(1),* 3–24.

Smith, A. (1973). *The Seasons: Rhythm of Life, Cycle of Change.* London: Pelican.

Snepenger, D., Houser, B., & Snepenger, N. (1990). Seasonality of demand. *Annals of Tourism Research, 17(4),* 628–630.

Soesilo, J. A., & Mings, R. C. (1987). Assessing the seasonality of tourism. *Visions in Leisure and Business, 6(2),* 25–38.

Somerville, J. (1987). Jamaican, Swiss, U.S. independents target new markets to beat seasonality. *Hotels and Restaurants International, 21(11),* 50–53.

Spotts, D. M., & Mahoney, E. M. (1993). Understanding the Fall tourism market. *Journal of Travel Research, 32(2),* 3–15.

Stynes, D. J., & Pigozzi, B. W. (1983). A tool for investigating tourism-related seasonal employment. *Journal of Travel Research, 21(3),* 19–24.

Sutcliffe, C. M. S., & Sinclair, M. T. (1980). The measurement of seasonality within the tourist industry: an application to tourist arrivals in Spain. *Applied Economics, 12(4)*, 429–441.

System Three, (1998). *Seasonality in Scotland, Final Report.* Edinburgh: Scottish Tourist Board.

Van der Werff, P. (1980). Polarising implications of the Pescaia tourism industry. *Annals of Tourism Research, 7(2)*, 197–223.

Wall, G., & Badke, C. (1994). Tourism and climate change: an international perspective. *Journal of Sustainable Tourism, 2(2)*, 193–203.

Wanhill, S. R. C. (1980). Tackling seasonality: A technical note. *International Journal of Tourism Management, 1(4)*, 243–245.

Witt, S., Brooke. M. Z., & Buckley, P. J. (1991). *The Management of International Tourism.* London: Unwin Hyman.

Watson, R. T., Zinyowera, M. C., & Moss, R. H. (1995), (eds) *Climate Change 1995:* Impacts, adaptations and mitigation of climate change: Scientific-technical analysis. Cambridge: Cambridge University Press.

WTO (World Tourism Organisation) (1999). World Tourism Statistics. WTO. Madrid.

Yacoumis, J. (1980). Tackling seasonality: the case of Sri Lanka. *Tourism Management, 1(2)*, 84–98.

Chapter 3

Measuring Tourism Seasonality

Svend Lundtorp

Part I. Measures for Tourism Seasonality

1. The Phenomenon

Seasonality in tourism is a well-documented phenomenon in tourism literature and particularly in relation to peripheral regions of Northern Europe and America. An often-quoted
source is Bar-On's (Bar-On, 1975) comprehensive study of seasonality in a serial of destinations. Butler (1994) describes tourism seasonality as *a temporal imbalance in the
phenomenon of tourism, and may be expressed in terms of dimensions of such elements as
number of visitors, expenditure of visitors, traffic on highways and other forms of transportation, employment and admission to attractions.*

There is no scientific theory on tourism seasonality. Obviously climate plays a major
role. In cold water resorts the tourists arrive in summer and only few want to visit the destination when it is cold and foggy in the off-season. Second, it is recognized that
institutional patterns play an important role as well, i.e., school holidays, industrial holidays and calendar holidays (Easter, Christmas etc.). Third, the destination may have
special characteristics influencing the shape of the seasonality curve. Thus, some skiing
resorts have both a winter and summer season. Fourthly, marketing including special
events may influence the season.

For the supplier — the destination and especially the tourism industry — seasonality is
a problem of efficient use of capacity. The destination has a certain amount of capacity —
hotels, restaurants and attractions. Only in the peak season there is a high capacity use.
Because of that many resorts try to expand the season.

To describe the nature of seasonality and for analysing the importance of seasonality it
seems evident to provide tools for measuring the phenomenon. That is the attempt in this
chapter.

Seasonality in Tourism, pp 23–50
© 2001 by Elsevier Science Ltd.
All rights of reproduction in any form reserved
ISBN: 0-08-043674-9

2. Why Measure Seasonality?

Reasons for Measuring

There are several reasons for measuring seasonality. The most important are presumably:

- seasonality has a great economic importance;
- seasonality influences pricing — high level prices in main season and discount rates in off season;
- to analyse the possibilities and the impacts of season extension one must be able to measure central characteristics of seasonality;
- the implication of seasonality must be taken into account for tourism forecasting;
- in this connection it is necessary to be able to test the stability or instability of seasonality.

The Economy of Seasonality

The tourism industry — or more specifically hotels — has a strong desire for seasonal extension. Looking at the economic structure of the hotel business it is easy to understand why. The main reason is overcapacity outside the peak season.

This is illustrated in Figure 1, where the curve depicts a hotel's contribution during the year. The contribution is equal to the turnover minus variable costs. So, if v_i is the number of visitors at time i, p_i is the room rate in month i and k the variable costs per visitor, the contribution in month i is $v_i(p_i-k)$. The curve C_1–C_1 denotes the minimum costs by opening up the hotel — expenses for minimum staff, heating, light etc. The curve C_2–C_2 shows the total monthly costs excluding the variable costs but including the weighty costs for depreciation and interests, i.e., the fixed costs.

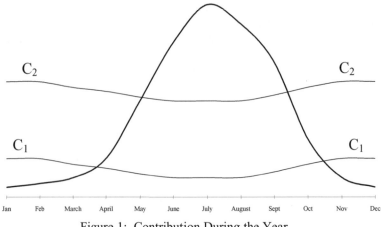

Figure 1: Contribution During the Year.

The curve C_1–C_1 is biggest in the winter due to the costs for heating. So, for the appointed hotel it does not pay at all to open up in the period from mid-October to mid-March, because the costs are higher than the contribution. Therefore, it is not surprising that many hotels in summer holiday destinations are closed during the winter. The figure also demonstrates the sensibility for energy prices. If the price for heating goes up, the curve C_1–C_1 is pushed up and so the opening up season will be abbreviated.

The period when the curve for contribution lies above C_2–C_2 specifies that part of the year with a positive profit. In the figure it includes the peak season and the shoulder season (May–October). The earnings in this period must be able to compensate the lack of income for the rest of the year.

This illustrates, evidently, that season has a decisive influence on the economy of a hotel and so, it is an obvious target for most hotels to increase the utilization of the capacity outside the peak season.

What is to be Measured

The intention in this chapter is first of all to point out a few simple measures for seasonality, i.e., to find a formula, which is able to describe the distribution of visitors during the observed period in one figure. As such, measures are introduced, the Gini coefficient and the seasonality indicator (See Section 4). Further it is the intention to give measures for the stability of seasonality, i.e., to give a measure for the variation of seasonality during a span of time (See Section 9).

3. Different Kinds of Season

Seasonality here is regarded as the fluctuations in tourism at a destination. Thus, the timing of meetings, conferences, and events are only included when they are linked to a certain geographical area. The annual meeting for the head of states in G7 is not a seasonal pattern, from a destination perspective, because the elected place for the meeting varies from year to year. But the annual general assembly in the United Nations is — for New York City — a seasonality phenomenon.

Further, the phenomenon of seasonality is inseparably connected with that period of time within which the seasonality moves takes place. So, seasonality has to be defined in relation to a certain time span.

Long Run Waves

These are not to be defined as seasonality. They figure the trend. In special cases it is possible to regard temporal imbalances in the phenomenon of tourism over more than one year as seasonality. This is the case for biennials taking place at the same destination and at the same time of the year.

Seasonality During the Year

Most often season is related to a period of one year and usually related to the calendar year. As examples, Figures 2–5 show for the period 1989 to 1997 the occupancy rate for hotel rooms in Denmark and in selected destinations in Denmark. Figure 2 shows the occupancy rate for all hotels in Denmark and Figure 3 for Copenhagen City. In both figures it is possible to see the trend: the demand fell from 1989 to 1993 and since then it has been increasing. But more spectacular is the yearly season with a peak in July–August and low season at mid-winter. Denmark is obviously a summer destination. As the extreme example, the occupancy rate for the Baltic island Bornholm is studied in Figure 5. This island is a typical holiday destination with very few visitors in the winter. The season for the island of Funen is pictured in Figure 4. On this island the differences between summer and winter are smaller, as Funen is not a typical summer holiday resort.

It is a remarkable feature that the shape is almost the same year for year and with special characteristics for each figure. That indicates a high degree of stability in seasonality.

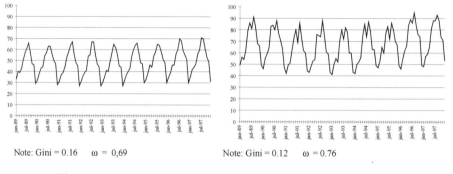

Note: Gini = 0.16   ω = 0,69   Note: Gini = 0.12   ω = 0.76

Figure 2: Denmark.   Figure 3: Copenhagen City.

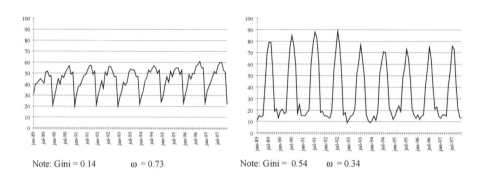

Note: Gini = 0.14   ω = 0.73   Note: Gini = 0.54   ω = 0.34

Figure 4: Funen.   Figure 5: Bornholm.

Month, Week and Day

The shifts in tourism demand during the month are usually of less importance in relation to seasonality. The period — a month — is too short to figure the total season and the move during the month is a cutting of the whole season.

Against it stands the variation of the numbers of visitors during a week. It can be quite substantial and so of great importance for the actual destination, attraction, hotel etc. Thus the number of visitors to the sea life centre "Kattegatcentret" in Jutland is taken as example in Figure 7. The low values show the number of visitors in April, i.e., an outseason week

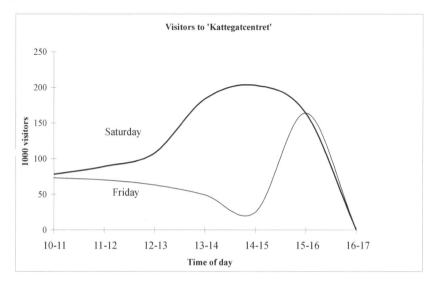

Figure 6: Visitors to "Kattegatcentret" Friday and Saturday.

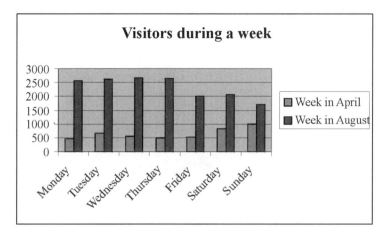

Figure 7: Visitors to "Kattegatcentret" During the Week.

and the high values are from August. Quite understandably there are in April most visitors at the weekend because they mainly are Danish one-day tourists or simply people from the region. Looking at a week in the peak season we have the opposite picture: The visitors are Danish and foreign tourists on holiday and they prefer to visit the fish on a weekday because weekend is time for arrival and departure.

Even the number of visitors during a day expresses a season. Thus Figure 6 shows the number of visitors to the sea life centre Friday and Saturday in April. On Saturday there is a maximum of visitors at two o'clock in the afternoon and this is exactly the time when there is a minimum of visitors on Friday. Saturday is characterized by local visitors and one-day tourists from nearby locations. They arrive in the early afternoon and leave a couple of hours before dinnertime. The Friday morning visitors are children from schools or kindergartens. In the afternoon they are families arriving after hours.

Public Holidays

Finally public holidays — Easter, Whitsun, Christmas etc. — shape their own seasons with a sudden increase in the number of visitors. In Figure 8 is shown the number of visitors to "Kattegat" 1997 for every day in the year. The high number of visitors on calendar days appears as peaks in the figure: Winter holidays for School children in February, Easter in April, Whitsun in May, October holidays and finally Christmas (closed two days) and New Year.

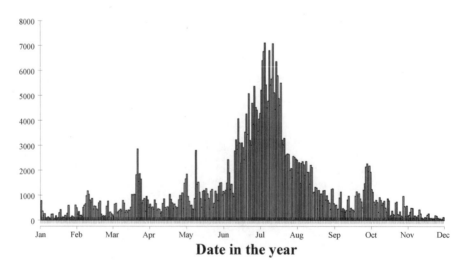

Date in the year

Figure 8: Visitors During the Year.

4. Measures of Seasonality

The basic unit for measuring tourism seasonality is usually the number of visitors. If the purpose is to measure economic impacts, the creation of incomes would be a better standard, but such figures are very seldom available. So the number of visitors — arrivals, departures, staying guests and so on — is used for practical reasons.

In the following, v_i is the number of visitors at time i, where i for instance indicates the month, the day in the week or the time of the day, depending of the kind of season to be looked upon. v_i can be measured as a flow, i.e., number of visitors per time unit or as a stock, i.e., number of visitors at a certain time. If the purpose is to restrict the number of visitors at peak time — for instance, in attractions or fragile areas — the stock is the appropriate measure. For statistical purposes, where the sum of visitors over time will be calculated, the flow is to be preferred. Further, for practical reasons, the flow is more often observed than the stock. So, the stock must be indirectly calculated, which is rather easy having the flow and an estimate of the average length of stay. To simplify, i indicates in the following the month in the year and v_i the number of visitors during the month i (the flow). It may be arrivals or overnights per month.

Both the trend and the season determine v_i. To eliminate the influence of the trend, v_i must be related to the total number of visitors during the year, the average number of visitors or the number of visitors in a given month.

Yacomis (1980) uses two measures to describe the importance of seasonality. The first he calls *coefficient of seasonal variation,* which is equal to the standard deviation of the seasonal indices, where index = 100 is the average number of visitors per month.

Evidently this coefficient describes the fluctuation of visitors during the year. Further it is an easy measure. But it is difficult to describe an appropriate interpretation of this coefficient. It is adopted from statistics, but seasonality is not — within the year — a stochastic variable.

The other measure is called the *seasonality ratio.* When v_0 is the total number of visitors (arrivals) during the year, i.e. $v_0 = \sum_{i=1}^{12} v_i$ and the average number of visitors is $\bar{v}$, the coefficient is calculated as seasonality ratio

$$R = v_n / \bar{v} \tag{1}$$

where v_n is the highest number of visitors

With the same number of visitors every month the ratio will be 1. If all visitors come in month n, the ratio is 12. So, with increasing seasonal variation the ratio increases. For the years 1967–1979, looking at the number of foreign tourists to Sri Lanka, Yacomis measures the seasonality ratio to values between 1.3 and 2.0.

Also this measure is easy and — by taking the maximum value in the numerator — it emphasises the influence of the peak season.

In the following the inverse value of the above mentioned ratio is used. It is named the *seasonality indicator* and thus defined as

$$\omega = \bar{v} / v_n \qquad 1/12 \leq \omega \leq 1 \tag{2}$$

This definition is chosen because of the interpretation. Let v_i be the number of overnights in a hotel and, for simplicity, v_n denotes not only the maximum but also the capacity of the hotel. Thus all rooms are occupied in the peak season. If so, ω shows the average number of overnights in relation to the capacity and so the average occupancy rate. Thus ω is a measure for capacity utilisation. By indicating the occupancy rate, ω also is a measure for the average use of rooms during the season. If for example $\omega = 0.5$ it means that in a year 50 percent of the capacity in the hotel is used and that means that a room on average is used 50 percent of the year or six month. So, the seasonality indicator is as well a measure for the width of the season. If v_n is smaller than the capacity, ω denotes the relative capacity use — relative to the use in the peak month.

Parallel to this, Yacoumis' seasonality ratio can be regarded as the *amplitude*, because the ratio measures the relation between the maximum value and the average value, which is the way the height of waves usually, is measured.

In a comment on Yacoumis' chapter, Wanhill (1980) finds that the measures have serious deficiencies when used as measures of inequality: they have different lower bounds and both of them have very high upper bounds. Both measures take no account of the skewness of the distribution and both are influenced by extreme values. Instead he recommends use of the *Gini-coefficient* which in economics is a well-known tool for measuring inequalities. It is derived from the Lorenz curve (King, 1999).

The Lorentz curve is traced in Figure 10, showing the cumulated frequencies in rank with the lowest frequency (winter month) to the left and the month with the highest number of visitors to the right. The figure is based on overnights per month. Examples used are a typical summer holiday destination (island of Bornholm) and a region without greater monthly variations (Western Zealand). With the same number of visitors every month, the Lorentz curve would be a straight line, the line of equality. The more unequal the seasonal distribution of visitors, the larger will be the area between the Lorentz curve and the line of equality. The Gini coefficient is calculated as the area between the curve and the 45-degree equality line divided by the entire area below the 45 degree line.

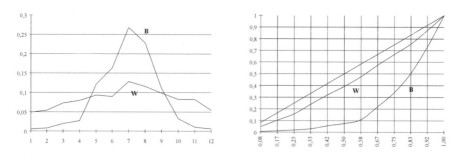

Figure 9: Seasonal Frequencies.   Figure 10: Lorentz Curves.

Note: B is the county of Bornholm — a summer holiday resort with many visitors during the peak season and almost non in the off-season. W is the county of West zealand with very little variation during the year. The figures are from 1997.

Western Zealand: $\omega = 0.75$ Gini = 0.13   Bornholm: $\omega = 0.34$ Gini = 0.54

Figure 10 shows for Bornholm that in 75 percent of the year (9 months) only 33 percent of the visitors are attracted and in 83 percent (10 months) only 50 percent. For West Zealand we have the reverse picture with 75 percent of its visitors in 10 months with the fewest visitors.

For simple fractiles the formula for the Gini coefficient is defined as

$$G = \frac{2}{n}\sum_{i=1}^{n}(x_i - y_i) \tag{3}$$

where

n = the number of fractiles (i.e. the number of month = 12 in the figure)
x_i = the rank of the fractiles (in the example 1/12, 2/12 ...). So $x_i = i/n$
y_i = the cumulated fractiles in the Lorentz curve.

The fractile for month i is defined as $f_i = v_i/v_0$. In this relation i indicates the rank of month i, so $f_i \leq f_{i+1}$. Hence we have:

$$y_i = v_1/v_0 + v_2/v_0 + + + v_i/v_0 = \sum_{j=1}^{i} f_j \tag{4}$$

and by definition

$$y_n = \sum_{j=1}^{n} f_j = 1 \tag{5}$$

Then

$$\sum_{i=1}^{n} y_i = \sum_{i=1}^{n}\sum_{j=1}^{i} f_i = f_1$$
$$+ f_1 + f_2$$
$$+ f_1 + f_2 + f_3$$
$$\dots \ \dots \ \dots \ \dots \ \dots \ \dots$$
$$+ f_1 + f_2 + f_3 - - - - - - - f_n$$
$$= \sum_{i=1}^{n}(n - i + 1)f_i = (n + 1) - \sum_{i=1}^{n} if \tag{6}$$

Further $\sum_{i=1}^{n} x_i = \sum_{i=1}^{n}\frac{i}{n} = \frac{n+1}{2}$

Thus we have from (3)

$$G = \frac{2}{n}\left[\frac{n+1}{2} - (n+1) + \sum_1^n if\right] = \frac{2}{n}\left(\sum_1^n if_i - \frac{n+1}{2}\right) \tag{7}$$

which is rather easy to compute.

5. Comparing the Gini Coefficient and the Seasonality Indicator

Wanhill (1980) finds it critical that Yacoumis' two measures take no account of the skewness of the distribution and they are both influenced by extreme values.

First, one single measurement — neither the Gini coefficient nor the seasonality indicator — can give a complete picture of the skewness. For this purpose you have to have more information as illustrated in Figures 9 and 10. Both figures give an impression of the shape of seasonality. But Figure 9 shows exactly the seasonal pattern within the year, while Figure 10 just displays their existence.

To examine the influence of extreme values, and to test the reliability of the two measurements, the sensitivity of changes in the fractiles may be analysed as follows:

For the seasonality indicator ω it is obvious that the magnitude of the number of visitors in the peak season is of great importance. Using the definition we have:

$$\omega = \frac{\bar{v}}{v_n} = \frac{\Sigma v_i}{m}\frac{1}{v_n} = \frac{1}{mf_n} \tag{8}$$

m is the number of time units. Counting in month that means $m = 12$.
So ω is inverse proportional with the biggest fractile. Further we have:

$$\frac{d\omega}{dv_1} = \frac{1}{mv_n} \qquad i \neq n$$

and

$$\frac{d\omega}{dv_n} = \frac{1}{v_n}\left(\frac{1}{m} - \omega\right) \qquad i = n$$

To estimate the sensibility for changes in v_i following elasticity is introduced. The first is the relative increase in the seasonality indicator in relation to the relative increase in the number of visitors:

$$E_{(')}^i = \frac{d\omega/\omega}{dv_1/v_i} = \frac{1}{mv_n}\frac{v_1}{\omega} = \frac{1}{mv_n}\frac{v_1}{v/v_n} = \frac{v_1}{v_0} = f_i \qquad i \neq n \tag{9}$$

$$E_{(')}^n = \frac{d\omega/\omega}{dv_n/v_n} = \frac{1}{v_n}\left(\frac{1}{m} - \omega\right)\frac{v_n}{\omega} = \frac{v_n}{v_0} - 1 = -\frac{v_0 - v_n}{v_0} = -1 + f_n \qquad i = n \tag{10}$$

Figure nine shows a positive elasticity which is exactly equal to the fractile. So, an increase in the number of visitors outside the peak season causes an increase in the seasonality indicator. For the peak month (10) the elasticity is negative and proportional with the difference between the total number of visitors and the highest number in relation to the total number.

Thus, the conclusion is that the seasonality indicator ω is virtually influenced by the number of visitors in the month where it is biggest.

A similar analysis of the Gini coefficient leads to following results:

From (7) we have

$$\bar{j} = \frac{2}{n}\left(\sum if_1 - \frac{n+1}{2}\right) = \frac{2}{n}\left(\sum i\frac{v_1}{v_0} - \frac{n+1}{2}\right)$$

$$\frac{dG}{dv_1} = \frac{2}{n}\left(i\frac{v_0 - v_1}{v_0^2}\right) = \frac{2i}{nv_0}(1-f_1) \tag{11}$$

Thus the elasticity is

$$E_G = \frac{dG/G}{dv_1/v_1} = \frac{2i}{nv_0}\left(1 - \frac{v_1}{v_0}\right)\frac{v_1}{G} = \frac{2i}{nG}(f_1 - f_1^2) = \frac{2if_1}{nG}(1-f_1) \tag{12}$$

Thus $E_G > 0$ and increases with i. So, the elasticity of the Gini-coefficient is also sensitive for variations in the biggest fractiles, but not only for the biggest.

By definition ω is a measure for capacity use. If v_n is equal to the capacity ω expresses the proportion of the capacity used in a year. If v_n is lower than the capacity, ω shows the the capacity use put in relation to the maximum use in the year.

If the number of visitors were the same every month, the Gini-coefficient would be zero. So, evidently, the Gini-coefficient is in the same way a measure for the unused capacity. Thus, when ω increases, G is decreasing. The relation between the two sizes can be derived from (7) and (8):

$$G = \frac{2}{n}\left(\frac{1}{\omega} + \sum_{i=1}^{n-1} if_1 - \frac{n+1}{2}\right) \qquad\qquad G = (n-1)/n \text{ when } \omega = 1/n \text{ and}$$

$$G = 0 \text{ when } \omega = 1$$

Even though both measures are between zero and one and both are expressing capacity use (or lack of use) the relation between ω and G is not simple. Which to prefer for use depends of the circumstances. If a well-known expression for inequality is preferred, G must be used. Further G is less dependent of the highest fractile and thus more sensitive for variations outside the peak season.

On the other hand, ω is more comprehensible by being a direct measure for capacity use.

Part 2: Empirical Study

6. The Applied Unit for Measurement

In the following empirical analysis, hotel overnights in Denmark 1989–1998 are used as the example for an analysis of seasonality patterns.

As the unit for measuring the number of overnights is used, i.e., the number of nights the hotel rooms have been occupied. This unit has an advantage over number of bed-overnights because the number of occupied rooms is the most important figure for the hotel owners.

The data is official Danish tourism statistics published by Statistics Denmark. The figures include hotels with more than 40 beds. This analysis uses monthly data for the period 1989–1998 for the 15 Danish counties. So, in the following, v_{it} denotes number of occupied rooms in a month i in the year t. For simplicity, v_{it} is called the number of visitors.

7. A Time-Series Model

Time-Series

It is assumed that the number of visitors is influenced by both trend and seasonal patterns. It is further assumed that those two parameters are independent so

$$v_{it} = \xi_t \delta_i + x_{it}$$
$$\mu_{it} = \xi_t \delta_i \tag{13}$$

Thus the parameter ξ_t indicates the trend, while δ_i is an expression for the season in month i. The two parameters are multiplied because it is assumed that the fluctuations due to seasonality varies proportional with the trend. x_{it} is a stochastic variable with the mean $E(x_{it}) = 0$. In consequence μ_{it} is the expected number of visitors in month i and year t, i.e. $E(v_{it})=\mu_{it}$.

Estimation of the Parameters

The parameter for seasonality δ_i indicate the influence of season for month i. Being independent of the trend the sum of δ_i's must be a constant, which in this relation is fixed to one. So

$$\sum_i \delta_i = 1 \tag{14}$$

Further we define v_{0t} as the sum of visitors in year t and v_{i0} as the sum of visitors in month i during the years. Thus we have defined

$$v_{0t} = \sum_i v_{it} \quad \text{and} \tag{15}$$

$$v_{i0} = \sum_t v_{it} \quad \text{and} \tag{16}$$

$$v_{00} = \sum_i \sum_t v_{it} \tag{17}$$

So we have

$$v_{0t} = \sum_i v_{it} = \sum_i (\xi_t \delta_i + x_{it}) = \xi_t \sum_i \delta_i + \sum_i x_{it} \approx \xi_t \tag{18}$$

The approximation is acceptable because $E(x_{it}) = 0$. So ξ_t is estimated by the total number of visitors in the year and thus simply expresses the amount of visitors that year. Further we have

$$v_{00} \approx \sum_t \xi_t$$

$$v_{i0} \approx \sum_t \xi_t \delta_i = \delta_i \sum_t \xi_t$$

$$\Leftrightarrow \delta_i \approx \frac{v_{i0}}{\sum_t \xi_t} = \frac{v_{i0}}{v_{00}} \tag{19}$$

Thus δ_i is simply interpreted as month's i's expected proportion of the visitors during the year.

8. Observations

Data

For the whole country and for the 15 regions in Denmark, the observations v_{it} are in the figures in Appendix A plotted against the estimated time series μ_{it}. The figures leave no doubt about the importance of tourism seasonality in Denmark. Carefully watched it is also possible to recognise a trend: The number of visitors is stable until 1993 and has been increasing since that year. This feature is more exposed for some regions than for others: for typically summer holiday resorts it is difficult to see the trend. They are the regions with high seasonal amplitude, i.e., Storstom, Bornholm, Southern Jutland, Viborg and Northern Jutland (with Bornholm as an extreme).

Furthermore, there is in most of the figures a surprisingly high coincidence between the observations and the estimate. In particular, this is the case for the whole country. That indicate a high validity of the model and so a great stability in the seasonal patterns. That will be examined below.

The Distribution of v_{it} and x_{it} χ^2 -test

The fluctuations in the number of visitors may be regarded as occasional and so v_{it} is a stochastic variable.

The poisson distribution is very often used to analyse the number of customers, visitors, arrivals etc. It is also reasonably to assume a poisson distribution for the variation in occupied hotel rooms. If so, the model (13) can be tested by a χ^2 -test of significance. But, a test gives χ^2 values far too great to accept a simple poisson distribution. The number of visitors is not only determined by random arrivals. It is also influenced by many other phenomena as weather conditions, events, different kinds of development for different market segments etc. Thus, the actual fluctuations may possibly be regarded as a sum of poisson distributions, with parameters changing during the time and different for incomparable regions. This is, however, not possible to test.

For larger values of the stochastic variable, which are the case here, the poisson distribution can be replaced by the normal distribution. Thus a more pragmatic and convenient approach is to regard the number of visitors as normally distributed, with the mean $\xi_t \delta_i$ and the variance σ^2, i.e.,

$$p\{ v_{it}\} = N(\xi_t \delta_i, \sigma^2)$$

As a consequence does also x_{it} follow the normal distribution as

$$p\{ x_{it}\} = N(0, \sigma^2)$$

The following statistical tests are based on this assumption.

Simple Tests

First the values of x_{it} are figured on a time axis in order to discover whether the values are displayed randomly round the zero value. Looking through the figures for the 15 regions there seems to be no systematic divergences from the random distribution. The divergences are further examined below. As an example, the figures for Denmark in total are presented in Figure 11.

There are for most regions some extreme values. Even for the entire country there are extreme values. Thus, in Figure 8.1 the value for May 1998 is extremely low.

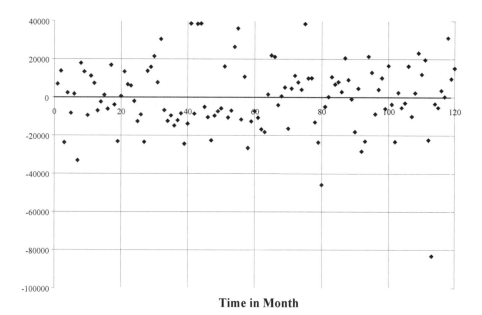

Time in Month

Figure 11: The Values of x_{it} (All Regions in Denmark).

Secondly, as a simple test, it is analysed whether there are many or great differences between the observed values and the estimate.

Some of the observations differ statistically significantly from the estimated curve. It could be expected that there would be quite many extreme values as a consequence of events, new attractions, opening new hotels and closing others. But the incidence of such extreme observations is actually not high. In fact, fewer than statistically expected. However, some of the extreme values differ so much from the curve, that a special explanation is needed to understand them. In many cases it is possible to relate some of these extreme figures to special events, for example, the closing down of an amusement park with its own hotel capacity.

Analysis of Signs

The next step is to examine the sign of x_{it}. If x_{it} is randomly distributed, we may expect 50 percent positive values and 50 percent negative values in all years. Actually, there must by definition be almost an equal number of positive and negative signs.

Therefore, it is more interesting to observe the number of changes of signs. The time series contains ten years covering twelve months. That gives 120 observations from each of the 15 regions. Looking at the changes from one year to the next, we have 108 observations, because we have twelve months less, when one year is compared with the previous.

For each region the expected number of changes in the sign of x_{it} is half of 108, i.e. 54. Actually, only one of the regions has more than 54. The rest have less. With great variations between the regions, the average is 46 and thus significantly lower than the expected 54. That indicates some kind of seasonal trends. In some years in succession the observed values are below the estimate followed by years above the curve, or the reverse.

9. Stability of Months

Above it is strongly indicated that seasonality patterns in general are very stable but the marginal demand seems not to show the same seasonal stability. For further investigation, the question for the analyses in this section is whether the number of visitors in the individual months is stable in relation to the estimated value of μ_{it}.

For this purpose the differences between observed values, vit and the estimated values μ_{it} i.e. x_{it} are examined for the same month, for each region during the time. To measure the variation over time is used the coefficient of variation, i.e. the standard deviation divided with the mean, STD/m, in the following abbreviated as *cv*. This is a measure for the stability of seasonality for a specific month. It is computed as

$$
cv_{month} = \frac{\sqrt{\sum_t (x_{it}^2)/10}}{\left(\sum_t v_{it}\right)/10} = \frac{\sqrt{\sum_t (x_{it}^2)/10}}{0.1 v_{i0}}
$$

The denominator 10 relates to the number of years (1989–1998). As *cv* is calculated as the standard deviation divided with the mean, a low value of *cv* indicates high stability and vice versa. If *cv* for instance is 0.03 the standard deviation is three percent of the mean, which usually is regarded as a moderate value and so *cv* expresses a little variation. The figures are given in Table 1.

Ignoring Bornholm, having extreme high values for all the months outside the season, the coefficients of variation are rather small and the variations throughout the year are not remarkable. The lowest value, and so the highest stability, is found in September (month = 9). The biggest values are for March, April and May, which presumably, in part, is due to the location in the year of Easter and Whitsun. Perhaps the most important observation is that the figures for the peak months of July and August are below mean for all important tourism regions. So, the figures suggest that variations in the peak season do not cause instability. Even for Bornholm, the coefficient of variation is rather low in July and August.

The mean varies from 0.036 in Northern Jylland (a summer holiday destination) to 0.90 on Bornholm (also a tourism destination). Ignoring Bornholm, the highest values are found in regions with relatively few visitors. Part of the reason for that is the uncertainty connected with statistical measures for small numbers.

Furthermore, Table 1 indicates that the coefficient of variation is a useful tool for a simple measure of seasonality stability, or more precisely, of the monthly variation over a span of time.

Table 1: Stability of Monthly Variations Measured by the Coefficient of Variation. For 15 Danish Regions.

Coefficient of Variation	Month												
	1	2	3	4	5	6	7	8	9	10	11	12	Mean
Cop. City	0.033	0.033	0.062	0.045	0.063	0.032	0.031	0.036	0.029	0.033	0.026	0.054	0.039
Cop. county	0.043	0.037	0.103	0.073	0.084	0.054	0.085	0.046	0.043	0.042	0.052	0.089	0.062
Frederiksborg	0.056	0.083	0.107	0.068	0.058	0.046	0.044	0.053	0.05	0.048	0.056	0.065	0.059
Roskilde	0.086	0.041	0.148	0.077	0.073	0.077	0.078	0.103	0.086	0.084	0.053	0.129	0.086
West Zealand	0.057	0.065	0.073	0.073	0.076	0.05	0.161	0.068	0.04	0.064	0.057	0.069	0.07
Storstrom	0.109	0.111	0.115	0.096	0.081	0.075	0.048	0.075	0.061	0.041	0.059	0.108	0.075
Bornholm	0.288	0.282	0.366	0.214	0.103	0.061	0.043	0.058	0.09	0.222	0.314	0.27	0.09
Fyn	0.056	0.051	0.063	0.075	0.058	0.046	0.058	0.028	0.029	0.046	0.044	0.043	0.049
Ribe	0.038	0.053	0.04	0.072	0.035	0.039	0.052	0.035	0.029	0.055	0.058	0.052	0.045
Southern Jutl.	0.042	0.067	0.042	0.076	0.067	0.051	0.066	0.038	0.056	0.07	0.055	0.05	0.057
Vejle	0.049	0.041	0.087	0.083	0.049	0.052	0.048	0.05	0.055	0.037	0.038	0.04	0.052
Arhus	0.053	0.036	0.037	0.071	0.057	0.046	0.044	0.053	0.03	0.032	0.042	0.064	0.046
Ringkobing	0.093	0.048	0.096	0.053	0.093	0.045	0.056	0.052	0.055	0.069	0.069	0.092	0.065
Viborg	0.054	0.078	0.072	0.06	0.078	0.065	0.08	0.048	0.055	0.057	0.04	0.058	0.062
Nordjylland	0.043	0.034	0.05	0.05	0.04	0.019	0.027	0.026	0.021	0.054	0.052	0.048	0.036
Denmark	0.033	0.027	0.047	0.026	0.051	0.025	0.029	0.031	0.017	0.031	0.024	0.031	0.031

Note: The mean is weighted according to the expected number of visitors in the months.

10. Growth and Seasonality

Since the study deals with seasonality it may be most important to look at the demand in the peak time. So, the share of visitors in July and August is shown in Table 2.

Being the inverse value of the modified seasonality indicator mentioned below (See Section 11), this table is also a way to demonstrate the importance of seasonality. Again, the high degree of stability is once more observed.

Looking at the marginal moves, the stability is, however, not visible any more. Thus, in Table 3. the increase in the peak season is related to the increase for the total year. The figures in Table 3 are calculated as

$$(v_{(July+August), t+1} + v_{(July+August), t}) / (v_{0, t+1} - v_{0, t})$$

So, the figures express the peak season's share of the total increase in the number of visitors.

In this table the variations are tremendous. Negative values occur if there is a positive growth in July and August while the total number of visitors is lower than last year or vice versa. When the figures are bigger than +100 percent it means that the increase in July and August is higher then the total growth for the whole year and that means a decline in the months outside the two peak months. For instance, in 1998 in Denmark as a whole, the growth in the peak season counts for 1752 percent of total growth. That covers up for an increase in peak season at 20.900 visitors while the total growth in 1996/1997 only was 1193.

Table 2: Number of Visitors in July and August as Percentage of Total Number of Visitors.

Region (county)	1989	1990	1991	1992	1993	1994	1995	1996	1997	1998
Copenhagen City	21	21	22	22	22	22	20	21	21	21
Copenhagen County	20	21	20	22	22	21	19	21	21	20
Frederiksborg	22	22	22	22	23	22	21	23	23	23
Roskilde	20	21	20	20	19	19	17	19	22	20
West Zealand	15	16	17	18	17	18	17	17	21	22
Storstoms County	27	28	28	31	27	27	27	28	28	30
Bornholms	46	43	43	45	42	41	41	43	45	47
Fyns	19	20	21	22	22	21	20	21	21	21
Ribe	25	25	27	27	27	25	25	25	24	25
Southern Jutlands	27	26	28	29	29	28	27	28	28	27
Vejle	20	20	22	22	21	20	20	20	20	22
Århus	22	21	23	23	23	22	21	21	21	22
Ringkobing	23	23	25	25	24	24	24	24	23	24
Viborg	24	24	25	27	27	24	24	25	25	26
Northern Jutlands	28	27	29	29	28	29	28	28	28	28
Denmark	24	24	25	25	24	24	23	24	24	24

The only relation possible to detect is the fact that most figures are positive, i.e., an increase (decrease) for the total year usually follows on an increase (decrease) in the peak season.

This feature is further examined by relating the increase (decrease) in July and August with the increase (decrease) in the rest of the year. There is a positive correlation between the two set of figures (not displayed in this chapter). The coefficient of correlation is 0.48 for the country and varies from 0.0 to 0.87 in the different regions. For the most visited regions the coefficient is round 0.50. This is a rather moderate correlation. Actually, almost one third of the figures, has different trends in the peak season and in the rest of the year.

This is a substantial indication of what is mentioned above: On the margin, the demand patterns in relation to peak season and the other seasons varies very much from one year to the next. An increase in the total number of visitors to the country is usually followed by an increase in all months. But the correlation between the total increase in the number of visitors and the corresponding increase in the different months and regions is very weak. So, on the margin it seems like every month is having it own pattern of demand (the exception is that there is a strong correlation between July and August and so there is one demand pattern for the peak season).

11. Seasonality Indicator and Gini-Coefficient

In Tables 4 and 5 the seasonality indicators and the Gini-coefficients are displayed for all regions during the observed period.

Table 3: Increase in the Number of Visitors in July and August Related to the Total Increase in Visitors During the Year.

	1989/ 1990	1990/ 1991	1991/ 1992	1992/ 1993	1993/ 1994	1994/ 1995	1995/ 1996	1996/ 1997	1997/ 1998
Copenhagen City	19	10	39	−33	23	−38	36	−349	−22
Copenhagen county	30	33	142	24	−1	−64	34	−77	−19
Frederiksborg	18	22	4	14	7	16	45	29	40
Roskilde	44	17	23	−30	16	−92	170	−150	−21
West Zealand	21	−62	11	−73	−87	0	11	−258	45
Storstom	34	30	−73	−55	34	26	8	2	−14
Bornholms	19	37	21	68	−29	35	−3	83	−27
Fyns	35	32	57	−5	8	−56	26	12	31
Ribe	32	36	117	50	−16	27	61	60	36
Southern Jutl.	142	47	9	21	−8	20	47	21	3
Vejle	20	58	14	−18	17	10	23	34	21
Århus	−10	49	22	32	7	14	22	21	54
Ringkobing	3	123	31	39	−96	62	20	−130	11
Viborg	25	31	44	19	−155	−6	28	11	57
Northern Jutland	123	46	27	62	800	−63	31	35	−46
Denmark	19	47	47	81	13	−12	36	1752	25

As expected the seasonality indicators are lowest and the Gini-coefficients biggest in typical summer holiday regions.

For both measurements, there is very little variation during the time, as indicated by the coefficient of variation in the last column. That confirms that the seasonal patterns are rather stable, just as the figures in Appendix A show.

The tables also answer the question whether there has been a seasonality extension or concentration. The answer is no. There has been neither extension nor concentration. There was a greater extension (low Gini value) in 1995 than in 1992. But the difference is small and looking at the entire span of 10 years there seems no substantial move in any region.

As expected the values of ω and Gini varies from region to region. Four regions with many summer holiday guests have Gini-values greater than 0.2, i.e., high degree of seasonality. Another four regions with rather few visitors all have values below 0.15. Also the regions in the capital area have low values, i.e., the four regions at the top of the table. Here the value is 0.13–0.15. That expresses a low degree of seasonality so the capital is not heavily dependent on summer holiday visitors.

Looking at the different regions, the coefficient of variation also varies, which means that the degree of stability varies accordingly. The figures give no evidence for the causes of this by no mean insignificant difference.

So the variations are marginal, but they are not randomly distributed over time and between the regions. In 1992, for instance, we can see a moderate concentration of

Table 4: Seasonality Indicators.

Region (County)	1989	1990	1991	1992	1993	1994	1995	1996	1997	1998	Mean	STD	Coeff. of var.
Copenhagen City	0.74	0.74	0.70	0.68	0.73	0.72	0.77	0.75	0.76	0.76	0.73	0.026	0.036
Cop. County	0.68	0.74	0.72	0.72	0.70	0.70	0.80	0.72	0.73	0.75	0.73	0.031	0.043
Frederiksborg	0.72	0.68	0.68	0.73	0.71	0.76	0.78	0.70	0.67	0.73	0.72	0.033	0.046
Roskilde	0.68	0.65	0.76	0.78	0.80	0.79	0.77	0.72	0.70	0.74	0.74	0.048	0.065
West Zealand	0.74	0.76	0.81	0.84	0.77	0.82	0.83	0.85	0.77	0.75	0.79	0.038	0.049
Storstrom	0.59	0.57	0.56	0.52	0.55	0.60	0.55	0.53	0.58	0.54	0.56	0.027	0.048
Bornholms	0.36	0.37	0.37	0.35	0.36	0.40	0.38	0.35	0.36	0.34	0.37	0.016	0.044
Fyns	0.78	0.76	0.76	0.75	0.75	0.78	0.80	0.79	.078	0.73	0.77	0.019	0.025
Ribe	0.65	0.65	0.63	0.61	0.62	0.65	0.64	0.64	0.65	0.64	0.64	0.014	0.022
Southern Jutland	0.61	0.62	0.57	0.56	0.51	0.57	0.58	0.58	0.58	0.59	0.58	0.028	0.049
Vejle	0.71	0.76	0.73	0.77	0.76	0.78	0.79	0.83	0.78	0.73	0.77	0.032	0.042
Århus	0.72	0.77	0.77	0.72	0.69	0.77	0.78	0.76	0.76	0.76	0.74	0.031	0.041
Ringkobing	0.63	0.66	0.63	0.60	0.66	0.68	0.68	0.68	0.70	0.67	0.66	0.029	0.044
Viborg	0.66	0.64	0.64	0.57	0.55	0.65	0.63	0.64	0.64	0.63	0.62	0.035	0.056
Northern Jutland	0.55	0.57	0.53	0.53	0.52	0.51	0.52	0.52	0.54	0.54	0.53	0.016	0.030
Denmark	0.68	0.69	0.67	0.66	0.66	0.69	0.72	0.69	0.69	0.69	0.68	0.017	0.025

Note: STD = Standard deviation.

Table 5: Gini-coefficients.

Region (County)	1989	1990	1991	1992	1993	1994	1995	1996	1997	1998	Mean	STD	Coeff. of var.
Copenhagen City	0.13	0.13	0.14	0.14	0.14	0.14	0.12	0.13	0.13	0.12	0.13	0.01	0.07
Cop. County	0.14	0.14	0.13	0.13	0.14	0.15	0.10	0.12	0.12	0.11	0.13	0.01	0.11
Frederiksborg	0.13	0.16	0.15	0.14	0.14	0.14	0.13	0.16	0.16	0.15	0.15	0.01	0.07
Roskilde	0.14	0.17	0.11	0.12	0.12	0.12	0.12	0.13	0.13	0.12	0.13	0.02	0.13
West Zealand	0.12	0.12	0.09	0.09	0.10	0.09	0.10	0.09	0.12	0.13	0.10	0.01	0.14
Storstrom	0.19	0.22	0.24	0.28	0.21	0.21	0.20	0.22	0.22	0.22	0.22	0.02	0.10
Bornholm	0.55	0.55	0.55	0.55	0.52	0.50	0.48	0.50	0.51	0.54	0.53	0.02	0.05
Fyns	0.12	0.13	0.13	0.14	0.14	0.13	0.12	0.13	0.13	0.14	0.13	0.01	0.05
Ribe	0.17	0.18	0.17	0.18	0.18	0.16	0.18	0.17	0.16	0.17	0.17	0.01	0.04
Southern Jutland	0.19	0.21	0.21	0.22	0.23	0.21	0.20	.21	0.20	0.20	0.21	0.01	0.05
Vejle	0.12	0.12	0.12	0.13	0.13	0.13	0.11	0.11	0.12	0.13	0.12	0.01	0.05
Århus	0.13	0.12	0.15	0.14	0.14	0.13	0.12	0.12	0.12	0.13	0.13	0.01	0.08
Ringkobing	0.14	0.14	0.17	0.18	0.16	0.15	0.16	0.13	0.14	0.15	0.15	0.01	0.09
Viborg	0.16	0.16	0.16	0.17	0.18	0.16	0.15	0.16	0.16	0.17	0.16	0.01	0.05
Northern Jutland	0.21	0.20	0.23	0.23	0.21	0.23	0.21	0.22	0.22	0.21	0.22	0.01	0.04
Denmark	0.16	0.16	0.18	0.18	0.17	0.17	0.15	0.16	0.16	0.16	0.16	0.01	0.06

overnights in the peak season indicated by a relatively high Gini coefficient and similarly a relatively low seasonality indicator. And that goes for almost all regions. Similarly the concentration eased off in 1994 and in 1995 for the great majority of regions. That indicates again that marginal moves in demand are due to different demand patterns over the year.

It is in particular noteworthy that both measures show high stability. As an immediate assumption, it would be natural to expect that the weaknesses of the seasonality indicator resulted in greater fluctuations. Actually, in the computations, there are as well used a modified seasonality indicator for both July and August and not only July as the denominator in equation (10). This modification does not change the figures significantly, evidently because the demand patterns in the two peak months are very much alike.

However, the seasonality indicator as well as the Gini-coefficient is a simple expression for the degree of seasonality. But the figures may cover up for different kinds of development in different months. To examine that, the increase in the number of visitors in each month from 1989–1998 is displayed for all regions in Table 6.

For the country as such the increase in the number of visitors has been 25 percent from 1989–1998. Looking at the different regions, it is observed that they have had different kinds of development (column 13, all year) . The figures offer no possibility of general explanations. The holiday resorts have had uneven increases (for example Bornholm and Northern Jutland). Also the regions dominated by urban settlements with more than five percent of the visitors have had different growth. It is understandable that Copenhagen County has had an increase greater than that of Copenhagen City. It is partly because the capacity limit often is reached in the city and so the hotels in the neighbourhood are used. Particularly when Copenhagen hosts a major conference. Apart from that, the only explanation for the differences seems to be that there has been a different development in demand for different regions. So, the explanation must be related to the specific regions.

The second observation is the different development for different months. This is included in the time series model giving each month a parameter δ_i and is in that way not causing divergences from the estimated value.

Also these differences are difficult to explain in any other way than differences in demand. In general there is a high growth in March, July and October and low in May, February and November. It is even not possible to define seasons with more than one month tracing an identical course.

This feature is reflected in neither the seasonality indicator nor the Gini coefficient. That is because there is a parallel increase in the peak month (July) and in off-season months. That means that the fractiles for the different months are changing, but they are only substituting for one another.

So, the two tools for measuring tourism seasonality do only measure the unequal distribution of visitors during the year. They tell nothing about the patterns for the individual months and in that way they express a non-existing stability because they cover up for unequal monthly development.

CHESTER COLLEGE LIBRARY

Table 6: Increase in the Number of Visitors 1989–1998.

Index 1989=100	1	2	3	4	5	6	7	8	9	10	11	12	All year	Visitors pct.
Copenhagen City	119	123	138	113	104	123	124	120	124	133	130	136	123	27
Cop. County	136	140	173	122	106	119	147	121	138	135	134	153	132	6
Frederiksborg	97	89	122	105	103	111	120	105	111	113	101	96	107	3
Roskilde	150	136	146	130	126	154	169	118	144	102	123	116	133	1
West Zealand	124	103	126	96	103	128	203	137	108	100	103	101	117	2
Storstrom	137	139	128	141	103	119	140	149	114	127	114	93	127	5
Bornholms	87	123	112	165	84	82	96	90	74	133	116	111	91	4
Fyns	142	121	153	113	132	148	159	146	142	139	121	128	138	8
Ribe	135	127	138	156	132	135	136	142	131	156	135	144	139	4
Southern Jutland	119	97	105	115	99	111	107	122	126	122	104	118	112	4
Vejle	163	132	172	108	136	160	166	133	144	156	164	145	148	6
Århus	127	125	138	105	117	144	132	120	121	134	124	128	126	9
Ringkobing	140	110	105	124	88	114	125	104	97	121	101	95	110	4
Viborg	130	110	92	102	97	115	127	113	112	118	119	115	113	3
Northern Jutland	139	137	143	140	131	129	135	132	129	146	115	120	133	13
Denmark	130	124	138	119	111	124	131	122	122	134	124	127	125	100

12. Conclusions

The Empirical Study

There are two sets of conclusions: The first relates to the empirical study. The second relates to the overall question — is it possible to measure seasonality in a simple way?

In general, the seasonality pattern of Danish hotel overnights is very stable. The figures and most of the tables demonstrate this. In the observed period there are trends: an increase from 1989 until 1992, then a decline from 1992 to 1993 and since then an upward trend. The number of overnights was in 1998 for Denmark 25 percent above the 1989 level. With variations from region to region and from month to month this trend is reflected in the figures for overnights for all regions and months. So, the trend is not caused by a few regions or by some selected months. This feature is statistically significant.

Although there is in general a great stability in the seasonality pattern, there are important marginal movements. Because of their sizes they cannot be ignored. Further, the hotels are in many cases heavily dependent on the marginal demand. The contribution relies on their share of that margin. So, the customers included in this margin are often the targets for marketing efforts. Therefore, these marginal variations are of interest as is the overall picture of seasonality.

The differences between the estimated and the observed values for number of visitors are not simply randomly distributed around the curve. There are trends in seasonality behaviour. Some years in succession, there is a concentration, i.e., more distinct seasonality and vice versa.

This is almost the only common feature discovered during the analyses. The fluctuations vary from region to region and from month to month without any visible pattern. It has been examined whether marginal increase or decrease for the country and for each region is reflected in a similar move for each month. Neither is the case. It has been particularly tested whether the peak season is the driving force in the movements, but it is not. In some years the total number of visitors increases overall while the number of guests in the peak season declines, and vice versa.

This indicates that each season marginally has it own pattern of demand. Even given that it is not possible to define seasons as groups of months with similar development. Only July and August — the peak season — seem to be significantly correlated.

A very concrete conclusion is that there has neither been a seasonality extension nor a concentration during the observed period.

Thus the final conclusion apparently has to be that each month is different in different regions in terms of its own demand, albeit involving marginal changes. Some, but very few, of the variations can be related to local circumstances, such as calendar days, special events and closing down of hotels. The impression is that each region has a separate market for each month. As a consequence a policy for extending the season — which is an objective for almost all destinations in the temperate zones — must attract new visitors for the off-season. It is not an adequate policy to try to convince visitors in the peak season to prefer another time of the year, because off-season visitors belong to another tourism segment.

The Measures

The seasonality indicator and the Gini-coefficient are used as a measure for the distribution of visitors during the year. Both measures show a great stability and they are both suitable for demonstrating the importance of seasonal concentration and dispersion. But they are simple measures and they fail in regard to developments over different months. In the example, they mask important seasonality changes within the year. To counteract this, the measurement ought to be related to a picture with a curve of the season.

The coefficient of variation is used as a measure for monthly stability. By applying this tool it is proved that some months show greater stability than others. As far as empirical data are applicable to this purpose, the measure seems useful.

References

Bar-On, R. V. (1975). *Seasonality in Tourism.* London: Economist Intelligence Unit.

Baum, T. & Hagan, L. (1997). *Responses to Seasonality in Tourism: The Experiences of Peripheral Destinations*, Peripheral Area Tourism. International Tourism Research Conference. Bornholm 8–12 September 1997, Unit of Tourism Research at the Research Centre of Bornholm.

Butler, R. W. (1994). Seasonality in tourism; issues and problems. In Seaton, A. V. *et al., Tourism. The State and the Art* (pp. 332–339). Chichester: John Wiley and Sons.

Faché, W. (1994). Short break holidays. In Seaton, A. V. *et al., Tourism. The State and the Art* (pp. 459–467). Chichester: John Wiley and Sons.

Frechtling, D. C. (1996). *Practical Tourism Forecasting.* Oxford.

Hartl-Nielsen, A., Rømer Rassing, & Wanhill, S. (1997). *Survey of Visitors to Bornholm. July 1995–June 1996.* Research Centre of Bornholm.

Hjalager, A.-M. (1996). *Turismens Arbejdssammensætning.* Memorandum for the Ministry of Industry, Copenhagen.

King, W. (1999). *Measuring Inequality in Income Distribution.* Http://william-king.www.drexel.edu.

More, T. W. (1989). *Handbook of Business Forecasting.* London.

Rafn, T. (1995). *Turismens økonomiske Betydning for Bornholm.* Research Centre of Bornholm.

Research Centre of Bornholm (1995/1996). *Survey of Visitors to Bornholm*, database.

Seaton, A. V. (1994). Are relatives friends? Reassessing the VFR category in segmenting tourism markets. In A. V. Seaton, *et al.* (eds) *Tourism. The State and the Art* (pp. 316–321). Chichester: John Wiley and Sons.

Sorensen, N. K. (2001). *Modelling the Seasonality of Hotel Nights in Denmark by County and Nationality.* Chapter in this book.

Twinning-Ward, L. & Twinning-Ward, T. (1996). *Tourist Destination Development. The Case of Bornholm and Gotland.* Research Centre of Bornholm.

Wanhill, S. C. R. (1980). Tackling seasonality: A technical note. *International Journal of Tourism Management.*

Yacoumis, J. (1980). Tackling seasonality — the case of Sri Lanka. *International Journal of Tourism Management.*

Data:

Statistics Denmarks' database on tourism statistics. 1999
Record of visitors to 'Kattegatcentret' — a sea life attraction in Jutland. Data from 1997.

Appendix A

Hotel overnights in different regions 1989–1998.

Denmark

Copenhagen City

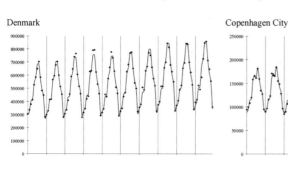

Copenhagen county

Frederiksborg

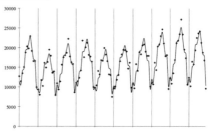
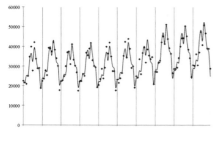

Roskilde

West Zealand

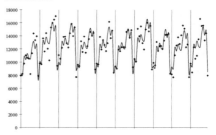
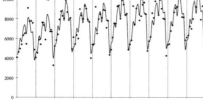

Storstrom

Bornholm

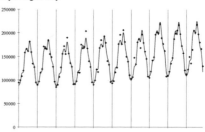

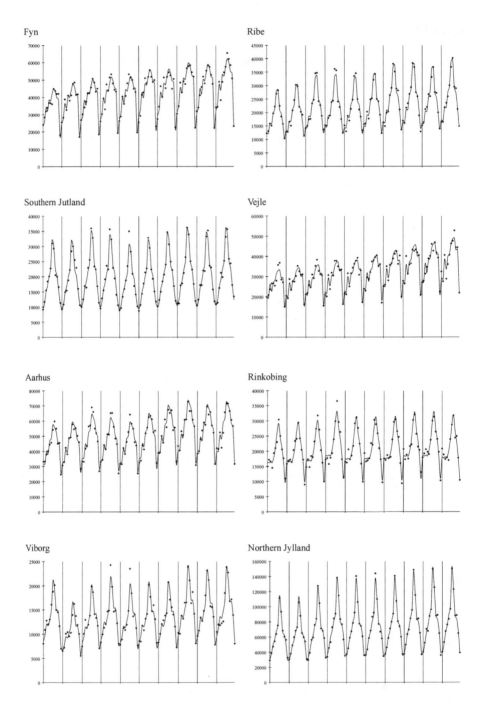

Note: The figures relate to hotels with more than 40 beds.
Source: Statistics Denmark.

Chapter 4

Seasonality in Irish Tourism, 1973–1995

Elizabeth Kennedy and James Deegan

Introduction

The improved performance of Irish tourism and its contribution to employment growth since 1987 can be attributed in part to a more focused concentration of government efforts, improved access transport policies, liberalization of air fares, more favourable external demand factors, and increased European input through structural funds and the resulting emphasis on tourism investment. A total of 5.534 million people visited Ireland during 1998, and figures show that 5.007 million visited in 1997. Consequently, the numbers have increased by eleven percent over the period.

This improved performance since the late 1980s, however, has failed to address adequately a long-term structural problem of Irish tourism, seasonality. The purpose of this paper is to provide a detailed analysis of seasonality in Irish tourism and in doing so to identify some salient policy issues that need to be addressed as a matter of priority. The structure is as follows. The first section provides a definition of seasonality in the Irish context, and outlines the nature of Ireland's main source markers. The next section discusses the seasonal distribution of overseas visitors to Ireland (1973 to 1995).[1] A brief discussion pertaining to the seasonal profile of the domestic market and regional distribution is also included in the analysis. The paper concludes with an outline of policy initiatives and implications of the trends for seasonality in Irish tourism.

A Statistical Profile

The importance of analysing seasonality in Irish tourism stems from the severity of the peaking of demand in July and August. Many businesses in Irish tourism experience long periods of low usage and short periods of high usage. These have implications for under-utilization and low profitability at one end and over-utilization of resources and congestion at the other. However, a review of the literature highlights a dearth of information pertaining to seasonality in Irish tourism and a consequent tack of understanding of the issues involved. This chapter seeks to bridge some of these gaps, with a view to providing

[1]The analysis begins in 1973 because this is the first year that comparable data are available.

This chapter was originally published in *Tourism Economics*, Vol. 5, No. 1 (March 1999).
© 1999 IP Publishing Ltd. Reproduced by permission.

suggestions for the amelioration of seasonality in Irish tourism. Various methods are taken to analyse the evidence of seasonality in Ireland and key areas addressed include: the absolute numbers arriving, the constituents of Ireland's major markets, and regions visited within Ireland. The major contributors to Irish tourism have changed over the last twenty-five years. This change in market mix has affected the seasonal profile of tourism in Ireland and the following discussion outlines the main causes of seasonality.

Defining Seasonality in the Irish Context

The definition of seasons (peak, shoulder and off-peak) has changed over the last decade due both to the evolutionary nature of tourism worldwide and to the changing nature of the market constituents of Irish tourism. This has resulted in numerous definitions being deployed for seasonality in the Irish context, particularly in terms of which months constitute different seasons. An international definition of seasonality as applied to the tourist industry asserts *that seasonality in the travel and tourism sector is usually seen in the strictest sense of peaking of demand at different times of the year.* In this definition, the peak and off-peak seasons were defined as July–August and November–April, respectively, while the shoulder seasons referred to the remaining four months. Due to the dispersion and increase in numbers of visitors arriving in Ireland in the different months, this definition is not adequate for analysing tourism in Ireland and there has been considerable debate on this issue in recent years.[2] These inconsistencies highlight the difficulty in defining and in resolving the seasonality problem. The difficulties in defining seasons on a monthly basis are compounded further by the way in which the data are collected.

The information used in the following analysis is based on official statistics from Bord Fáilte, including, for example, the Survey of Travellers (SOT),[3] in which the data are divided into eight monthly periods. Seasonality in Irish tourism is defined in this study using official Irish data. These definitions are generally accepted though not officially defined and are outlined in Table 1.

Table 1: Seasons Defined by Monthly Series for the Purpose of this Study.

Seasons Defined by Monthly Series for the Purpose of this Study

Seasons	Months
Peak Season	July, August
Shoulder Season	April, May, June, September
Off-Peak Season / Off-Season	October to March

[2]The peak season in Irish tourism was defined in the months of July and August until the 1990s. In the National Development Plan (1994, 1999), the peak season was redefined as July through to September but the Department of Tourism have since been advised to define the peak as only July and August (Department of Tourism and Trade, 1994b). The Operational Programme for Tourism (1994–99) defines October through to April as the off-peak.

[3]The SOT (administered since 1972) monitors the passenger flows through sea and airports of entry to the Republic (excluding cross-border traffic on a continuous basis throughout the year, administered through personal interviews. Minor modifications and improvements have been made to the surveying procedures since 1972.

Nature of Ireland's Main Markets: Visitors and Holidaymakers

Before assessing the seasonal distribution of Irish tourism (1973–95), it is important to ascertain growth patterns over the period coupled with the changing nature of Ireland's main source markets.

Overseas visitors are defined by Bord Fáilte as: "Tourists may visit Ireland for many reasons — some purely for holidays, others combine a holiday with visits to friends and relatives, while others may combine a business visit with a holiday." (Bord Fáilte, 1996a. 2)

Overseas holidaymakers are a subset of overseas visitors and are defined by Bord Fáilte as "those tourists whose purpose in visiting Ireland is for a holiday." (Bord Fáilte, 1996a. 2)

Between 1973 and 1995, the numbers of overseas visitior arrivals in Ireland increased frrom 1.28 million to 4.23 million, while the numbers on holiday alone increased from 1.14 million to 2.243 million, as illustrated in Figure 1.

Figure 4.1 outlines the phenomenol growth which occurred in Irish tourism between 1973 and 1995. Compared with relative stagnation in the 1970s, the total number of overseas visitors to Ireland increased by 119 percent between 1981 and 1984, from 1.680 million to 3.679 million (Deegan & Dineen, 1997). While much of this growth took place during the latter half of the period, the annual average growth rates for specific sub-periods are outlined in Figures 2 and 3.

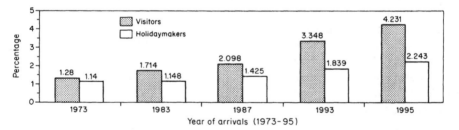

Figure 1: Arrivals of Overseas Visitors & Holidaymakers in Ireland, 1973–1995.
Source: Derived from Borde Fáilte data

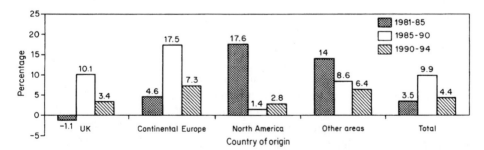

Figure 2: Annual Average Percentage Change in Overseas Visitor Numbers to Ireland by Country of Origin, 1981–1994.
Source: Deegan & Dineen, 1997

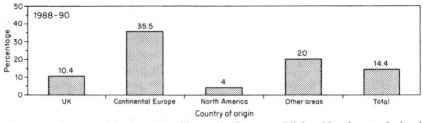

Figure 3: Annual Average Percentrage Change in Overseas Visitor Numbers to Ireland by
Country of Origin, 1988–1990.

Source: Deegan & Dineen, 1997

In 1995, overseas visitors to Ireland increased by 15 percent on the previous year (ITIC,
1996). Between 1994 and 1995, long-haul markets, assisted by developments in the peace
process, showed the greatest growth, with the North American market to Ireland growing by
30 percent and other long-haul markets (notably Australia and New Zealand) by 38 percent,
albeit from a low base. British visitor arrivals rose by twelve percent and that of mainland
Europe by eleven percent (Bord Fáilte, 1996). Given the data results and the evidence of
massive growth of number over the 22 year period in question, it is important to view the seas-
sonal trends of Ireland's major markets. Britain, the United States, Germany and France were
chosen for analysis because these countries constitute Ireland's major source markets.

The acceleration in overall growth rates is noted in the three-year interval 1988 to 1990,
with the compound average annual 15 percent growth rate target (equivalent to the doubling
of numbers over five years) set out in the Programme for National Recovery being almost
achieved during this period alone. These data are outlined in Figure 3, which also highlights
the phenomenal growth in visitors from continental Europe to Ireland over the period. The
evidence thus shows that there has been a significant increase in Continental European visitors to Ireland towards the end of the 1980s, while the number of visitors from North
America declined in relative terms up until 1994 (Deegan & Dineen, 1997).

Despite the recent decline in overall percentage share, Britain continues to be the most
important single market in terms of visitor numbers, accounting for more than half of the
arrivals (54%) in 1995, as shown previously in Figure 2. Over the same period the relative
importance of Continental European visitors has increased significantly and they now
account for one in four visitors. Due to rapid growth over the past two years, the US market
has recovered to represent 15 percent of total visitor arrivals in Ireland. It is important to note
that 1995 may have been an exceptional year for Irish tourism, which is not unrelated to the
"peace process". Table 2 outlines revenue figures from Ireland's major markets and shows
that while Britain constitutes Ireland's major market, Britain's contribution to Ireland's
foreign exchange earnings has declined from 32 percent in 1973 to 30 percent in 1995.

The table shows that North America's contribution to Ireland's foreign exchange earnings
has declined from 23 percent in 1973 to 16 percent in 1995, even though this market is the
country's second largest. The greatest growth has come from the mainland European market
whose contribution share has increased from a low base of eight percent in 1973 to 25 percent
in 1995. Both the British and mainland European markets have remained static since 1994 with
respect to their contribution to foreign exchange earnings, while the North American market
has gained two percent at the expense of the "other" overseas markets during the same period.

Table 2: Revenue of Ireland's Markets, 1973–1995.

Year	Total Revenue IR (£M)	Total Foreign Exchange Earnings IR (£M)	Britain's Share (%)	North America (%)	Mainland Europe (%)	Other (%)
1973	158.9	110.1	32	23	8	37
1983	804.2	520.3	25	24	12	39
1987	1021.7	731.0	29	22	14	40
1993	2008.7	1367.0	27	13	20	35
1994	2177.7	1497.0	30	14	25	31
1995	2302.2	1677.0	30	16	25	29

Source: Bord Fáilte Data

Table 3 summarizes the percentage distribution of Ireland's main markets in terms of numbers and revenues and shows that while British is our biggest market and accounts for 30 percent of revenue spent, revenue earned from the "rest of world" is substantial at 29 percent, particularly considering that arrivals from this market account for only six percent of all overall visitor numbers to Ireland.

In light of the above, the next section discusses the seasonal distribution of arrivals in Ireland over the period 1973 to 1995.

Seasonal Distribution of Arrivals in Ireland, 1973–1995

There has been a substantial change in the seasonal distribution of arrivals of all overseas visitors to Ireland over the 22-year period. Forty percent of all overseas visitors arrived in Ireland during the peak season in 1973. In 1995, 30 percent of overseas visitors arrived during July and August, representing the steady decline in peaking of demand over the period under discussion. At the same time, however, the actual number of overseas visitors arriving in Ireland on an annual basis has grown dramatically over the period. Figure 4 depicts these seasonal changes.

Table 3: Percentage Distribution in Ireland's Main Markets by Number of Visitors and Revenue, 1995.

Year	% of overall visitors	% of revenue spent
Britain	54	30
Mainland Europe	25	25
North America	15	16
Rest of world	6	29
Total	100	100

Source: Derived from Bord Fáilte data

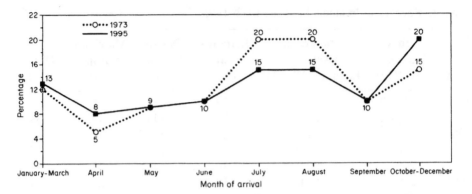

Figure 4: Seasonal Distribution of all Overseas Visitors Arrivals in Ireland, 1973 & 1975.
Source: Derived from Bord Fáilte data

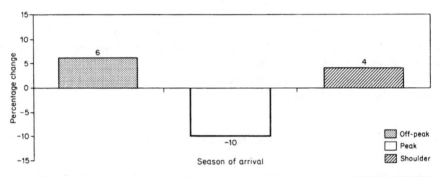

Figure 5: Change in Seasonal Distribution of all Overseas Arrivals 1973–1995 (%).

The percentage change in seasonal arrivals in Ireland between 1973 and 1995 is depicted in Figure 5 and shows that the off-peak months of October to December have gained most from this seasonal change. The figure illustrates that six percent more overseas visitors arrived in Ireland during the off-peak months and four percent more arrived in the shoulder months of 1995 than in 1973. Table 4 shows that this movement has been a gradual one during the period in question.

Table 4: Seasonal Distribution of Overseas Visitors Arivals in Ireland, 1973–1995.

	1973	1983	1995	% change 1973/1995
Off-peak (October–March)	27	28	33	↑6
Peak (July–August)	40	35	30	↓10
Shoulder (April–June/September)	33	37	37	↑4
Total	100	100	100	

Source: Derived from Bord Fáilte data

Table 4 shows that much of the movement in the 1970s and 1980s has been from the peak months to the shoulder months, while in the 1980s and 1990s the movement has been from the peak to the off-peak months. The percentage of overseas visitors arriving in the shoulder months has remained more or less static since 1983. While the peaking of demand has diminished, a substantial 30 percent of all visitors who arrived in Ireland did so between July and August in 1995. These visitors have a more significant impact on resources than the 40 percent who arrived during the same months in 1973, because absolute numbers have more than tripled in the 22-year period under observation. The changes that have taken place in the seasonal profile of Irish tourism and which are depicted in Figure 5 and Table 4 probably reflect international outbound trends and trends in Ireland's major tourism markets, rather than any Irish tourism policy. In light of these changes, it is interesting to question the effectiveness of any policy initiatives.

Seasonal Distribution of Visitor Arrivals by Major Origins

The seasonality of demand for overseas visitors thus appears to have been alleviated somewhat, falling from 40 percent in 1973 to 30 percent in 1995, albeit gradually. The data in this section have been recalculated to illustrate the percentage share of the contribution by overseas arrivals to the peaking of demand in July and August; they are weighted to take account of the numbers associated with each market. An example of how the weighting was achieved is given in Table 5 which shows how Britain contributed 67.4 percent to Ireland's peaking of demand in 1973, yet only 41 percent of British visitors arrived in Ireland between July and August 1973.

Table 6 (below) takes account of this weighting and highlights visitor arrivals in Ireland in July and August as a percentage of total visitor arrivals in those two months, by origin market, 1973–1995.

Table 5: Example of Weighting: Seasonal Distribution of Visitor Arrivals in Ireland.

Total UK Visitor Arrivals (1973) vs British British Peak Demand for Visitor Arrivals July/August (1973) **Arrivals in July/August (1973)**
= **67.4%**
1,284, 000 x 40% = 513,600

Seasonal Distribution of British Visitor Arrivals in Ireland. From the data presented in Table 6 it emerges that the British visitor market to Ireland was much less seasonally peaked in 1995 than 1973, with 26 percent of British visitors arriving between July and August compared with 41 percent in 1973. In 1995, of the total peaking of demand in July and August (30%), 47 percent of this figure can be attributed to peak British visitor arrivals. This figure is in stark contrast to the 1973 figure of 67.4 percent. Both of these figures are weighted to allow for numbers arriving in any given year. In 1973, 845,000 British overseas visitors arrived in Ireland and the respective figure for 1995 is 2.28 million. The yearly data in Table 6 shows

Table 6: Contribution of Visitors from Origin Markets to the Seasonal Distribution of Demand in Ireland, 1973–1995.

Year	Overseas visitor arrivals July & August %	Visitor Arrivals in Ireland July & August as a % of total visitor arrivals in July & August by origin market (1973–1995)[4]				
		Britain %	USA %	Germany %	France %	All other Overseas %
1973	40	67.4 (*41*)	16.0 (*36*)	5.2 (*51*)	3.2 (*48*)	8.2
1974	38	66.5 (*39*)	15.4 (*34*)	5.2 (*42*)	3.1 (*40*)	9.8
1975	39	61.7 (*38*)	16.6 (*38*)	6.3 (*50*)	3.9 (*46*)	11.5
1976	37	61.4 (*37*)	16.1 (*34*)	5.0 (*36*)	5.7 (*54*)	11.8
1977	38	58.8 (*38*)	16.2 (*34*)	5.9 (*43*)	5.3 (*45*)	13.8
1978	36	58.4 (*35*)	16.3 (*37*)	6.1 (*41*)	6.6 (*50*)	12.6
1979	33	60.0 (*33*)	15.2 (*34*)	7.4 (*43*)	6.0 (*38*)	11.4
1980	33	61.6 (*33*)	14.7 (*36*)	7.3 (*44*)	4.7 (*32*)	11.7
1981	32	56.2 (*30*)	17.6 (*38*)	7.5 (*45*)	4.2 (*25*)	14.5
1982	34	58.2 (*33*)	18.3 (*37*)	5.6 (*38*)	7.3 (*46*)	10.6
1983	35	57.7 (*33*)	17.6 (*37*)	6.1 (*40*)	4.7 (*35*)	13.9
1984	34	53.8 (*29*)	18.6 (*39*)	6.0 (*42*)	4.8 (*38*)	16.8
1985	32	52.2 (*29*)	22.0 (*35*)	5.2 (*33*)	6.7 (*44*)	13.9
1986	31	54.3 (*28*)	16.4 (*31*)	6.6 (*39*)	6.4 (*42*)	16.3
1987	30	55.0 (*28*)	16.9 (*29*)	6.3 (*39*)	5.9 (*33*)	15.9
1988	30	58.0 (*28*)	15.3 (*29*)	6.3 (*41*)	5.7 (*38*)	14.7
1989	30	55.0 (*27*)	13.2 (*29*)	6.5 (*36*)	5.9 (*36*)	19.4
1990	30	52.0 (*27*)	12.5 (*29*)	6.3 (*33*)	8.5 (*40*)	20.7
1991	30	49.5 (*26*)	10.8 (*31*)	7.5 (*34*)	8.6 (*36*)	23.6
1992	30	48.1 (*26*)	11.7 (*30*)	9.4 (*39*)	9.0 (*39*)	21.8
1993	31	44.7 (*25*)	12.2 (*31*)	9.4 (*29*)	9.1 (*39*)	27.6
1994	29	46.0 (*24*)	13.4 (*32*)	9.8 (*39*)	7.9 (*37*)	22.9
1995	30	47.0 (*26*)	17.6 (*38*)	9.8 (*39*)	7.0 (*38*)	18.6

Source: Derived from *Survey of Travellers* (various issues), Bord Fáilte; *Trends in Irish Tourism (1973–1989);* Bord Fáilte (1995a): *Perspectives on Irish Tourism, Markets, 1990–1994,* Bord Fáilte (1996b); *Tourism Pacts, 1995.* Bord Fáilte Eireann, Dublin, 1996.

that this decline in Britain's contribution to Ireland's peaking of demand problems was a gradual development. This table takes into account the absolute volume arriving from this

[4]The unweighted data (in brackets) outlines the trends in timing of arrival of Ireland's major origin markets and refers to the seasonal distribution of visitor arrivals in Ireland between July and August in any given year. The seasonal distribution of Italian visitor arrivals in Ireland is not yet available and so cannot be included in the analysis in Table 6 "All other overseas" refers to all other arrivals from countries other than Britain, the USA, France and Germany.

market. Even though the British market is least seasonally peaked, it contributes most to Ireland's seasonality problem because it constitutes an enormous share of overall visitor arrivals in Ireland. The British visitors accounted for over half of all visits to Ireland in 1995. This will have important implications in shaping the overall seasonality profile of Irish tourism from overseas markets.

Transport policies[5] and institutional reasons (i.e., changes in school holidays in Britain) may partly explain this improvement in the seasonal peaking of demand. In addition, Irish emigrants who are now working in Britain are in better paid and flexible jobs (paid leave) in Britain and are therefore, in a better position to return home more frequently throughout the year. Current international trends, including social factors, current lifestyle habits and expectations, are conducive to more frequent year round travel demand. Also, the increased number of business passengers to Ireland over the period was seen to contribute to the overall spreading of arrivals in Ireland since these travellers, by their nature, travel to Ireland outside of the peak season. VFRs constitute approximately 50 percent of the British visitor market. Weekend breaks are also very popular, for example, stag-nights in Dublin. This type of demand assists in alleviating seasonality. On balance, however, great care must be taken with any future policies which try to understand and influence the British market because of its absolute size.

Seasonal Distribution of US Visitor Arrivals in Ireland . From Table 6, it can be seen that the US[6] visitor market in Ireland is less seasonally peaked in 1994 than 1973, with 32 percent of US visitors arriving in July and August compared with 36 percent in 1973. However, the corresponding figure for 1995 is 38 percent. A number of important trends must be noted. In 1995, of the total peaking of demand in July and August (30%), 17.6 percent can be attributed to peak US visitor arrivals. This figure corresponds to the 1973 figure of 16 percent and highlights the fact that there has not been any major movement in the seasonal distribution of US visitor arrivals in Ireland when the two years are compared. However, if 1994 figures are taken, Table 6 shows that the US visitor market contributed 13.4 percent to the overall peaking of demand, substantially less than the 1973 figure of 16 percent. In 1973, 227,000 US visitors arrived in Ireland and the respective figure for 1994 was 449,000 with 587,000 arriving in 1995. Hence the size of the US market in Ireland proportionately affects the degree to which it contributes to Ireland's seasonality problem. This of course is true for every market.

Table 6 shows that the change in 1985–86 saw a relatively large improvement in the seasonal dispersion of US visitors to Ireland. This continued in the late 1980s and 1990s, but the percentage of US visitors arriving in July and August increased to 38 percent in 1995, close to the level in 1984 (39%). In 1995, 38 percent of US visitors arrived in Ireland during the July–August period and, in the same year, they accounced for 17.6 percent of the total peaking of demand, compared with an average of twelve percent for 1992 to 1994. The increase in the

[5]Transport policies include liberalization of air fares, improvements in surface and air transports in terms of more departure and arrival points, increased frequency, capacity and real prices.
[6]For the purpose of this research it was decided to analyse the US market because it constitutes over 92 percent of the North American market, and the small Canadian market is so extremely peaked it would distort the overall data. Possibly, the main reason for the peaking of Canadian demand is lack of access transport outside the peak season.

overall volume of arrivals in 1995 is partly attributable to the IRA cease-fire and the media coverage which accompanied it. In addition, the US economy was performing well and in the absence of their involvement in wars (with the exception of Bosnia), the propensity to travel outbound increased, with 587,000 US visitors arriving in Ireland in 1995. White there is no definite trend in the seasonal distribution of US travellers, the figures demonstrate a critical concern for the sustainability of Irish tourism. While there have been some improvements in the seasonal distribution of US visitors to Ireland and their contribution to the seasonality problem from 1985 to 1991, there has been a growing trend towards contributing more to Ireland's seasonal peaking of demand since then. This contribution reached an all-time high in 1995.

Seasonal Distribution of Visitors from Mainland Europe. In 1973, the Federal Republic of Germany (FRG) constituted 4.1 percent of total overseas visitors to Ireland. This had increased to 7.5 percent in 1995 (for a unified Germany). Whereas 2.6 percent of total overseas visitors to Ireland originated in France in 1973, by 1995, French visitors accounted for 5.5 percent of Ireland's total overseas market. Throughout the 1970s and 1980s, the share held by the two markets alternated. Since 1991, the percentage share of the German market to Ireland's total arrivals has been higher than the French market. The German outbound market exhibits a broad seasonal spread. On average German visitors to Ireland have contributed more to Ireland's foreign exchange earnings than French visitors to Ireland.

An analysis of the data in Table 6 demonstrates that the German market is less seasonally peaked in both 1995 and 1994 when compared with 1973 arrivals (i.e. 39 percent compared with 51 percent). However, in 1995, due to the increased number of Germans arriving in Ireland, of the total peaking of demand occurring in July and August (30%), 9.3 percent can be attributed to peak German visitor arrivals. This figure is in stark contrast to the 1973 figure of 5.2 percent. In 1973, 53,000 Germans arrived in Ireland and the respective figure for 1995 is 319,000. Consequently while the seasonal peaking of arrivals of the German market has declined somewhat (albeit sporadically), German visitors contribute more to Ireland's seasonality problem than at any time in the past. This is due to the overall numbers arriving. While there has been a significant overall reduction in the peaking of demand from 51 percent in 1973 to 39 percent in 1995, the change has been slow, inconsistent and haphazard. Notwithstanding this, Germany's percentage share contribution to seasonality in Irish tourism from overseas has increased significantly since 1990. The Germans have a high propensity to travel abroad and, more importantly, a high propensity to travel year-round. These trends are not reflected in the statistics. Thus, policy urgently needs to address the issue of peaking of demand of the German market.

Taking the unweighted seasonal distribution of French visitor arrivals to Ireland in July and August, outlined in Table 6, the overall reduction in peaking of demand between 1973 and 1995 fell from 48 percent to 38 percent. While the seasonal profile of the market has improved, this figure has fluctuated throughout the period somewhat similarly to that of the German market. Table 4.6 shows that French visitors contributed 7.1 percent to the peaking of demand in 1995. compared to 3.2 percent in 1973. Consequently, French visitors' contribution to Ireland's seasonality problem has more than doubled over the 22-year period. In 1973, 34,000 French visitors arrived in Ireland, compared with 234,000 in 1995. Also their contribution to Ireland's seasonality problem is by no means consistent, and this makes it difficult for policy makers to ascertain a definitive explanation for the pattern of demand.

Perhaps the dissatisfaction with passenger ferries in the 1980s has had a role to play in the differences which have occurred in the seasonal peaking of demand of both Germany and France. This dissatisfaction was related to inadequate capacity and poor quality in the mid-1980s. The increase in air traffic on the Continental European routes does not appear to have made a dramatic improvement in the seasonal distribution of European visitors to Ireland. These markets have not shown dramatic improvements in associated seasonal distribution since the mid-1980s, in line with their rate of growth in volume. Hence there have been improvements in most markets in terms of seasonal spreading, but the real problem of seasonality is caused simply by the sheer volume of numbers. This would imply that policy growth should be aimed only at those who travel off-season. A number of other factors are also outlined below.

Seasonal Distribution of all Other Overseas' Visitor Arrivals in Ireland. The origin mix of the "all other overseas" market has changed considerably between 1973 and 1995. Table 6 demonstrates that in 1973 this market contributed 8.2 percent to the seasonal peaking of demand. By 1995, this had more than doubled to 18.6 percent. It is very difficult to outline which country within this segment has contributed most to seasonal peaking of demand of Irish tourism since the 1970s because the constituents (i.e., arrivals from different countries of origin) of the market have changed constantly throughout. With such restrictive data one must look at the global travel behaviour of Irish source markets. For example, it has only been since 1992 that the Japanese market has reached the quota for inclusion in the *Survey of Travellers* (SOT). While it is difficult to speculate to what extent the Japanese arrivals contribute to the seasonal peaking of demand of Irish tourism, they do nevertheless tend to travel to Europe in the months between September and November and in February and March, and so they should assist in alleviating the problem of seasonality, even if only to a very small extent. The Italian market is highly seasonal (59 percent arriving in July and August in 1995) and, even though it is small, the volume has been contributing to Ireland's seasonal peaking of demand.

Implications of the Data for Seasonal Trends: Overseas Visitors to Ireland. Between 1973 and 1995 overseas visitor arrivals to Ireland during July and August have shown a 25 percent drop from 40 percent to 30 percent. In conjunction with this change, Ireland's major markets have also seen a decline in their contribution to Ireland's peaking of demand. Given the reasonable assumption that the seasonal distribution of all overseas arrivals in Ireland is spread across all markets and given that the expected value of a proportionate 25 percent decline in the seasonal peaking of demand is also spread across all markets, it is important to ascertain the degree to which each market is performing relative to this overall decline in peaking of demand. Table 7 shows expected and observed values of seasonal distribution of overseas visitors to Ireland.

The Table contains data that are weighted to take account of numbers arriving from each market. Given the hypothesis, Table 7 demonstrates the change in Britain's contribution to Ireland's seasonality problem and shows that this is consistent with the overall position since there is no significant difference between observed and expected values. The seasonal peaking of demand by the British market has been consistent in proportion to the overall trends throughout the period.

Table 7: Seasonal Distribution of Overseas Visitor Arrivals: Expected and Observed Values, 1973–1995 (weighted data).

Overseas visitor arrivals	Expected	Observed
British	51	47.0
USA (1995)	12	17.6
USA (1994)	12	13.4
Germany	4	9.8
France	2	7.0
All other overseas (1995)	6	18.6
All other overseas (1994)	6	22.9

Source: Derived from Bord Fáilte data.

For the US market there has been a significant difference between expected and observed values for 1995, as depicted in Table 7, with the seasonal distribution of the US market substantially more peaked in 1995 than would otherwise he expected, given the assumption. Taking 1994 figures, the US market is less peaked relative to overall average trends. The US pattern of arrivals to Ireland has fluctuated between 1973 and 1995. This market has been performing favourably (ie less seasonally peaked) with respect to the seasonal distribution of arrivals between 1989 and 1993. However, much of the low seasonal peaking during this time might be due to the lull in arrivals and Ireland's poor performance in attracting Americans during the period.

The German and French markets are extremely peaked. This is due to changes in the overall numbers arriving which amounted to 319,00 and 234,000 respectively in 1995, compared to 53,000 and 34,000 respectively arriving in 1973. Perhaps the greatest change can be seen in the "all other overseas" market, whose seasonal distribution was three times more peaked in 1994 and almost four times more peaked in 1995 than would otherwise be expected given the assumption. Perhaps this is the result of generic marketing which specifically fails to give substantial representation to holidaying in Ireland during the off-season. Table 8 below summarizes the differences which have taken place in the seasonal distribution of visitor arrivals in Ireland (the data are not weighted to take account of numbers).

Table 8: Seasonal Distribution of Visitor Arrivals in Ireland (expected and observed values), 1973–1995 (unweighted data).

Overseas visitors arrivals	Expected	Observed
British	31	26
USA (1995)	27	38
USA (1994)	27	32
Germany	38	39
France	36	38

Source: Derived from Bord Fáilte data.

Given the hypothesis that the 25 percent reduction in the seasonal peaking of demand is spread across all markets, the seasonal distribution of the British market should be 31 percent. This figure, however, is lower than the expected value which shows that the British market is performing satisfactorily with respect to its seasonal pattern of arrivals in Ireland. While the British market has performed a little better than the assumptions suggest, visitors from Britain are not as likely to travel throughout the country. In 1994, 41 percent of British visitors to Ireland were concentrated in Dublin, 21 percent in the South West, while only 15 percent visited the Mid-West (ITIC, 1996a).

Further to the hypothesis and the overall reduction of 25 percent in the peaking of demand, seasonal peaking for the US visitor market should have been 27 percent but was actually at 38 percent in 1995 and 32 percent in 1994. The observed seasonal distribution of visitor arrivals from Germany and France is exactly what one would expect in terms of seasonal distribution, given the assumption. It is important to discuss these data in conjunction with the projected criteria in the latest Operation Programme for Tourism (1994–1999) which proposed to:

> "… concentrate growth in the shoulder/off-peak periods so that by 1999, 75 per cent *of* visitors will arrive to Ireland outside the July/August season, compared with 70 percent at present."

In other words, the Operational Programme projects that by 1999 only 25 percent of over-seas visitors to Ireland will arrive during the months of July and August, compared with 30 percent at present. When the data are analysed between 1973 and 2005, using the "half life concept" (see Table 9), one would expect there to be great movements in the initial period.

Taking the data in eight yearly periods, between 1973 and 1981, the seasonal distribution of arrivals fell from 40 percent arriving in the peak to 32 percent, as expected. With consistent policy the seasonal distribution of arrivals in Ireland should have changed from 32 percent to 28 percent between 1981 and 1989. However, during this time the percentage of visitors arriving in the peak months never fell below 30 percent. Using the hypothesis that any changes in the seasonal distribution of arrivals is spread across markets, between 1989 and 1997 the seasonal distribution of arrivals should have reached 26 percent, and by the year 2000 it should reach 24 percent. However, since 1989, the distribution of seasonal arrivals in Ireland in the peak season has fluctuated between 29 percent and 30 percent.

Table 9: "Half Life Concept" (over 32 years): Percentage of Overseas Visitors Arriving in Ireland between July and August, 1973–2005.

First year		Mid-term				
		Final year				
40%	32%	**28%**	26%	25%	24%	22%
1973	**1981**	**1989**	**1997**	**1999**	**2000**	**2005**
1 Year	**8 years**		**16 years**		**24 years**	
		32 years				

Projecting onwards, using the "half life concept", by the year 2000 the seasonal distribution of arrivals should be at 24 percent, and 22 percent by 2005. This would correspond favourably with the projected 25 percent (to arrive in the peak season in 1999) outlined in the Operational Programme for Tourism (1994–99). However, due to the period of stagnation which occurred in the seasonal distribution of arrivals in the late 1980s and early 1990s, the problem required a more structured approach.

In summary, the above evidence shows that the British market has been contributing less to Ireland's seasonality problems. However, since it is Ireland's largest overseas market, Britain still contributes the most to Ireland's peaking of demand problems. On the other hand, the US market was actually more peaked in 1995 than in 1973 (17.6% compared with 16%). Both the German and French markets have more than doubled their respective percentage contribution to Ireland's seasonality problem. The "all other overseas" market accounts for an increasing share of seasonality in Irish tourism, reaching a record high of 27.6 percent in 1993. In light of the fact that the overall seasonal profile of Ireland's tourism industry has improved since 1973, this raises the question of what caused this improvement, and whether the answer lies with demand-side or supply-side considerations or with a combination of both.

Change in the Market Mix of Visitor Arrivals in Ireland and Seasonality

It is important to ascertain whether there is any relationship between the seasonal trends of Ireland's major source markets and the change in Ireland's market dependencies as a percentage of the total number of visitor arrivals in Ireland in a given year (see Table 10).

Yearly data indicate that British visitors arriving in Ireland contributed 53.3 percent of the total volume of visitors to Ireland in 1995, which is a fall of 12.5 percent since 1973. The former figure represents an all-time low and highlights the growing significance of Ireland's other main markets. The data are summarized in Table 11 and are weighted to take account of the proportionate share of each market in the given years, as outlined.

The composition of Ireland's market share has altered considerably throughout the period. However, the change in the market mix of visitor arrivals does not portray any clear discernible trend which would indicate that this is the main explanatory factor for the overall improvement in seasonality. Table 11 illustrates that between 1973 and 1979 the percentage of overseas visitors arriving in Ireland between July and August declined from an average of 37.3 percent, to 30 percent between 1989 and 1995.

Table 10: Example of Weighting: Visitors by Market as a Percentage of Total Visitors.

Total British visitor arrivals (1973)		
Total visitors overseas (1973)		
845,000	=	**65.8%**
1,284,000		

Table 11: Market Mix of Visitor Arrivals in Ireland and Seasonality, 1973–1995.

Years	Overseas Arrivals in July & August %	Origin market to Ireland as an average of Ireland's total number of visitor arrivals (%) (1973–1995)			
		British %	**North America %**	**Continental Europe %**	**All other overseas %**
1973–79	37,3	62.0	15.8	15.8	2.9
1980–87	33.0	60.3	18.1	18.0	3.7
1988–95	30.0	57.3	14.2	24.8	3.8

Source: Derived from Bord Fáilte: *Survey of Travellers* (various issues); Bord Fáilte: *Trends in Irish Tourism (1973–1989),* Bord Fáilte: *Perspectives in Irish Tourism: Markets 1990–1994,* Bord Fáilte (1996b): *Tourism Facts (1995)*

The only country experiencing a drop in market share was Britain (Ireland's highest volume market). However, the seasonality profile of British visitors has improved in line with the overall seasonality of Irish tourism. As already outlined, there has been an overall improvement in the seasonal dispersion of German and French visitors to Ireland.[7] This has contributed to reducing the overall seasonality in Irish tourism from overseas markets and has coincided with a dramatic growth in the market share of arrivals from "all other overseas"; a market characterized as very seasonal.

Any analysis of the seasonal distribution of tourism warrants the inclusion of a discussion on the domestic market. Typically peaked, worldwide, the Irish domestic market is particularly peaked towards the months of July and August.

Seasonal Distribution of the Domestic Holiday Market

Though it is often posited that the domestic market is underestimated due to data collection deficiencies, the size of this market is still very significant. It is estimated that in 1994 7.42 million trips were taken by the domestic market, 3.12 million of which were holidays and 2.84 million VFR trips. Much of the rest of the market can be accounted for by business trips. The seasonal spread of domestic tourism is more difficult to gauge than any other market but the estimates available show that Irish tourism is highly seasonal. This is illustrated in Figure 6.

The figure shows that August is the most popular month for domestic holidaymakers, accounting for 29 percent of all holidays in 1994, (Bord Fáilte, 1995a). Almost half of domestic holidays were taken in the peak months of July and August in 1994. Compelling reasons therefore exist for staggering school and work holidays in Ireland. At present, school holidays are not staggered and the implementation of such a policy is unlikely in the near future due to the power of the unions. Staggering could help to alleviate problems of

---

[7]The seasonal profile of German holidaymakers is more peaked than would otherwise be expected.

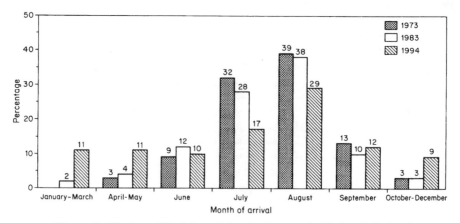

Figure 6: Timing of Holidays Taken by Domestic Market in Ireland.
Source: Derived from Bord Fáilte data.[8]

congestion experienced on Irish road networks in September and June. A large proportion of the construction ndustry still closes for the first two weeks of August, adding another dimension to the problem of seasonality. The trend of domestic holiday-taking in Ireland during the peak season months is as much due to traditional patterns as to institutional constraints.

One of the underlying causes of Ireland's seasonality problem is the age-old preoccupation with climate. Only 20 percent of domestic holidays were taken between October and March in 1994. This does not explain, however, the difference in seasonal patterns that occurs in other countries which have broadly similar weather conditions (e.g., Britain and the Netherlands) but which tend to have a better seasonal spread than Ireland. These countries have implemented strategic policies to stagger holidays and implement effective marketing campaigns, addressing both the demand and supply-side considerations. In many instances, the domestic market appears to have been ignored in areas of tourism research, particularly that pertaining to seasonality. However, the extent of holiday-taking by the indigenous market is substantial. When this is taken in conjunction with the seasonal pattern of holiday-taking (68% between June and September in 1994) it can be realized that it is perhaps the domestic market which contributes to the greatest peaking of demand in Ireland. However, clear improvements can be detected from the table.

Regional Distribution of Overseas Arrivals

Seasonal peaking of demand must also be analysed in terms of regional distribution and while this study does not concentrate specifically on this area, it is important to analyse the

---

[8]There is no figure to depict the off-season domestic market in 1973. Data pertaining to 1973 and 1983 relate to "long" holidays. 1994 data relate to all domestic holidays. In comparison with data pertaining to the seasonal distribution of other countries, the data for the domestic market is not robust.

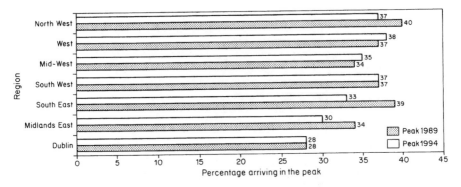

Figure 7: Regional Distribution of Holidaymakers in Ireland during July – August, 1989 & 1994.

Source: Data derived from ITIC (1996b)

regional disparities in the Irish case because of the differences that exist and their consequences. Figure 7 outlines the regional distribution of holidaymakers to Ireland during the peak season.

The Figure shows that the North West is seen to be the most peaked of the regions in 1989 with 40 percent of visitors travelling during July and August. However, this improved in 1994 with the shoulder months (May, June, September, October)[9] growing from 39 percent to 42 percent while the off-peak (November–April) remained unchanged and the peak months became less peaked, with 37 percent per cent arriving in 1994.

The Midlands/East and South East were seen to achieve a more even distribution. The South West resulted in greater peaking of demand than otherwise expected. The numbers arriving in the South East during the off-peak season, however, grew from 20 percent to 25 percent for the period, while the peak season in the Midland/East region was reduced with corresponding growth in the shoulder season. Seasonal distribution of numbers arriving in the West and Mid-West remained relatively unchanged. These regional trends of arrivals for 1994 can be seen more clearly in Figure 8.

Implications of Seasonal Trends for Irish Tourism by Major Market

The general trends discussed above suggest a favourable climate for promoting an effective tourism policy with respect to seasonal spreading across the tourism industry on an annual basis. This is because long-haul markets, for example, which showed an increased propensity to travel between 1994 and 1995, tend to be more evenly spread in terms of both time of arrival and geographical dispersion. Attention must be paid to the absolute numbers arriving and the control of them.

---

[9]Note the differences in seasonal definitions outlined by ITIC (1996a, 19996b) in their study on regional distributions.

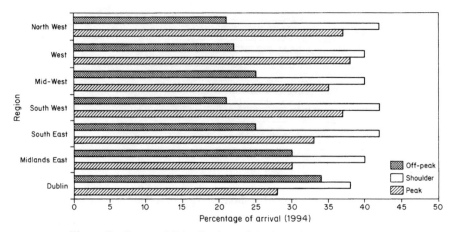

Figure 8: Seasonal Distribution of Arrivals by Region, 1994.
Source: Data derived from ITIC (1996b)

A number of criteria have been outlined for assessing the future of a sustainable development of the tourism industry in Ireland. These include absolute numbers arriving, expenditure of Ireland's major markets (per diem), length of stay, seasonality of arrivals and regional distribution. Attention should thus be paid to those markets that have a high propensity to travel out of the peak season, spend the most money per capita, stay the longest and travel throughout the country while they are here on holiday. In an Irish context this is represented by the following:

- British market, Ireland's largest market, is the most seasonally spread, spending an average of eight nights and accounting for 39 percent of total expenditure in 1995. This market was also highly concentrated in Dublin (41% in 1994) and the South West (21% in 1994). Only 15 percent of British visitors to Ireland in 1994 travelled to the Mid-West region. This could partly reflect the uncompetitive nature of the region's airport, compared with that of Dublin.
- Mainland Europe is Ireland's second biggest market, but it is also the most seasonally peaked. However, mainland European travellers tend to spend an average of twelve nights and they accounted for 32 percent of total overseas expenditure in 1995. Continental Europeans also have a high tendency to travel throughout the regions. In 1995 over 55 percent visited Dublin, while 40 percent and 35 percent visited the South West and West respectively. The high percentage share of arrivals in Dublin is accounted for by the large numbers arriving and departing through Dublin. Only 28 percent said they had travelled to the Mid-West (reflecting, among other things, the lack of access transport to the region).
- The North American market accounted for 21.4 percent of total overseas expenditure in 1995. They stayed on average ten to eleven nights in 1994 (this has since increased). Statistics for 1994 show that 64 percent travelled to Dublin, 44 percent travelled to the South West and 44 percent travelled to the Mid-West. The number of arrivals in Dublin and in the Mid-West is influenced by the use of Dublin and Shannon Airport as points of entry and exit, both of which are used interchangeably by Americans.

Review of Statistical Profile

From the above, attention needs to be paid to the mainland European market, which has the highest regional distribution and longest stay but which tends to be concentrated in the peak periods. However, as was illustrated in Figure 4, 38 percent of all visitors still arrived in the shoulder months in 1995. Marketing should focus on those markets in Europe which have a high propensity to travel year-round, namely the Dutch and Germans. The British also have a high seasonal distribution, relatively high expenditure (due to the numbers travelling) but tend to be concentrated in Dublin and have a short stay propensity. Both of these are inter-related due to the development of short breaks and city breaks. However, they are also indicative of the importance of access transport in alleviating regional and seasonal disparities.

Overview of Seasonality in Irish Tourism Policy

Formulation of tourism policy in Ireland historically has suffered from the absence of a strategic plan, and until the 1980s there was no formal attention paid to tourism. On balance, government policy on tourism until the 1990s appears to have been aimed at increasing profitability (as a means of recouping investment). Consequently, extension of the season was incidental (but complementary) to the achievement of this overall objective. Throughout the last forty years, numerous Irish government policy documents and statements have recognized the seasonality problem, yet little concrete action has been undertaken to alleviate it. Many of the strategies being discussed in the 1990s were addressed in the 1950s — a fact which highlights the lack of commitment to finding an adequate solution to the problem. The tourists who did visit Ireland until the 1980s appeared to do so without the stimulus of planned advertising or promotion campaigns.

While tourism policy in the early 1980s was criticized for its lack of clear objectives, the late 1980s saw the realization by government of the tourist industry's potential to make a significant contribution to economic and social development, in terms of export earnings and regional development and in the provision of employment Deegan & Dineen, 1992). Fortified by the availability of structural funds for tourism development through the European Regional Development Fund (ERDF), government authorities focused on tourism policy objectives for the first time in the late 1980s (National Development Plan, 1989–1993). Notwithstanding that fact, extension of the tourist season was not high on the government's attempts to reconstruct and build a successful tourist industry.

The first Operational Programme for Tourism (OP) 1989–93 was a milestone in the development of Irish tourism policy. Recognizing the importance of seasonality-engendered difficulties, the Programme did not, however, specify the reduction of seasonality as one of its main objectives. The lack of resources devoted to overall tourism policy formation and implementation curtailed the development of tourism in Ireland until the 1990s (SIS, 1992). The OP relied on a tripartite arrangement of public, private and European sector funds in the attainment of its objectives.[10] While the Operational Programme 1989–93 was seen as a success, in that many strategic targets were met, it did little to reduce the peaking of demand. In the OP, the government failed to give environmental considerations priority.

The unprecedented increase in overall numbers arriving in Ireland in the late 1980s and early 1990s was attributed by government authorities to the initiatives outlined in the first OP. Improvements which took place in tourism in the 1980s, however, were more a result of international developments (changes in consumer trends and the liberalization of air fares) than indigenous policies in the area. This attitude reflects the casual relationship which tends to exist between policy and performance in Irish tourism. The increased numbers of Europeans arriving, for example, were assisted by growth in second holidays across Europe and the renewed emphasis on the environment and quality tourism (Deegan, 1995). Justification for the improved performance in Irish tourism appears to emanate from a combination of international and indigenous factors. The arrival of air competition (through the introduction of Ryanair) and the huge reduction in fares that resulted from it, appear to have made a greater contribution to Irish tourism in two years than all the spending and effort that had gone into tourism promotion for many years previously. While this was the initial intention of the government, the changes in air transport legislation did realize growth in the Irish tourism industry throughout the year.

The close attention which the second Operational Programme for Tourism (1994–1999) has paid to the extension of the tourist industry in the government's latest economic programme is a welcome development. The second Operational Programme for Tourism (1994–1999) proposes a wide-ranging, integrated set of measures relating to key aspects of tourism development, which are designed to build upon the partnership between the European Union and the public and private sectors. The government's emphasis is on providing a high-quality tourism industry through the development of activity-based facilities (and special-interest holidays). Initiatives proposed for improving seasonality include the development of off-season events with international appeal and the marketing of tourist products suitable for year-round high-yield business (conference, incentive, quality, niche and activity markets).[11] Support was thus made available in the second OP for extending the season, expanding sea and air access and developing special-interest tourism, in the form of, for example, equestrian, language learning, cultural, heritage and angling holidays.[12] Cultural and heritage products were thus prioritized for development as one of the more popular forms of all-weather tourist facilities in the Irish product range.

The maximum aid rate for those attracting designated segments[13] in the peak season is 20 percent and in the off-peak season 50 percent. The programme states that it is necessary

---

[10]ERDF funds accounted for 53 percent of a total of £380 million compared with 17 percent given by the Irish exchequer.

[11]One of the main measures is to develop key aspects of the tourism product base with emphasis on developing a range of products for the high spending specialist segments of the international market.

[12]57 percent and 13 percent of the support came from EU funds and from the National Exchequer, respectively, the latter of which is lower than OP (1989–1993). However, the total investment of £652m shows that the Government is committed to the development of the tourism (Deegan: 1995).

[13]Access, product development, niche markets and high yield business, as outlined in the OP, 1994–99.

to identify specific marketing themes and to focus on the key objectives — season extension and access — both of which are inextricably linked. In the 1994–99 programme, marketing assistance, administered by Bord Fáilte (in consultation with the Department of Tourism and Trade, and public and private sector tourism interests) is to be given to those initiatives which aim to generate increased tourist traffic in the off-peak and shoulder seasons. Along with innovative, creative pricing and the development of quality products which enhance Ireland's attractiveness as a holiday destination on a year-round basis, extending the season will require target marketing. In addition to the normal range of Exchequer-assisted marketing activities, there is a separate measure in the new Programme to assist Bord Fáilte with initiatives to extend the tourism season (OP, 1994–1999).

The Overseas Tourism Marketing Initiative (OTMI), is a key element in the overseas marketing of Ireland in 1996. However, OTMI does not have a specific policy targeting those who are most amenable to travelling off-season. Perhaps all public sector marketing efforts could have been focused on selling the off-peak season only, rather than distributing the funds in generic marketing. In their attempts to improve the off-season domestic market, Danish authorities, for example, have devoted all their marketing efforts towards selling the off-season to those most amenable to travelling at that time (i.e., households without schoolchildren; seniors) (CEC, 1993a). On the other hand, some European countries have discovered that marketing the shoulder season has led to more numbers arriving in the peak season, resulting in the associated environmental problems of congestion (Deegan, 1995).

Congestion and environmental degradation are inextricably linked to seasonality. In this regard, EU authorities have placed emphasis on the staggering of school and work holidays as a means of alleviating seasonality-engendered problems. While EU pressure may have resulted in the development of discussions in this area at governmental level in Ireland, these talks may never develop into anything more than window-dressing initiatives to appease the European authorities. Irish education and industrial authorities are venomously opposed to the staggering of holidays and the power of unions serve to reinforce these oppositions (Department of Tourism and Trade, 1994).[14] While the latest OP does not address the "staggering" issue, its focus on seasonality incentives is nonetheless an important development.

Analysis of the first programme highlights that it did nothing to abate seasonality peaks and troughs. Access transport, product development and marketing incentives set out in the second OP aim to reduce the seasonal concentration of demand, The reduction of seasonality was cited as a major objective of the programme. In spite of this, the government does not appear to have a strategic plan specifically addressing the problems of seasonality. Development in the industry appears to be implemented in an *ad hoc* and uncoordinated fashion. The principal drawback of the second OP is the lack of attention it gives to the importance of the environment and the domestic tourism market. This is also a reiteration of the limited emphasis placed on those issues in the first OP. The latest OP and

---

[14]The absence of a representative from the Irish Department of Education at the "Staggering of School Holidays" Conference in 1994, serves to define this apathy.

Irish tourism policy have also failed to address the peaking of demand in certain regions and the ensuing regional imbalances which are taking place across the country. There is a widely held perception that the shift in regional distribution of tourists in recent years can be attributed to one determining factor — access. However, an analysis of available data has not proven conclusively that a direct causal relationship exists with any one factor which would account for the changes that have occurred (ITIC, 1996). The disparate regional performance is the result of a complex combination of factors, rather than a single cause (ITIC, 1996). The same report outlined six determinants which impact on regional distribution. These include access transport, mode and port of arrival, mobility within Ireland, length of stay, seasonality of demand, growth in city tourism and marketing, promotion and distribution. In addition, it suggested that investment in product and pricing strategy are factors that could not be substantiated directly from the data, though they do have an important role to play. This would suggest that all aspects of the industry are inextricably linked and it highlights the need for greater cooperation across all sectors.

The increasing concentration of arrivals through the East Coast gateways has had a major impact on changing travel patterns within Ireland. The growth of traffic on high-density scheduled air and sea services into Dublin/Dun Laoghaire has been largely driven by carrier strategy. The impact of concentration on access can he seen in the travel patterns of several important market segments. This is all the more obvious when combined with factors such as shorter lengths of stay, lower incidences of bringing a car to Ireland and a greater seasonal spread. The impact would appear to be most significant in respect to the regional dispersion of Europeans, the short break market from British and tour operators routing dual destinations for US visitors. Tour operators appear to have changed their gateway ports and itineraries to reflect the concentration of capacity into East Coast gateways. The cause of the downturn in British and Continental European holiday bed-nights in the South West and West can also be partly attributed to the relative decrease in share of arrivals by sea. While Dublin and its hinterland have been the main beneficiaries of increases in bed-nights from British holidaymakers, assisted further by growth in short break city tourism, the development appears to have benefited most regions but at varying rates of growth. The West and Mid-West regions would appear to have been losing a share of the growing concentration of European arrivals through Dublin Airport (ITIC, 1996).

Summary and Conclusions

While overall tourist numbers in Ireland are increasing, the historical profile of seasonality in Irish tourism highlights the lack of an effective, comprehensive governmental approach to the problem. There has been a traditional absence of year-round traffic to Ireland due to the cyclical nature of Ireland's major markets and the relative absence of significant promotional effort and resources to extend the season. Bord Fáilte acknowledges that a major deterrent has been the relative absence of significant resources to market off-season programmes and the consequent absence of knowledge or perception that such programmes and holiday opportunities exist (Bord Fáilte, 1994a). In 1992, Tansey Webster and Associates identified two major and related weaknesses in Ireland's tourism industry: excessive seasonality and low profitability. Without higher rates of return on tourism assets, the industry can neither attract new investment funds to the sector nor generate sufficient funds internally to finance investment programmes from own resources. The latest OP has paid much attention to these measures and is a welcome development. Despite the recent focus on seasonality, much remains to he achieved to secure the industry's future. One area which demands immediate attention is the problem with access transport. As an island economy, more direct and cost-effective year-round access is necessary to ensure that Ireland continues to increase its market share of the international tourist industry.

Despite the major investment in the industry and the phenomenal growth in numbers arriving and revenue earned, it has been only in the last two or three years that the Irish government has made any attempt to address the issue of seasonality in Irish tourism. In certain instances the awareness has come too late, and some areas are already suffering from saturation of resources during the peak season, notably the South West. A fundamental contradiction exists between promoting Ireland as a natural unspoilt destination and the growth of numbers arriving in Ireland during the peak months. The government must address this structural problem in a strategic fashion and not with the fragmented approach which has applied to date.

References

Bord Fáilte, (1996a). *Perspectives on Irish Tourism Markets 1991–1995*. Dublin: Bord Fáilte Eireann.

Bord Fáilte, (1995a). *Perspectives on Irish Tourism Markets 1990–1994*. Dublin: Bord Fáilte Eireann.

Bord Fáilte, (1996b). *Tourism Facts, 1995*. Dublin: Bord Fáilte Eireann.

Bord Fáilte, (1994a). *The Marketing Plan Framework 1994–1999*. Dublin: Bord Fáilte Eireann.

Bord Fáilte, (1990). *Trends in Irish Tourism, (1973–1989)*. Dublin: Bord Fáilte Eireann.

Bord Fáilte. *Survey of Overseas Travellers*, Various years, 1973–1995. Dublin: Bord Fáilte Eireann.

Bord Fáilte. *Tourism Facts*, various years, Dublin: Bord Fáilte Eireann.

Commission of the European Communities (1993). *The Experience of Products and Suitable Clientele for all Seasons Travel*, December, 1991. Report for the Tourism Unit of the BC Commission, DO XXIII, Luxembourg: Office for Official Publications of the European Community.

Deegan, J. (1995). Planning for Visitors. *Business and Finance,* December 21, 15–19.

Deegan, J. (1994). *Hospitality Delivers Jobs: The Tourism Dimension*, paper presented to The Irish Hotel and Catering Institute. National Conference. Cork, 21 October 1994.

Deegan, J., & Dineen, D. (1997). *Tourism Policy and Performance: The Irish Experience*. London: International Thomson Business Press.

Deegan, J., & Dineen, D. (1992). Tourism policy: Targets, outcomes and environmental considerations. In B. O'Connor & M. Cronin (eds) (pp. 115–117). *Tourism in Ireland: A Critical Analysis*. Cork: Cork University Press.

Department of Tourism & Trade (1994a). *Report of Conference on Staggering of Holidays*. Unpublished (internal).

Department of Tourism and Trade (l994b). *Memorandum by Tourism Council, 1994*. Unpublished (internal).

Ireland (1994). *National Development Plan. 1994–1999*. Ch. 6. Dublin: Stationery Office. 63 –68.

Ireland (1993). *Operational Programme for Tourism 1994–1999*. Dublin: Stationery Office.

Irish Tourism Industry Confederation (ITIC) (1996a). *Regional Distribution of Tourism in Ireland — Responding to Changing Market Trends*. Dublin: Tourism and Leisure Partners for ITIC.

Irish Tourism Industry Confederation (ITIC) (1996b). *Analysis of Regional Distribution of Overseas Tourism 1989–1994*. Dublin: Tourism Development International Ltd for ITIC.

McEniff, J. (1992). Seasonality of tourism demand in the EC. *EIU, Travel and Tourism Analyst, 3*, 67–88.

Structure Intermediare de Support (SIS) (1992). *Tourism and Regional Development in Ireland*. Report for the Commission of the European Communities (DCIXVI). Brussels: Structure Intermediare de Support.

Tansey, Webster and Associates (1992). *A Strategic Framework for Tourism Enterprises*. Dublin: Irish Tourist Industry Confederation.

Chapter 5

Modelling the Seasonality of Hotel Nights in Denmark by County and Nationality

Nils Karl Sørensen

Over the past few decades preferences for holidays have changed. Today people are more inclined to separate their holidays into several sub-periods, giving them the opportunity for summer as well as winter breaks. When people are on holiday, they consume accommodation such as residential house nights, camping nights, hotel nights, etc. Therefore, a change in their preferences should be reflected in the seasonal pattern of the type of accommodation under consideration. In the present case, the seasonal variation of hotel nights in Denmark will be examined.[1]

Such an analysis may be important for several reasons. Consider, as an example, the hotel demand for labour. During the peak season demand will be high, with an increasing wage rate, and off-season the unemployment rate will increase. In an economy with low mobility and partly public financed unemployment benefits, as is the case in Denmark, this situation is surely not optimal. Due to the lack of monthly labour market statistics for the sector, the presence of reliable monthly statistics on hotel nights provides the point of departure for the present analysis.[2]

This change in the preferences of holiday makers has not only occurred for Danes, but throughout the world. Consequently, the data set used on hotel nights for Denmark is divided into 13 different nationalities. In order to consider the regional dimension, data are divided into the counties of Denmark. The period examined ranges over nearly 30 years with monthly observations.

Traditionally, the seasonal variation has been modelled by assuming deterministic seasonality, i.e., setting up a simple univariate model in which the variation is explained by seasonal dummies. Implicitly this method assumes that the seasonal variation expressed by

---

[1]People using hotels are by definition tourists. However, the material presented in this analysis is *not* equivalent to an examination of the total Danish tourist nights. Tourism nights may take many forms other than hotel nights — for example, residential house nights, camping nights, etc. For a recent analysis of the impact of tourism at county level in Denmark, see T. Rafn, *Turismens økonomiske betydning for de danske amter*, Report 2/1996. Research Centre of Bornholm, Denmark, 1996 (in Danish); or T. Ahmt and L. Eriksen, *The Building of a Tourism Databank and a Regional Economic Tourism Model*, AKF Publishing, Denmark, 1997 (in Danish with an British Summary).

[2]The seasonal pattern of hotel nights can, for example, be related to input-output based coefficients on hotel demand for labour.

This chapter was originally published in *Tourism Economics*, Vol. 5, No. 1 (March 1999).
© 1999 IP Publishing Ltd. Reproduced by permission.

the estimates of the dummy variable coefficients is constant in time. However, this model-ling procedure may be inconsistent with the commonly used definition of seasonality in economics proposed in Hylleberg.[3] Here seasonality is defined as follows:

> Seasonality is the systematic, although not necessarily regular, intra-year movement caused by the changes of the weather, the calendar, and timing of decisions, directly or indirectly through the production and consumption decisions made by the agents of the economy. These decisions are influenced by endowments, the expectations and preferences of the agents, and the production techniques available in the economy.

If seasonality is *systematic*, and also *not regular* in nature, this should be reflected in the choice of the model used for analysing seasonality. The unit root model captures these features. Here seasonality is modelled in a stochastic manner. Hylleberg, Jørgensen and Sørensen,[4] for example, used this stochastic univariate approach, and examined a large number of quarterly and monthly macroeconomic time series covering many variables and OECD countries. They found that a varying and changing seasonal component is a common phenomenon in many time series.

The paper is organized as follows. The second section, below, presents a test for seasonal unit roots at the monthly frequency. The subsequent section is the empirical application. It also gives a description of the data set used and presents some graphical tools to accompany the analysis. In the final section, conclusions are drawn.

Theoretical Considerations[5]

A time series model with seasonal unit roots is an approximation that allows for changes in the seasonal pattern, ie integration at the seasonal frequencies. A test for seasonal unit roots in the quarterly case is developed by Hylleberg, Engle, Granger and Yoo,[6] and extended to the monthly case by Beaulieu and Miron[7] and Franses.[8]

[3]Hylleberg, S. (1986). *Seasonality in Regression*. New York: Academic Press.

[4]Hylleberg, S., Jørgensen, C. M. & Sørensen, N. K. (1993). Seasonality in macroeconomic time series. *Empirical Economics*, *18*, 321–335.

[5]This heading should be understood in an econometric sense. The present analysis is purely empirical, and no attempt is made to set up a theoretical model to explain preferences for choosing hotel nights over alternative types of nights during holidays and other stays. The present text is written especially with tourism economists in mind, with technical explanations kept to a minimum.

[6]Hylleberg, S., Engle, R. F., Granger, C. W. J., & Yoo, B. S. (1990). Seasonal integration and cointegration. *Journal of Econometrics*, *44*, 215–238.

[7]Beaulieu, J. J., & Miron, J. J. (1993). The seasonal cycle and the business cycle. *Journal of Political Economy*, *97*, 503–535.

[8]We rely here on Franses, who gives a more formal theoretical deviation of the test: P. H. Franses, *Model Selection and Seasonality in Time Series*, Tinbergen Institute Series No. 18, Thesis Publishers, Amsterdam, 1991. The test presented in this section is also known as the HEGY-test (see Hylleberg *et al., op cit*, Ref. 6).

For a given time series variable x_t a univariate model integrated at all the seasonal frequencies as well as the long-run frequency is $(1-B^{12})x_t = \epsilon_t \sim i.i.d(0,\sigma^2)$, $t = 1,2,..,T$, where B is the lag operator defined as $B^n x_t = x_{t-n}$. Franses[9] proved that an AR(p) process of the form $\phi(B)x_t = \epsilon_t$, using a proposition given in Hylleberg, Engle, Granger and Yoo[10] defining the form of $\phi(B)$, in the monthly case can be written as

$$(1 - B^{12})x_t = y_{8t} = \pi_1 y_{1t-1} + \pi_2 y_{2t-1} + \pi_3 y_{3t-1} + \pi_4 y_{4t-2}$$
$$+ \pi_5 y_{4t-1} + \pi_6 y_{4t-2} + \pi_7 y_{5t-1} + \pi_8 y_{5t-2}$$
$$+ \pi_9 y_{6t-1} + \pi_{10} y_{6t-2} + \pi_{11} y_{7t-1} + \pi_{12} y_{7t-2} + \phi^\Delta(B) y_{8t} + \mu_t + \epsilon_t \quad (1)$$

In this equation x_t is a linear combination of the variables y_i, $i=1,...,8$. These variables are all various transformations of x_t. In all there are 12 coefficients π_j, $j=1,...,12$ to be estimated by applying OLS to equation (1). The coefficients of the π's correspond to the 12 solutions of the equation $(1-B^{12})=0$ all lying on the unit cycle.

The test for monthly seasonal unit roots can then be performed as a test of whether or not the coefficients are lying on the unit cycle. There will be *no* seasonal unit root if the coefficient to a given π is significantly different from zero. If the coefficient is insignificant, a unit root is present showing a changing seasonal component.

Consider as an example a situation in which *all* the π's are significantly different from zero. Consequently, no seasonal unit roots are present, and the data have a deterministic or constant seasonal pattern. Only in this case is the dummy variable model appropriate; ie by applying the filter $(1-B^{12})$ the time series x_t, will become stationary.

The transformations y_i $i=1,...,8$ of x_t remove the seasonal unit roots at certain frequencies while preserving them at other frequencies. For example $y_{1t} = (1+B)(1+B^2)$ $(1+B^4+B^8)x_t = (1+B+B^2+.....+B^{11})x_t$ is a transformation which removes the seasonal unit roots and preserves the long-run or zero-frequency unit root.

The remaining transformations are $y_{2t} = -(1-B)(1+B^2)(1+B^4+B^8)x_t$, which preserves the frequency 6/12 corresponding to a six month period; $y_{3t} = -(1-B^2)(1+B^4+B^8)x_t$, which retains the frequency 3/12 (9/12) corresponding to a four month period; $y_{4t} = -(1-B^4)(1-\sqrt{3}B+B^2)(1+B^2+B^4)x_t$, which leaves behind the frequency 5/12 (7/12); while $y_{5t} = -(1-B^4)(1+\sqrt{3}B + B^2)(1+B^2+B^4)x_t$, $y_{6t} = -(1-B^4)(1-B+B^2)(1-B^2+B^4)x_t$, $y_{7t} = -(1-B^4)(1+B+B^2)(1-B^2+B^4)x_t$ retains the frequencies 1/12 (11/12), 4/12 (8/12) and 2/12 (10/12). Finally $y_{8t} = (1-B^{12})x_t$. A survey of the data transformations and test hypothesis is given in Table 1.

The test for seasonal unit roots at the relevant seasonal frequencies can then be performed either as t-tests for the estimates of $\pi_3,...,\pi_{12}$ or as joint F-tests for sets of parameters, ie π_3 and π_4 etc. The t-ratios corresponding to the estimates of π_1 and π_2 follow the Dickey-Fuller distributions. All critical values of the test have a non-standard distribution and have to be simulated by Monte Carlo experiments. Critical values are obtained from Franses and Hobijn.[11]

[9]Franses, *op cit*, Ref 8.
[10]Hylleberg *et al.*, *op cit*, Ref. 6.
[11]Franses, P. H., & Hobijn, B. (1997). Critical values for unit root tests in seasonal time series. *Journal of Applied Statistics, 24*, 25–47.

Table 1: Testing for Seasonal Unit Roots in Monthly Data.

No.	Frequency		Transformation	H_0: Unit Root	H_1: No Unit Root
0	0	long-run	$y_{1t} = (1+B+B^2+..+B^{11})x_t$	$\pi_1 = 0$	$\pi_1 < 0$
1	6/12	semi-annual	$y_{2t} = -(1-B)(1+B^2)(1+B^4+B^8)x_t$	$\pi_2 = 0$	$\pi_2 < 0$
2	3/12 (9/12)	quarterly	$y_{3t} = -(1-B^2)(1+B^4+B^8)x_t$	$\pi_3 \cap \pi_4 = 0$	$\pi_3 \cup \pi_4 \neq 0$
3	5/12 (7/12)	monthly	$y_{4t} = -(1-B^4)(1-3\sqrt{B}+B^2)(1+B^2+B^4)x_t$	$\pi_5 \cap \pi_6 = 0$	$\pi_5 \cup \pi_6 \neq 0$
4	1/12 (11/12)	monthly	$y_{5t} = -(1-B^4)(1+3\sqrt{B}+B^2)(1+B^2+B^4)x_t$	$\pi_7 \cap \pi_8 = 0$	$\pi_7 \cup \pi_8 \neq 0$
5	4/12 (8/12)	monthly	$y_{6t} = -(1-B^4)(1-B+B^2)(1-B^2+B^4)x_t$	$\pi_9 \cap \pi_{10} = 0$	$\pi_9 \cup \pi_{10} \neq 0$
6	2/12 (10/12)	monthly	$y_{7t} = -(1-B^4)(1+B+B^2)(1-B^2+B^4)x_t$	$\pi_{11} \cap \pi_{12} = 0$	$\pi_{11} \cup \pi_{12} \neq 0$

Note: Critical values can be obtained from Franses, P.H. & Hobijn, B. (1997), "Critical values for unit root tests in seasonal time series", *Journal of Applied Statistics*, 24, 25–47.

Equation (1) is an extension of the Dicky-Fuller auxiliary regression for a zero-frequency unit root with augmented lagged values of the left-hand side variable.

Finally, two more points concerning equation (1) should be made. First, μ_t is the included deterministic component such as a constant, a trend, and seasonal dummy variables. The test can be performed without these components, but the critical values will then change. Also, in this case critical values can be found in Franses.[12]

Second, equation (1) has to be augmented by lagged y_{8t}. This is done in order to make the residuals white noise, and leaves the asymptotic distribution unaffected. The power is negatively affected if too many nuisance parameters are used in the augmentation. In the present case, a strategy to determine $\phi^4(B)$ has been to start with 24 lags equalling two years, and then test down the significant augmented variables by carefully inspecting the test statistics for autocorrelation.

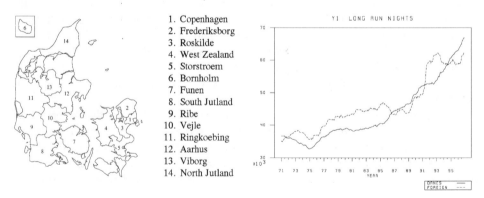

1. Copenhagen
2. Frederiksborg
3. Roskilde
4. West Zealand
5. Storstroem
6. Bornholm
7. Funen
8. South Jutland
9. Ribe
10. Vejle
11. Ringkoebing
12. Aarhus
13. Viborg
14. North Jutland

Figure 1: Counties of Denmark and Hotel Nights Attributable to Danes and Foreigners.

[12]Franses, *op cit*, Ref 8.

Testing for Seasonal Unit Roots in Danish Hotel Nights

A databank has been set up covering monthly series from 1970.1 to 1996.12 by use of material from the regular publications on hotel nights supplied by Statistics Denmark. All series contain 324 observations. Data are divided into 16 geographical areas (counties), and 14 different nationalities. Before 1970 the geographical areas of many counties of Denmark were different. A map with the geographical location of the counties of Denmark is provided in Figure 1 above.

In 1996 the total number of hotel nights in Denmark amounted to about 12.9 million, equivalent to an increase of about 80 percent since 1970. With regard to nationality, half the hotel nights are attributable to Danes, and half to foreign nationals. The graph in Figure 1 displays the long-run transformation y_{lt} of hotel nights by Danes (solid line) and foreigners respectively. The division of hotel nights between Danes and foreigners has remained relatively constant throughout the period. Notice also that the number of hotel nights has been affected by external events such as the slump in the mid-1970s. From the mid-1980s the pattern of hotel nights consumed by foreigners seems to have become more volatile, perhaps due to variations in taste or fluctuations in the exchange rate for some important foreign visitors. Tables 2 and 3 give some summary statistics.

Hotel Nights by County

From Table 2 below it can be seen that more than one-quarter of the hotel nights recorded are in the Copenhagen city area. Here, there are conference facilities as well as major Danish tourist attractions (for example the Tivoli amusement park, the royal residence Amalienborg, and the Little Mermaid). In addition, hotel accommodation is the natural choice in a larger city. Other counties with significant shares of hotel nights are Storstroem, Bornholm, Funen, Aarhus and North Jutland. Storstroem, Bornholm, and North Jutland are rural areas with beaches, etc, whereas the second and third largest cities of Denmark are located in the counties of Aarhus (Aarhus) and Funen (Odense — the birthplace of the Danish fairytale writer H.C. Andersen) respectively.

As stressed earlier, the number of hotel nights has increased by about 80 percent during the period. Above-average increases have taken place especially in the rural counties, whereas growth has been almost non-existent for the Copenhagen city area. However, compared with the county population, Copenhagen city is still very significant. But the most important area is the island of Bornholm with more than twelve hotel nights per inhabitant annually. In sum, the division of hotel nights has become more regional.

The evolution of the number of hotel nights is further investigated in Figure 2, which shows the long-run transformation y_{lt} for the two most important areas of Denmark, Copenhagen city and the county of Bornholm. The picture is very diversified. For Copenhagen city the economic crisis in the 1970s surely affected the number of hotel nights. This could be due to the large number of foreign visitors (see below). Since the end of 1980s the number of hotel nights has increased quite dramatically. The peak in the mid-1980s could be due to variations in the US dollar exchange rate. As can be seen from the right-hand

Table 2: Summary Statistics on Hotel Nights in Denmark by County, 1970.1 to 1996.12.

County	Share Average, %	Growth, 1996 Index	Nights, 1996 Relative to county	1970.1– 1979.12	1980.1– 1989.12	1990.1– 1996.12	1970.1– 1996.12
Denmark total	100.0	181	2.46	0.49	0.46	0.45	0.50
Copenhagen city	26.8	112	5.05	0.37	0.31	0.33	0.34
Copenhagen	4.9	141	0.97	0.35	0.38	0.36	0.37
Frederiksborg	2.9	121	1.06	0.48	0.39	0.40	0.44
Roskilde	1.1	210	0.69	0.36	0.33	0.32	0.44
West Zealand	1.5	132	0.67	0.42	0.39	0.21	0.42
Storstroem	5.5	419	4.04	0.54	0.60	0.49	0.89
Bornholm	6.4	183	12.31	1.35	1.20	1.09	1.22
Funen	7.2	176	1.92	0.43	0.38	0.39	0.44
South Jutland	4.5	187	2.25	0.54	0.58	0.58	0.62
Ribe	4.5	254	2.94	0.61	0.47	0.54	0.59
Vejle	4.3	225	1.93	0.39	0.36	0.40	0.47
Ringkoebing	4.4	262	2.02	0.60	0.51	0.46	0.61
Aarhus	8.8	164	1.79	0.37	0.37	0.42	0.43
Viborg	2.8	254	1.78	0.54	0.55	0.52	0.60
North Jutland	14.3	339	4.65	0.66	0.62	0.57	0.72

Note: The percentage shares are computed on the mean values for the full period, and consequently do not sum to 100 percent. The computations in the second and third columns are on annual data cumulatively aggregated from the monthly observations. In the second column the growth index is with the 1970 set equal to 100. In the third column the figures measure the number of hotel nights relative to the total population in the county. In the last four columns, CV is the coefficient of variation computed using the non-transformed data and defined as: CV = standard deviation divided by the mean.

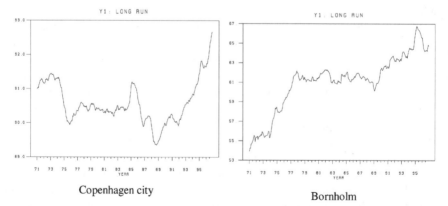

Copenhagen city   Bornholm

Figure 2: The Logarithm of Hotel Nights: Copenhagen City and Bornholm, Long-run, y_{1t}.

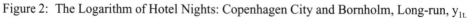

graph of Figure 2, the island of Bornholm, located in the Eastern Sea, was not affected at all by the oil crises in the 1970s. This could be due to the fact that Danes, Swedes, and Germans substituted a holiday closer to home for their usual trip to the Mediterranean region. For both counties an increased growth in the number of hotel nights is evident at the end of the 1980s.

The coefficient of variation indicating the relative variation of the time series takes the highest value for the county of Bornholm. This could suggest large variations between summer and winter — ie a very significant seasonal pattern. As shown later in Figure 4, this in fact proved to be the case. Compared with the sub-periods for the whole of Denmark, the coefficient of variation has remained almost constant throughout the period. At county level the coefficient of variation has decreased in nine cases, remained constant in five cases, and increased in only one case (for the county of Aarhus). This decrease in seasonal variation could be taken as an indicator of changed preferences for holidays, ie a decrease in the seasonal variation. As is evident from Table 2 above this change took place in many counties from the 1970s to the 1980s.

Hotel Nights by Nationality

Turning to the number of hotel nights divided by nationality, this is shown in Table 3 below.

The most important foreign consumers of hotel nights in Denmark are Germans, Swedes and Norwegians; in other words people from the neighbouring countries. Tourists from these three nations account for more than half the foreign hotel nights. Overall, the number of hotel nights consumed by foreigners has doubled over the period. Interesting exceptions are observed for Norwegians, who show an increase of over 300 percent, and the decreased significance of hotel nights consumed by Americans.

Figure 3 (left-hand graph) shows the long-run transformation y_{lt} of the hotel nights (solid line) by Americans and the US dollar exchange rate.[13] The decrease in hotel nights was already in evidence at the beginning of the 1970s. This pattern should not necessarily be taken as an indicator of a decreasing number of foreign visitors, but alternatively as an indicator of a shorter visiting period. Notice the close similarity between the exchange rate and the number of hotel nights, suggesting a cointegrating relation at the long-run frequency. Particularly noticeable is the increase in hotel nights in the mid-1980s due to the market power of the strong US dollar.

The finding that economic changes in the home county affect the number of hotel nights in Denmark is also applicable to many other nationalities. For example, the right-hand graph of Figure 3 above depicts the long-run transformation y_{lt} of the hotel nights (solid line) by Finns and the exchange rate of the Finnish Mark. The impact of the Finnish depression following the break-down of the trade with the former Soviet Union at the

---

[13]Data on exchange rates have kindly been supplied by Dan Knudsen from the Danish National Bank. The cointegrating relationship between the exchange rate and the number of hotel nights, ECM-modelling, periodic cointegration, etc, will be considered in future work.

Table 3: Summary Statistics on Hotel Nights in Denmark by Nationality, 1970.1 to 1996.12.

Nationality	Share Average, %	Growth, 1996 Index	Nights, 1993 Relative to home	Coefficient of variation, CV 1970.1– 1979.12	1980.1– 1989.12	1990.1– 1996.12	1970.1– 1996.12
Danes	48.8	182	1.089	0.25	0.24	0.26	0.32
Foreigners, total	51.2	179	0.165	0.72	0.71	0.69	0.73
Swedes	11.2	226	0.165	0.65	0.65	0.65	0.73
Norwegians	6.0	421	0.182	0.91	1.19	1.15	1.29
Finns	1.1	121	0.015	0.59	0.79	0.80	0.76
Germans	13.4	239	0.021	1.10	0.96	0.85	0.99
British	3.3	149	0.005	0.42	0.50	0.49	0.50
Dutch	1.4	191	0.012	0.83	0.68	0.90	0.88
French	0.9	94	0.001	0.71	0.57	0.48	0.62
Italians	1.1	201	0.002	0.62	0.94	1.08	1.02
Rest of Europe	3.2	148		0.48	0.50	0.49	0.52
Americans (USA)	5.1	34	0.001	0.86	0.75	0.69	0.87
Japanese	1.0	205	0.008	0.46	0.52	0.65	0.57
Rest of world	3.7	200		0.49	0.45	0.38	0.48

Note: The percentage shares are computed on the mean values for the full period, and consequently do not sum to 100 percent. The computations in the second and third columns are on annual data cumulatively aggregated from the monthly observations. In the second column the growth index is with the 1970 set equal to 100. In the third column the figures measure the number of hotel nights relative to the total population in the home country. In the last four columns CV is the coefficient of variation computed using the non-transformed data and defined as: CV = standard deviation divided by the mean.

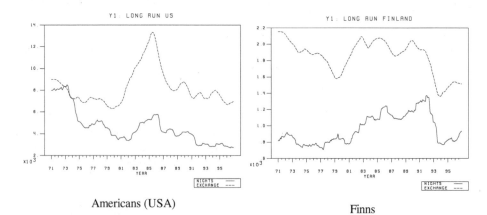

Americans (USA)   Finns

Figure 3: Hotel Nights and Exchange Rates: Americans and Finns, Long-run, y_{1t}.

beginning of the 1990s is clearly demonstrated. In addition, very similar patterns in the two series can be observed.

For many nationalities, a relationship between the number of hotel nights and the exchange rate can be found. However, this depends on the exchange rate relationship between the relevant currency and the Danish Kroner. For example, the German Mark is found not to be influential on the number of hotel nights consumed by Germans in Denmark, perhaps due to the fixed exchange rate system between the two currencies. On the other hand, a shift in preferences away from Denmark in the 1980s is discernible.[14] In general, economics is of more importance in foreigners' consumption of Danish hotel nights than the climate. It can be shown that a variable such as the average temperature turns out to be a poor indicator of the hotel nights.

Overall, the coefficient of variation for foreigners exceeds that for Danes for the full period as well as for the sub-periods. This is not surprising. Foreigners' demand for hotel nights is high during the holiday season, and is also affected by their domestic economy, travel distance etc, whereas Danes can easily visit another part of the country throughout the year. For the full period, the highest coefficient of variation is found for Norwegians, Germans and Italians.

Comparing it with the evidence presented in Table 2 above, the evolution of the coefficient of variation within sub-periods is quite different. Of the twelve nationalities considered, the coefficient of variation has increased in six cases, remained constant in three cases, and decreased in three cases. An increase could be taken as indicative of a more significant season — ie that people only want to visit Denmark during the summer, at Easter, and so on. This is the case for Norwegians and Finns, but also for visitors from a number of countries further away, including Japan and Italy. As for German, French and American visitors, the season seems to have become longer.

Results of Testing for Monthly Seasonal Unit Roots

The results of applying the auxiliary regression (1) are set out in Table 4. The test strategy for augmentation has been applied along the lines described earlier.

It is evident from the material that a varying and changing seasonal pattern is a common phenomenon with regard to both counties and nationality. The seasonal pattern has varied considerably in six of the counties investigated and for six nationalities.

For the counties in which the number of hotel nights is concentrated, the seasonal pattern is varying for Copenhagen city, Storstroem, and North Jutland, whereas the pattern is quite constant for the island of Bornholm. Given that it is a rather isolated rural area this could be a problem for the island, which over the past decade has faced a decreased population and increased unemployment rate.[15]

---

[14]See also Jensen, T. (1998). Income and price elasticities by nationality for tourists in Denmark. *Tourism Economics*, *4*, 101–130.

[15]See also Schønemann, S. (1996). *Bornholm: Economic structures and development*, Report 6/1996. Research Centre of Bornholm, Denmark (in Danish).

Table 4: Results of HEGY-Tests for Monthly Unit Roots in Hotel Nights in Denmark.

Nights by county	Unit roots at:	Nights by nationality	Unit roots at:
Denmark total	0, 2, 4, 5, 6	**Danes**	0, 2, 4, 5, 6
		Foreigners, total	0, 2, 4
Copenhagen city	0, 2, 4, 6		
Copenhagen	2, 4	Swedes	0, 2, 4, 6
Frederiksborg	0, 1, 2	Norwegians	0, 1, 2, 4
Roskilde	2, 4	Finns	0, 1, 2, 4
West Zealand	0, 2, 4, 6		
Storstroem	0, 1, 2, 3	Germans	0, 2, 4
Bornholm	0, 2	British	0, 1, 2, 4, 6
Funen	0, 2	Dutch	0, 1, 2, 5
		French	0, 2, 4
South Jutland	0, 1, 2, 3	Italians	0, 1, 2, 4, 6
Ribe	0, 2, 4	Rest of Europe	0, 2, 4
Vejle	0, 1, 2, 4		
Ringkoebing	0, 2, 4	Americans (USA)	0, 2, 4
Aarhus	0, 2	Japanese	1, 2, 4
Viborg	0, 4	Rest of world	2, 4
North Jutland	0, 2, 4,5		

Note: See Table 1 for a description of the frequencies. Results from the auxiliary regression of equation (1) include a constant term, trend, and 11 seasonal dummies. Estimation period 1970.1 to 1996.12. Detailed regression results with augmentation, etc can be obtained on request from the author.

With regard to nationality, the seasonal pattern has been most varying for all the Scandinavian nationalities, and for British and Italian visitors. The most stable pattern is observed for Germans, Americans, and Japanese using hotels in Denmark.

Finally, it should be noted that the seasonal pattern of the aggregated series for hotel nights in Denmark seems to preserve the seasonal unit roots found at county level, whereas the picture is unclear with regard to nationality.

Graphical Analysis

The question of whether the seasonal component in a time series is best described by a model with non-changing seasonal patterns — ie a dummy variable model — or by a model which allows the seasonal pattern to change is difficult to resolve. It may therefore pay to rely on other means of analysis than the test presented.

It is recommended that the test should be accompanied by a full graphical analysis of the transformed data — i.e., the transformations y_{1t} to y_{8t}. The Appendix presents a full graphical analysis of the logarithm of the hotel nights for Denmark total. As seen from Table 4 above, seasonal unit roots are present at many frequencies. Here pictures looking like ARCH processes are observed (i.e., a process with a positively autocorrelated variance and

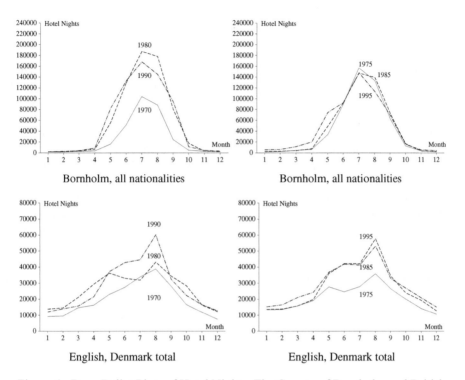

Figure 4: Bays-Ballot Plots of Hotel Nights: The County of Bornholm and British Visitors.

changing amplitude). In a case in which seasonal unit roots were not present one would expect the graphs to depict very regular processes with a quite constant amplitude.

There are two ways to simplify the graphical analysis. First, as proposed by Franses,[16] one could use a graph of the first quarter, second quarter, etc. However, in the monthly case, with $q_{i\tau}$ $i=1,2,....,12$, $\tau=1,2,...,T/12$ this complicates matters.[17] Consider as an alternative the use of the so-called Bays-Ballot plots, in which the series are depicted against the number of the month.[18] Figure 4 above shows two examples — for the island of Bornholm, and for British visitors to Denmark. In the case of a constant seasonal pattern the yearly lines should be almost parallel. Evidently, and consistent with the test results reported in Table 4 above, the seasonal pattern for Bornholm is more stable than the seasonal pattern for the British. With regard to British visitors, the seasonal pattern seems to vary especially during the spring. Compared with Bornholm the travel season for the British is much longer, and concentrated over the spring and summer with the peak in August. For Bornholm, the peak is constant in July with a large range of variation over the year consistent with the results in Table 2 above.

[16]Franses, *op cit*, Ref. 8.
[17]Full sets of such plots for all the time series being considered are available on request from the author.
[18]See, for example, Hylleberg, S. (1992). *Modelling Seasonality*. Oxford: Oxford University Press.

Conclusions

It is found that a varying and changing seasonal component is a common phenomenon in many time series for hotel nights for Denmark covering the period from 1970.1 to 1996.12. This observation is found for hotel nights divided by counties as well as for hotel nights divided by nationality. Consequently seasonality is more frequently of a stochastic than of a deterministic nature. This feature should be understood and taken into account in the modelling procedure.

In 1996 the total number of hotel nights amounted to about 12.9 million, equivalent to an increase of about 80 percent since 1970. During the period the division of hotel nights has shifted away from the Copenhagen area. However, Copenhagen is still by far the most important region. Other important counties are Bornholm, Storstroem, Funen, Aarhus and North Jutland. Throughout the period, around half of the nights were demanded by foreigners, and Germans, Swedes, and Norwegians were the most important nationalities in this respect.

Hopefully the analyses will provide tourism economists with an incentive to investigate the literature on seasonal unit roots, and make use of the technique in their applied work.

Appendix: Plots of Hotel Nights, Denmark Total, 1970.1–1996.12.

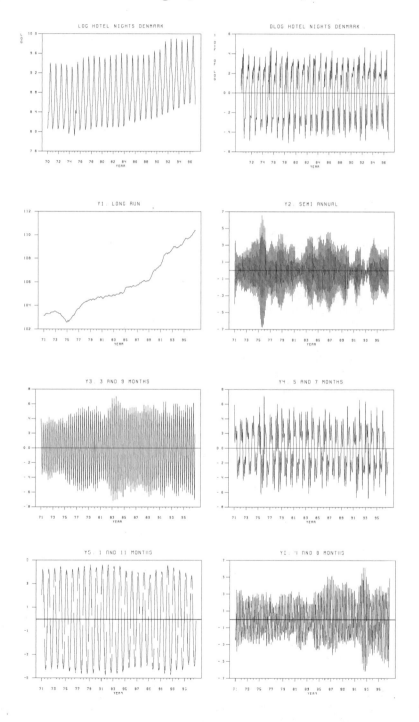

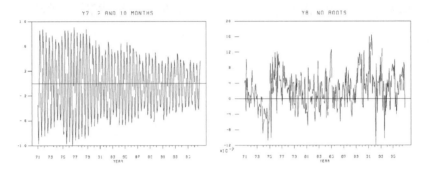

Acknowledgement

The work discussed here benefited from a grant from the Unit of Tourism Research hosted by the Research Centre of Bornholm, Denmark. Earlier versions of the paper were presented at the European Congress of the European Regional Science Association (ERSA) held in Rome, Italy, 26–29 August 1997 and Vienna, Austria, 28 August–1 September 1998, the International Tourism Research Conference organized by the Unit of Tourism Research at the Research Centre of Bornholm, Denmark, 8–12 September 1997, the Danish Society of Applied Statistics Conference, University of Aarhus, Denmark, 26–28 January 1998, the Fourth International Forum on Tourism Statistics, Copenhagen, Denmark, 17–19 June 1998, and at various seminars during the summer of 1998. The author wishes to thank the participants for their comments, which resulted in improvements to the paper.

Background material, in the form of the data set used and detailed plots of all series, is available from the author.

Chapter 6

Off-Season is No Season: The Case of Bornholm

Svend Lundtorp, Charlotte R. Rassing and Stephen Wanhill

The Phenomenon of Seasonality

Seasonality in tourism is a well documented phenomenon in the literature, particularly in relation to peripheral regions of Northern Europe and America. It is generally recognized that seasonality not only can be explained by climate variations. It is obviously one of the main reasons, but also institutional conditions have a major influence on the time of the holiday. The school-holiday and, in connection with this, the industrial holidays are of vital importance. Thus Butler defines five main reasons for seasonality (Butler, 1994):

- regular temporal variations in natural phenomena, particular those associated with climate and the true seasons of the year;
- human decision factors — the institutionalized seasonality;
- social pressure and fashion;
- sporting season;
- inertia and tradition.

Baum and Hagen (1997) and Frechtling (1996) have a similar classification of the causes:

- climate/weather (= Butler's first);
- social customs (= Butler's second);
- business customs (conventions, sport events etc. Very much like Butler's third cause but Butler does not mention seasonality in business tourism);
- calendar effects (number of weekends in a month, Easter, Christmas);
- supply constraints (availability of labour, alternative use of facilities).

Thus, seasonality in tourism is not only due to the holidaymakers' wish to spend the vacation in midsummer, but also to constraints making it complicated or even impossible to take off-season holidays. Actually, in spite of the well described phenomenon, we know very little about what is most important, the desire or the constraints. It is not known with any certainty whether tourists travel in the peak season because they want to, they have to or they have been conditioned to (Butler, 1994). In summary we have both push and pull factors, as shown in Table 1.

This chapter was originally published in *Tourism Economics*, Vol. 5, No. 1 (March 1999).
© 1999 IP Publishing Ltd. Reproduced by permission.

Table 1: Causes of Seasonality for Holidaymakers — Push and Pull Factors.

Push-factors	Pull-factors
Institutional (school holidays, industrial holidays)	Climate
Calendar — Easter and public holidays	Sporting seasons — hunting, fishing, golfing, skiing
Inertia and tradition	Events
Social pressure or fashion	
Access — transport costs and time	

Source: Based on Baum (1997), Frechtling (1996) and Butler (1994).

Although destinations even on the Equator experience seasonality, all findings prove that problems caused by seasonality in tourism are most difficult to overcome at high latitudes and particularly in peripheral regions in the north (Bar-On, 1975; Butler, 1994*)*.

Both the tourism industry and the local community usually regard seasonality as a problem: first of all the industry feels it needs a longer season to gain enough profit to pay capital costs, i.e., interests and repayments. It may also suffer from lack of labour in the peak season, especially skilled workers. In some countries, it is also difficult to hire and fire staff in time with the demand. For the local community one of the main problems is high unemployment in off-season and lack of labour in the main season. That problem can be reinforced by the competition for labour in the peak season because workers are not available for traditional jobs such as agriculture. Thus, the historic reason for school holidays is to give leave to children during the harvest.

Much attention has been paid and much effort has been made to reduce seasonality. To overcome seasonality there are different ways to go, such as launching additional seasons, diversifying markets, reduced prices and providing off-season activities (Baum & Hagen, 1997). The true nature of the problems experienced and the possible solutions — if any — will be discussed in the conclusion section of this paper.

The intention in this chapter is to explain the phenomenon of seasonality from the demand side, using a survey from Bornholm as a case. Therefore Baum and Hagen's and Butler's classifications are not used systematically. However, they are of fundamental importance for the understanding of tourism demand behaviour during the year.

Bornholm and the Visitor Profile

Bornholm is the most easterly part of Denmark and the island is located 150 km from Denmark's capital Copenhagen and 35 km from Sweden. Bornholm is the smallest county in Denmark with a landmass of 588 km^2 and a population of 45,000. Every year 485,000 tourists (Research Centre of Bornholm, 1997), mainly from the other part of Denmark, Germany and Sweden, visit the island.[1]

Figure 1 below illustrates where Bornholm is located in the Baltic.

The results presented in this chapter were collected by the Research Centre of Bornholm in the period July 1995–June 1996 (see Appendix 1 for further information about the methodology used in the survey). As Figure 2 below indicates, Bornholm experiences a main season, a shoulder season and an off-season. The seasonality Bornholm experiences is a very common form of institutionalized seasonality (Butler, 1994). The seasonality is to a great extent caused by the school holiday and the industrial holiday in the two main markets; the rest of Denmark and Germany. The main season on Bornholm covers July and August. The shoulder season consists of May, June and September and the off-season covers the rest of the year (January, February, March, April, October, November and December). During the main season Bornholm is visited by 197,000 tourists, in the shoulder season the number is 129,000 and off-season the island is visited by 159,000 tourists.

As shown in Table 2 below, the majority of the tourists in all three seasons find the nature, atmosphere and landscape the most important factors in making the decision to visit Bornholm. That they attach importance to nature, atmosphere and landscape is also

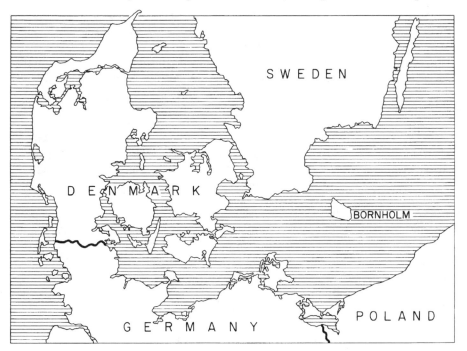

Figure 1: Map of Denmark and Surrounding Countries.

[1]If the results presented in this paper are compared with data from other countries it is important to remember that the data does not include Bornholm residents visiting other areas of the island.

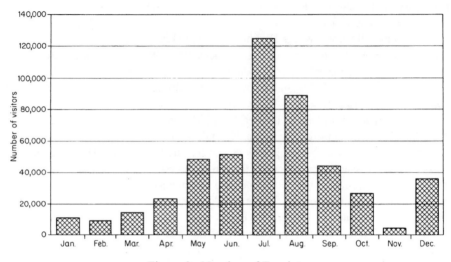

Figure 2: Number of Tourists.

reflected in the participation in different activities. Some 90 percent of all tourists to Bornholm have been walking on their own, 84 percent have been to the beach, 85 percent have just been relaxing and driving around.

The Danish Baltic Island of Bornholm is a holiday destination. Almost two third (64%) of the visitors come to the island for holiday purposes. People visiting friends and relatives

Table 2: Aspects of Bornholm.

Evaluation Base: All visitors	Main season 1226		Shoulder season 798		Off- season 1005		All Year 3029	
	Score	Ranking	Score	Ranking	Score	Ranking	Score	Ranking
Beaches	3.04	5	2.89	6	2.85	7	2.97	5
Landscape	3.61	3	3.71	2	3.72	2	3.66	2
Cycle routes	2.46	9	2.54	9	2.40	10	2.47	8
Walking	2.68	7	3.04	5	2.94	5	2.82	6
Fishing towns	3.15	4	3.28	4	3.23	4	3.20	4
Nature	3.67	1	3.75	1	3.77	1	3.71	1
Golf courses	1.19	13	1.18	13	1.26	13	1.20	12
Fishing	1.39	12	1.45	12	1.54	12	1.43	11
Cultural history	2.79	6	2.83	7	2.92	6	2.82	6
Restaurants	2.38	11	2.36	10	2.50	9	2.40	9
Craft/art workers	2.54	8	2.74	8	2.82	8	2.65	7
Atmosphere	3.64	2	3.62	3	3.58	3	3.62	3
Variety of activities	2.39	10	2.32	11	2.30	11	2.35	10

Note: The range was "Very Important"=4 to "Unimportant"=1

while on holiday account for twelve percent, business visitors count for seven percent, visitors solely travelling to visit friends and relatives count for eight percent and people with other reasons for their visit count for eight percent.

Figures 3a to 3e below show how the different purposes are distributed over the months (be aware of the different scales on the vertical axes).

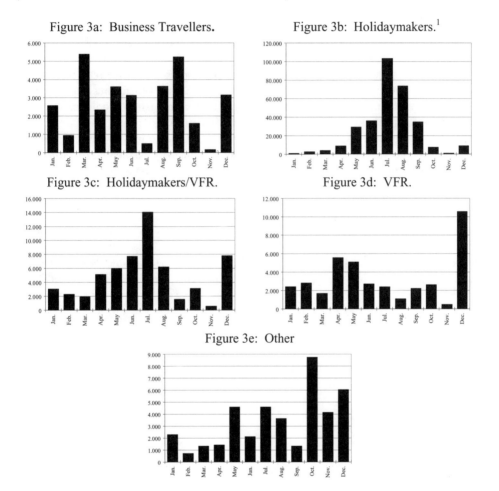

Figure 3a: Business Travellers.

Figure 3b: Holidaymakers.[1]

Figure 3c: Holidaymakers/VFR.

Figure 3d: VFR.

Figure 3e: Other

[1]Includes holidays only and holidays plus other reasons for the visit.

As is seen, people visiting Bornholm for business purposes mainly prefer March and September, while people travelling solely to visit friends and relatives to a great extent come in December in connection with Christmas. People travelling for 'other purposes' mainly choose October and December. The category 'other purposes' is mainly composed of shopping, education and sport events.

The distribution of the holidaymakers (Figure 3b) and people visiting friends and relatives while on holiday (Figure 3c) underlines the seasonality on Bornholm.

Business Travellers

Bornholm is visited every year by 33,000 business travellers. Some (53%) of those travellers visit Bornholm in the off-season, 14 percent business travellers come in the main season leaving the remaining 33 percent to visit the island in the shoulder season.

The majority of business travellers in the off-season as well as in the main season visit Bornholm because of general business (see Table 3 above). In the shoulder season business travellers mainly come to the island for conferences, meetings etc. Such travellers are mainly from Denmark.

Figure 4 above shows how business travellers are dispersed over the months and how they are distributed between conferences, meetings etc. and general business. In total, March is visited by most business travellers; some 17 percent visit Bornholm in March.

As can be seen people travelling for conferences and meetings mainly visit Bornholm in September; that is, in the shoulder season. A conference is never just business. It is almost always taken into account that people wish to have a chance to see their surroundings and because of the unstable weather on Bornholm the shoulder season is preferred before the off-season.

Table 3: Business Travellers by Purpose.

Purpose Base: Business travellers	Main season (%) 45	Shoulder season (%) 107	Off- season (%) 222	All year (%) 374
Conference, meetings, exhibitions	42	68	39	48
General business	58	32	61	52

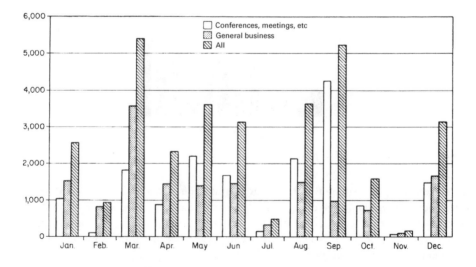

Figure 4: Business Travellers by Month.

March is the preferred month for people travelling for general purposes (buying, selling, etc.). One explanation could be that people travelling for general business prefer to trade with their customers before the season begins.

Holidaymakers

Every year 310,000 visitors come to Bornholm for holiday purposes, 22 percent of them in the off season. In the main season, the corresponding share is 90 percent and in the shoulder season the share is 78 percent.

The holidaymakers are very satisfied with Bornholm as a holiday destination (see Table 4 above). There is no significant difference between the three seasons. For the three seasons 98 percent of the visitors find Bornholm good/excellent as a destination for holidays. When it comes to value for money, it is especially the visitors in the off-season who find it excellent (see Table 5 below). If excellent and good is put together there is no significant difference between the evaluation of value for money.

The holiday market in the shoulder season is characterized by many German visitors (Table 6). Almost two-thirds of the visitors to Bornholm in. the shoulder season are from

Table 4: Bornholm as a Holiday Destination.

Evaluation Base: Holidaymakers	Main season (%) 779	Shoulder season (%) 465	Off- season (%) 208	All year (%) 1452
Excellent	79	77	82	78
Good	20	21	17	20
Average	1	1	1	1
Not good enough	0	*	0	*
Poor	*	*	0	*

Note: * means less than 0.5 percent

Table 5: Value for Money.

Evaluation Base: Holidaymakers	Main Season (%) 752	Shoulder Season (%) 438	Off- Season (%) 190	All Year (%) 1380
Excellent	26	20	29	25
Good	39	46	46	42
Average	29	29	20	28
Not good enough	5	4	3	4
Poor	1	1	2	1

Note: * means less than 0.5 percent

Table 6: Holidaymakers by Country.

Country Base: Holidaymakers	Main season (%) 814	Shoulder Season (%) 483	Off- Season (%) 239	All Year (%) 1536
Denmark	39	26	36	34
Sweden	15	8	23	14
Germany	41	64	33	47
Others	5	2	8	5

Notes: 1. The base includes multiple accommodation use
        2. * means less than 0.5 percent

Germany. In total 47 percent of the holidaymakers during the year are from Germany. The reason why German visitors dominate the shoulder season is the wide variation in the school holiday in Germany. The Danish school holiday falls in July and August, while the German school holiday is in the period June to September.

In the shoulder season many holidaymakers use a hotel/guesthouse as their accommodation (see Table 7 below). In total, 36 percent of holidaymakers in the shoulder season stay in a hotel/guesthouse compared with 30 percent in the main season and 22 percent in the off-season. However, there is no significant difference in the distribution between summer houses and hotels/guesthouses in the main and shoulder season. The share that prefers summer houses

Table 7: Accommodation Usage.

Accommodation Base: Holidaymakers	Main Season (%) 771	Shoulder Season (%) 467	Off- Season (%) 184	All Year (%) 1422
Hotel	24	32	18	26
Guesthouse	6	4	4	5
B & B/Private home	2	1	*	1
Farmhouse	3	2	3	3
Youth hostel	3	1	0	2
Holiday Centre	7	6	13	7
Friends and relatives	3	3	4	3
Summer house	32	38	49	36
Camping	10	4	*	7
Caravan	6	4	1	5
Other	4	5	7	5

Notes: 1. The base includes multiple accommodation use
        2. * means less than 0.5 percent

and the share that prefers hotels/guesthouses are increasing from the main to the shoulder season because the demand for other types of accommodation, such as camping and caravan, naturally is reduced.

In the off-season, almost half of the holidaymakers stay in a summer house. The corresponding share in the main season is 32 percent and in the shoulder season the share is 38 percent.

In total two-thirds of holidaymakers use a hotel/pension or a summer house as accommodation on their visit to Bornholm. The more cool types of accommodation, such as camping and caravan, only attract twelve percent of holidaymakers. Even in the main season camping and caravan are only preferred by 16 percent of them.

It is characteristic of the off-season that 71 percent of the holidaymakers are repeat visitors compared to about half of the visitors in the two other seasons (see Table 8).

In general short break holidays tend to be taken in the off-season (Faché, 1994). If the one-day visitors, who travel mainly to shop, are left out of account, almost three-quarters of the holidaymakers on Bornholm in the off-season stay for less than eight days (see Table 9 below). In the off-season, the average length of stay is 6.87 days compared with 9.60 days in the main season and 10.10 days in the shoulder season. A two-sided Chi-square test shows that there is no significant difference between the number of days the holidaymakers spend on Bornholm in the two seasons.

Table 8: Holidaymakers by Type of Visit.

Type of Visit Base: Holidaymakers	Main season (%) 814	Shoulder season (%) 482	Off-season (%) 237	All Year (%) 1533
First	45	49	30	44
Repeat	55	51	71	56

Note: Up to three days (one-day visitors left out).

Table 9: Holidaymakers by Length of Stay.

Length of Stay Base: Holidaymakers	Main season (%) 793	Shoulder season (%) 478	Off-Season (%) 199	All Year (%) 1470
Short stay	8	8	14	9
Up to one week	41	40	59	43
One–two weeks	40	37	25	37
Two–three weeks	10	13	2	10
More than three weeks	1	3	0	2
Average (days)	9.60	10.10	6.87	9.39

Note: Up to three days (one-day visitors left out).

The importance of different aspects of Bornholm when the holidaymakers decide to visit the island is shown in Tables 10a to 10g. In all three seasons the holidaymakers mainly choose to visit Bornholm because of the landscape, nature and atmosphere. The activity of "walking" is closely related to nature and landscape and therefore also important to holidaymakers in the three seasons. The beach (see Table 10a below) is quite important throughout the year even though there are different activities associated with the beach in the different seasons.

Holidaymakers coming to Bornholm in the off-season seem to be more interested in cultural history and craft/art work than those in the main and shoulder seasons. Actually three-quarters find cultural history an important/very important aspect when they choose to visit the island in the off-season. In both the main and the shoulder season, the corresponding

Table 10a: Importance of the Beach.

Beach Base: Holidaymakers	Main season (%) 722	Shoulder sason (%) 388	Off- Season (%) 180	All year (%) 1290
Very important	36	31	30	34
Important	35	35	24	34
Less important	24	26	32	26
Unimportant	5	8	13	7

Table 10b: Importance of the Landscape.

Landscape Base: Holidaymakers	Main Season (%) 750	Shoulder Season (%) 430	Off- Season (%) 194	All Year (%) 1374
Very important	68	73	76	71
Important	29	26	23	27
Less important	3	*	1	2
Unimportant	*	1	1	*

Note: * means less than 0.5 percent.

Table 10c: Importance of Walking.

Walking Base: Holidaymakers	Main Season (%) 671	Shoulder Season (%) 381	Off- Season (%) 168	All Year (%) 1220
Very important	24	38	35	30
Important	37	38	36	37
Less important	25	16	19	22
Unimportant	15	8	10	12

Table 10d: Importance of Nature.

Nature Base: Holidaymakers	Main Season (%) 745	Shoulder Season (%) 432	Off- Season (%) 199	All Year (%) 1376
Very important	73	80	82	76
Important	25	18	15	21
Less important	2	1	1	2
Unimportant	1	1	2	1

Table 10e: Importance of Cultural History.

Cultural history Base: Holidaymakers	Main Season (%) 690	Shoulder Season (%) 386	Off- Season (%) 185	All Year (%) 1261
Very important	19	21	25	20
Important	49	47	50	48
Less important	26	27	20	26
Unimportant	6	5	5	6

Table 10f: Importance of Craft/Art Work.

Craft/Art work Base: Holidaymakers	Main Season (%) 380	Shoulder Season (%) 378	Off- Season (%) 176	All Year (%) 1234
Very important	14	20	23	17
Important	42	42	44	42
Less important	31	32	28	31
Unimportant	13	6	6	10

Table 10g: Importance of the Atmosphere.

Atmosphere Base: Holidaymakers	Main Season (%) 734	Shoulder Season (%) 402	Off- Season (%) 190	All Year (%) 1326
Very important	68	67	68	68
Important	30	31	26	30
Less important	1	2	4	2
Unimportant	1	1	2	1

share is 68 percent. In the off-season, two-thirds find craft/art work important/very important compared with 56 percent in the main season and 62 percent in the shoulder season.

It was expected that families visiting Bornholm outside the main season had a lower household income and in general were elderly. When it comes to income among the holidaymakers, a two-sided chi-square test shows that there is no difference between the three seasons (see Table 11 below).

A two-sided chi-square test shows that the holidaymakers in the shoulder-season in general are significantly older than those in the main season and the off-season (see Table 12 below). It is convenient for families with children to travel during the industrial holiday, the children's holiday and the Christmas holiday while the older generation is more free to choose the time of their holiday.

Conclusions

Seasonality in tourism demand is one of the biggest challenges faced by the tourism industry in general as well as on Bornholm. A good part of the industry is operating at near or full capacity during the main season, with facilities and services idle at other times of the year (Baum & Hagan, 1997). For Bornholm, as for all cold water resorts, it is a dream to expand the season.

Table 11: Holidaymakers by Income.

Income Base: Holidaymakers	Main season (%) 734	Shoulder season (%) 402	Off- (%) 190	All Year (%) 1326
Less than 200,000 DKK	68	67	68	68
200,000–400,000 DKK	30	31	26	30
400,000–700,000 DKK	1	2	4	2
Greater than 700,000 DKK	1	1	2	1

Table 12: Holidaymakers by Age.

Age Base: Holidaymakers	Main season (%) 783	Shoulder Season (%) 463	Off- Season (%) 214	All Year (%) 1460
16–24 years	5	3	1	4
25–34 years	16	10	17	14
35–49 years	35	24	29	31
50–59 years	25	29	27	27
60–69 years	14	22	16	17
Over 69 years	5	11	10	8

Demand

In literature (Baum & Hagen, 1997), it is often mentioned that people visiting a holiday destination in different seasons have different preferences. The data about visitors to Bornholm does not support that statement. People visiting Bornholm in all three seasons wish to experience the nature, landscape and atmosphere of the island. Holidaymakers mainly visit Bornholm in the main season and business travellers and people visiting friends and relatives mainly visit the island in the off-season, but by and large they all find the same aspects about Bornholm important.

There is no evidence indicating an unreclaimed market for *off-season* tourism on Bornholm. The holidaymakers are a group of fanatics with an intense love of the island. They come every year for a short break holiday. They stay in summer houses and walk in the loneliness of nature. The very few, who have not visited the island before, have heard about the beautiful place from friends and relatives. Their visit is not a result of professional marketing. This indicates that nothing can be gained through targeted marketing. The best tool is satisfied customers returning home with fairytales of the Baltic Paradise. Evidently you have to be rather convincing to persuade people to come off-season.

In principle the shoulder season should provide better opportunities. The visitors in this season are remarkably similar to guests in the main season. There are some more seniors and, for obvious reasons, the beaches are of less importance. There are more Germans than in the main season because of the time of the school holiday in Germany. In almost all other respects the main and shoulder seasons are very much alike. The visitors have the same attitude towards the location, they participate in the same activities and they are predominantly staying in summer houses.

The literature often mentions that out-of-main-season, travel is more likely to consist of short break holidays (Baum & Hagen, 1997). This is true for those holidaymakers who visit Bornholm in the off-season. In the main season and the shoulder season, there is no significant difference between average length of stay. It is the main holiday for tourists in the shoulder season who are taking on the island. It is apparently not a short break season for them.

The question is consequently: why is it not possible to attract more visitors in the shoulder season? Speaking frankly, it is a weakness of this survey that only this small proportion of mankind who has visited Bornholm, has been questioned. However, there is one obvious reason: It is another market than that of the main season. For several reasons the demand is limited and there is strong competition with many destinations trying to attract visitors just in the shoulder season.

Naturally it might be a possibility to attract more business tourists for conferences, seminars and exhibitions. Actually the figures show that the preferred season for meetings is in the shoulder season (May and September) and in March. Through professional marketing it might be possible to increase the number of that kind of arrangement, although it is a market with heavy competition. Bornholm is not the obvious place for a conference or a meeting to take place. The island is peripheral and only possible to reach by sea or air.

Incentive travel which — for reasons of taxation — is a very small market in Denmark may also be a possibility. There are three golf courses on the island and splendid facilities for fishing.

At the same time nothing indicates much of a possibility for attracting conference guests during the winter. The main purpose for a visit may be learning and talking. However, visitors also want to enjoy the landscape, nature and the fishing villages during their breaks. This peripheral Danish island in the Baltic is not particularly attractive when it is dark, cold and wet.

Supply

The heart of discussions on tourism seasonality is that it is regarded as a problem. And the problem is to find out how to deal with it. The problem is obviously perceived, but to what degree is it real? In relation to a peripheral destination in a welfare state in Northern Europe, the problem may not be as heavy as it is often expressed.

For the tourism industry and for society as a whole, an extended season can be an advantage. Achieving a positive contribution while you have idle capacity is an economic gain. But this is not a special precept for tourism. It is a general condition for all economic activity. Other industries also suffer from seasonality. Perhaps it is more difficult to manage in tourism than in other trades, especially because it is impossible to store the products. On the other hand, seasonality can never be a surprise to managers in the tourism-related sectors. The seasons of the year are not random fluctuations but are a very predictable phenomenon. Other industries would envy establishments with such visible conditions.

For many tourism facilities it is a heavy challenge to pay capital costs within a short season. The fixed costs for a hotel room in Denmark are about £5000 a year. The fixed costs per overnight are thereby high and can be prohibitive. But that does not apply to all facilities dependent on tourism. Camping sites, caravan parks and many attractions cannot be used off-season. The capital investment does not rely on long period usage. The capital costs are either small or the profit is sufficient to cover the costs in the short season. As mentioned earlier, summer houses are a very popular type of accommodation in Denmark. They tend to be individually owned, used by the owner, lent out to friends or let out through an agency. Very few owners can hire their house out with profit, and in any case that is not the idea of having a house. It is for own use, and letting out is a perquisite. The real capital cost problem among the different types of accommodation is that of hotels, particularly those in tourist destinations. No wonder, that no new hotels have been built on Bornholm for ages.

Another major expressed problem is seasonality in employment, but this seems to be overstated in regard to a destination like Bornholm:

- In Denmark 32 percent of the employees in hotels and restaurants are students. That is a fine solution for both the students and the enterprises;
- Many people concentrate a whole year's work in a short season. A man-and-wife camping site often demands more than 100 hours work per week in 16–20 weeks. Off-season they use time for planning, preparation and maintenance. Some even have another job during the wintertime;
- Only a smaller proportion of tourism-related workers are in the tourism industry as such. Many are employed in travel, transportation, shops and other enterprises where tourism seasonality does not strike so hard (T. Rafn, 1995);

- On a destination like Bornholm, fishing and the fishing industry have a low season when the tourists arrive, i.e., workers in the fishing industry can take a summer job in tourism;
- Possibly some people are not bored with a break at Christmas time living on unemployment benefits.

Final Comments

If Bornholm can be used as a typical example of a tourist destination in a peripheral region in Northern Europe all evidence is against any serious attempt to promote a resort as an off-season destination. The tourism industry has taken the consequences. The attractions are closed down. This is also the case with most of the restaurants. As at other places of high latitudes the weather is unpredictable, it is early dark, there is a limited number of ferry departures and the autumn storms may add special excitement to the journey. It requires little explanation to prove how so few tourists invade the island off season. To open the destination in off-season would cost a lot of effort and collaboration between all the actors on the spot, and with very poor prospects. The shoulder season has a better chance. Particularly for conferences, seminars and other meetings.

It is not the goal in this paper to provide solutions. As a minor recommendation a more intensive collaboration between the hotels could be suggested. If, for instance, there are three hotels, each with 100 beds and with 100 visitors in total, there will be an occupancy rate of 50 percent if one of them is closed. If they compete the rate is only 33 percent.

The major recommendation is to accept seasonality as a fact — not as a problem. As do most of the people involved. The Baltic island Bornholm has adapted itself to the seasonality and is able to offer the needed product and services to different types of visitor in the different seasons. There is no reason to believe that more activities and attractions will mean more visitors in the shoulder season and the off-season.

References

Bar-On, R. V. (1975). *Seasonality in Tourism.* London: Economist Intelligence Unit.

Baum, T., & L. Hagen (1997). *Responses to Seasonality in Tourism: The Experiences of Peripheral Destinations.* Peripheral Area Tourism. International Tourism Research Conference. Bornholm 8–12 September 1997. Unit of Tourism Research at the Research Centre of Bornholm.

Butler, R. W. (1994). Seasonality in Tourism; issues and problems. In A. V. Seaton *et al.,* (eds) *Tourism. The State and the Art* (pp. 332–339). Chichester: John Wiley and Sons.

Faché, W. (1994). Short break holidays. In A. V. Seaton, *et al.,* (eds) *Tourism. The State and the Art* (pp. 459–467). Chichester: John Wiley and Sons.

Frechtling, D. C. (1996). *Practical Tourism Forecasting.* Oxford.

Hartl-Nielsen, A. C., Rassing, R., & Wanhill, S. (1997). *Survey of Visitors to Bornholm. July 1995–June 1996.* Research Centre of Bornholm.

Hjalager, A.-M. (1996). *Turismens arbejdssammensætning.* Copenhagen: Memorandum for the Ministry of Industry.

More, T. W. (1989). *Handbook of Business Forecasting.* London.

Rafn, T. (1995). *Turismens økonomiske betydning for Bornholm.* Research Centre of Bornholm.

Research Centre of Bornholm (1995/1996). *Survey of Visitors to Bornholm*, database.

Seaton, A. V. (1994). Are relatives friends? Reassessing the VFR category in segmenting tourism markets. In A. V. Seaton, *et al.,* (ed.) *Tourism. The State and the Art* (pp. 316–321). Chichester: John Wiley and Sons.

Twinning-Ward, L., & Twinning-Ward, T. (1996). *Tourist Destination Development. The Case of Bornholm and Gotland*. Research Centre of Bornholm.

Appendix 1

Overview of applied questions from the survey

⇒ **What is your country of usual residence?**

⇒ **How many people are in your personal party?**

⇒ **In total, how many days have you spent in Bornholm?** _____

⇒ **What is the *main* purpose of your visit?**
Please mark only one option.
Business conference/meeting/exhibition ❐
General business — buying, selling, installation or other ❐
Holiday ❐
Holiday/visiting friends or relatives ❐
Visiting friends or relatives solely ❐
Sporting event ❐
Education/school event ❐
Cultural event ❐
Other _____
      (please specify)

⇒ **How important were the following aspects of Bornholm in making your decision to visit the island?** *Please look at all aspects.*

	Very important	Im- portant	Less important	Un- important
Beaches	❐	❐	❐	❐
Landscapes	❐	❐	❐	❐
Cycle routes	❐	❐	❐	❐
Walking routes	❐	❐	❐	❐
Fishing villages and towns	❐	❐	❐	❐
Nature	❐	❐	❐	❐
Golf courses	❐	❐	❐	❐
Fishing	❐	❐	❐	❐
Cultural history	❐	❐	❐	❐
Restaurants	❐	❐	❐	❐
Craft/art workers	❐	❐	❐	❐
Atmosphere	❐	❐	❐	❐
A variety of activities	❐	❐	❐	❐
Family/friends/ relatives in Bornholm	❐	❐	❐	❐

⇒ **Type of accommodation used during your stay: Please state all places of accommodation and the number of days spent in each.**

Accommodation	Days	Nearest towns or villages
Hotel/Guesthouse/Pension, please give name		
Youth hostel		
Rented summer house through agency		
Rented summer house through other than agency		
Borrowed summer house from friends etc.		
Stayed with family/friends		
Farmhouse		
B&B/private home		
Camp site:		
* Tent/camplet ❐		
* Cabin ❐		
* Own caravan ❐		
* Rented caravan ❐		
Holiday Centre		
Other (please specify)		
None / on a day visit ❐		

⇒ **Overall, what is your opinion of Bornholm as a destination to visit?**

	Excellent	Good	Average	Not good enough	Poor
For holidays and recreation	❐	❐	❐	❐	❐
Value for money	❐	❐	❐	❐	❐

⇒ **Which of the activities mentioned below did you participate in?**
Please look at all activities mentioned.

	Participated this trip	Participated before	Not Participated at all
Going to the beach	❐	❐	❐
Swimming			
a) in the sea	❐	❐	❐
b) in a pool	❐	❐	❐
Windsurfing	❐	❐	❐
Cycling	❐	❐	❐
Guided coach tour	❐	❐	❐
Guided walks	❐	❐	❐
Walks on my/our own	❐	❐	❐
Scenic air flight	❐	❐	❐
Boat trips	❐	❐	❐
Fishing	❐	❐	❐
Golf	❐	❐	❐
Horseracing	❐	❐	❐
Music recitals	❐	❐	❐
Going to the cinema	❐	❐	❐
Eating out	❐	❐	❐
Shopping	❐	❐	❐
Just relaxing	❐	❐	❐
Driving around	❐	❐	❐
None of these	❐		
Other (please specify)			
_____	❐	❐	❐
_____	❐	❐	❐
_____	❐	❐	❐
_____	❐	❐	❐

⇒ **Which age group do you belong to?**
16-24 years ❐
25-34 years ❐
35-49 years ❐
50-59 years ❐
60-69 years ❐
over 69 years ❐

⇒ **Which of the following best describes your total family/household income?**
Less than 200,000 DKK per year ❐
200,000-400,000 DKK per year ❐
400,000-700,000 DKK per year ❐
More than 700,000 DKK per year ❐

Appendix 2

Background Information about the Applied Data

The survey used in this paper is undertaken by the Unit for Tourism Research, Research Centre of Bornholm, as a part of a wider and much larger investigation into the role of Tourism in the Peripheral Areas of Europe. For this instance, the survey is being conducted in order to assess the nature of tourism demand in peripheral areas, using Bornholm as a case example for the purposes of fieldwork.

The limited number of source markets for Bornholm indicated that the working sample size need not be large. But the paucity of information about visitors to the island, commended a strategy of over-sampling so as to ensure results that were robust. A pilot questionnaire was run among tourists visiting the island by ferry and aeroplane in early June with a sample of 50 respondents and a target of 6,000 visitor contacts (arrivals and departures). It was set within the allotted time span, with a screen questionnaire to filter out local residents. It was anticipated that the chosen method of interviewing would lead to some wastage in the form of unusable returns, but this could be accommodated within the target. Six different questionnaires were made up in four different languages (Danish, Swedish, German and English). Over the year, 6,071 visitor questionnaires were collected among tourists visiting Bornholm by ferry and aeroplane, with a wastage rate of just over three percent, together with 3,296 screen responses containing basic information about the trip movements of the residents of Bornholm.

At the beginning it was agreed that the survey should run for a complete year, from 1 July 1995 to 30 June 1996. Interviewing arrangements were structured so as to guarantee that, at a minimum, every day of the week and each week in any one month for every quarter of the year was surveyed. This was done so as to ensure that no systematic bias could arise in the quarterly reporting of information. Contacts would only be adults, using as the definition 16 years of age and upwards. Later on it was decided to let the survey continue until June 1999.

Interviewing is carried out at the main points of exit and departure so that data collection takes place mostly on BornholmsTrafikken's ferry departures to Copenhagen, Ystad (Sweden) and Neu Mukran (Germany) and DFO's to Saßnitz (Germany), and on Maersk Air's route between Bornholm and Copenhagen as well as the air-departures during the main season to Germany. The length of the questionnaire and terminal arrangements make it necessary for the interviewers to conduct the survey on the ferries and the aircraft. Cost dictates that respondents are introduced to the questionnaire and thereafter complete it themselves, with interviewers on hand to deal with any issues that may arise.

Chapter 7

Long-Term Positive Adjustments to Seasonality: Consequences of Summer Tourism in the Jotunheimen Area, Norway

Thor Flognfeldt

If there were a complete worldwide holiday and short trip survey available, it would be reasonable to believe that this would show a pattern of strong seasonality. Everyone is not able to travel during holidays, but among those who do travel the high seasons must be summer and Christmas. In some countries Easter and additional weeks during winter and autumn are school holidays. In the Nordic countries where this author lives, many persons will be travelling to the Sunshine Belt during low seasons. This means that we cannot get rid of seasonality problems ourselves, especially not in the rural areas. For some destinations, however, the local tourism producers could invent new products to reduce the seasonality problems at their specific sites.

The overall seasonality pattern of taking holidays and short trips would be tough to change. It will, however, locally often be possible to present "solutions" to some seasonality problems, most of those only lasting for a short time and forgetting about those others who lose their customers.

Seasonality of tourism demand is often regarded only as a *problem* and much effort has been devoted to developing a season widening demand (Baum & Hagen, 1997). Since off-season markets seldom are expanding, the main problem of such a creative view is that it might act as a zero-sum-play moving demand from one destination to another. One destination creates an "Art and Jazz weekend" with many visitors. After some years these visitors move to another destination to attend their "Theatre weekend", and so on. At a regional level a few creative and expansive efforts could be successes — more than just for a while. But such products never will be *the* solution of seasonality problems, either for companies or for employees.

A recent Delphi study of future German, Austrian and Swiss holidays (Müller, 1997) shows that efforts to spread the general holidays might lead to more long-haul travel, especially during the winter season. For those markets Müller's studies show that destinations like Australia, New Zealand and, most of all, South Africa will gain visitors, and many European destinations, depending on German markets, will lose traffic. The problem is, however, that this additional traffic will be added to the top seasons down there.

Only a few writers have tried to focus on the tourism seasons in a wider sense (Flognfeldt, 1988; Butler, 1994), looking at both advantages and disadvantages of seasonality.

Seasonality in Tourism, pp 109–117
© 2001 by Elsevier Science Ltd.
All rights of reproduction in any form reserved
ISBN: 0-08-043674-9

The aim of this chapter is to present some answers of how to live with strong seasonality-based tourism. The examples will show how a region with more than a century's experience of strong seasonality, has been adjusting its production and living conditions. How could the people living in a region, the local tourist trade and local authorities adjust to this "problem", or will there be groups or firms that are better off because of seasonality?

A recent study by Hull & Milne (1998) views employment possibilities in another marginal region, the North Shores of Lower Quebec in Canada. The traditions of work in this area are in a way similar to our regions, but both the seasonality pattern of fishing and the decline of this occupation have to be adjusted better to the tourism markets to be part of a real sustainable employment option.

In this author's opinion there would be better chances of developing sustainable seasonal tourism if able to fit different types of tourism production into the seasonal patterns of other production activities, including an adjustment of some public services.

Modelling to Explain How to Live with Seasonality Tourism

In this author's opinion there will always be a strong dependency on seasonality if marginal areas outside the Sun Belt want tourism to be an important source of local income as well as employment. Seasonality, therefore, has to be looked at through a set of figures, before we are able to explain the complex structures. Figures 1 to 3 below show three different ways of illustrating seasonality. The three figures are constructs based on the author's experience from 25 years of studies and consultancy in sparsely populated tourism regions in the Norwegian mountain and coastal regions.

If we are able to measure grocery store income, we could divide this into three groups of spenders: tourists, business travellers including commuters, and locals. Figure 1 is an example of the monthly variation of this expenditure pattern in a typical tourist destination heavily dependent on summer season traffic.

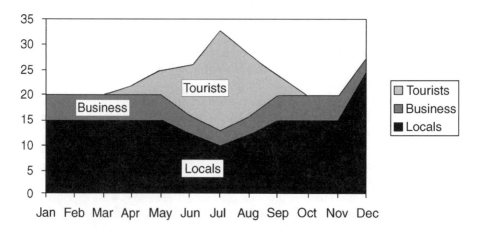

Figure 1: Grocery Store Income in the Ottadal Region During a Year.
Source: Flognfeldt, 1988

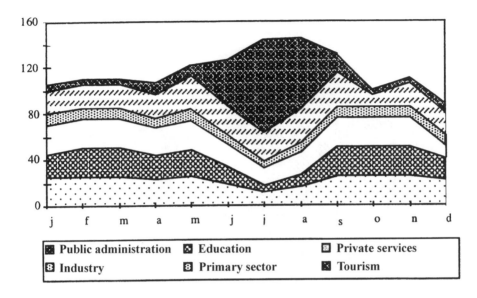

Figure 2: The "Example Marginal Region's" Need of Workforces During the Year.
Source: Flognfeldt, 1988

We should, of course, be able to add the direct income caused by own expenditures of tourism firms to this figure, and this might expand the income from tourism in the high seasons even more.

Based on the same consumption pattern as in Figure 1, Figure 2 above shows the monthly need of a work force to serve the tourists. Jobs are actually measured as an average monthly time-use, based on needs, not on actual employment. The tourism sector includes transport workers and those additional workers in tourism-based trades. The figures are based on the need of a work force in a tourism destination area — without any hint of where this work force might be coming from.

Figure 3 below shows two dimensions: first, the work force needed to supply visitors in the area with services, and second, to show the potential of using core tourism workers to export goods and knowledge during low seasons. This total work force might be divided into:

- The "core workers" are those who at least have an all-year-round part time employment in a tourism firm;
- Migrant workers, i.e., those working in the region every high season, but leaving for other work as soon as the season is over;
- Locals, i.e., those living in the community who get seasonal work in tourism, either in addition to another job or for students as a seasonal job. In Norway, those who have been on summer jobs are placed on an entrance list to the "stable job market" as an alternative to showing recommendations from seasonal employers;
- Summer workers from outside are either students or seasonal workers hired for a short seasonal job, or Summer commuters from outside systematic employment;

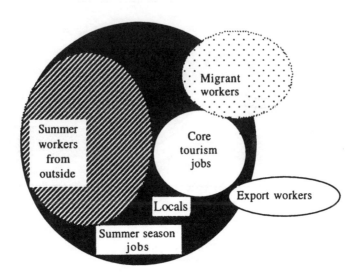

Figure 3: An Attempt to Show Different Groups of Workers Engaged in a Seasonal Tourism Area.

- Export work is not based on a separate work force, but on additional work provided to secure core workers.

In addition to these groups there is another group of visiting workers, such as coach drivers and tour guides who depend on a region's tourism for their livelihood , but are based in other parts of the country or abroad.

A Case Study from Jotunheimen Area in Norway

Even though tourism is generally regarded as a young industry, there are areas in Norway with at least 150 years of experience as a receiver of tourists during the short summer season. What adjustments to seasonality are made in areas that have been developing seasonal tourism for a long time? And why are attempts at widening the seasons restricted to a few producers?

Our examples are from the region of Ottadalen, the eastern part of the Jotunheimen mountain area in Norway, the highest mountain range of Scandinavia. The first tourists arrived here in the middle of the nineteenth century and in the classical book *Three in Norway — by two* (Lees & Clutterbuck, 1882) there is a special description of tourism life.

For more than a century seasonal tourism activities have played an important part in the occupation and income of those living in that part Norway. This area is located along the roads between the western Fjords and the valleys and forest areas in the eastern part of the country. The most important tourism road, Sognefjellsvegen, has its highest point at a level of 1400 metres above sea level and is only been accessible during summer. One of the most important attractions, driving from the Fjords and up to snow-covered mountains and glaciers in a short time, will therefore not be available outside the seasons.

Seasonal employment is available *in the Ottadal region* as follows:

- *Fossheim mineral centre* — a combined gem shop and museum — takes pupils from the age of 14 until they leave school or university, also housewives returning every summer and ready to step in during the rest of the year. In addition some key workers with specialized skills in gem polishing;
- *teachers acting as theme guides* during the Summer holidays, especially conducting glacier and mountain hikes;
- *the camping sector* must always play an important role in areas of seasonality. This sector will have a much lower investment in housing than other accommodation units and might therefore be economically viable based on a 100 days season. If there will be additional use of the site throughout the rest of the year, the camping site owners might be prosperous or at least be able to finance improvements without borrowing money;
- *summer hotels of high class* aiming at tour operated coach market. Long-term investment. Pre opening work, summer season, general maintenance — half year holiday combined with personal marketing;
- *tourist lodges* located inside or outside the Jotunheimen National Park area. These are lodges based on big sleeping rooms with up to 20 beds, a large number of extra beds, some traditional meals served and hard work during a short season. For some there will be another very short season around Easter time;
- some like *to work hard one period* and then go into longer holidays by travelling far away. Agreements with trade unions have reduced such opportunities until recently. Mainly due to oil production work on platforms out in the North Sea, a willingness to try out different working hours exists today. But the staff then has to be hired on a more permanent basis. There are examples of allowing up to 12 working hours a day during the summer period, but paid on a monthly basis for a longer time.

There will also be *staff moving solutions,* as between ski and seaside resorts, well known in Scandinavia, Italy, Spain and France. During the last few years, staff movements have started to take place between the Northern and Southern Hemisphere to the same types of resort but at the opposite time of the year.

To summarise, there are different occupational solutions for the summer seasonal working force. They could either move over to a different job in off-seasons, move to re-education or move to another site or focus on small-scale farming. The list below shows some recognized personal or collective adjustments to seasonality found in the municipality of Lom during the years 1995–98:

1. Normal Procedures

These are the ways firms or persons have adjusted themselves to seasons over a long time span.

1. Importing students and pupils in the high season;
2. Offering jobs in the high season to local pupils and housewives;
3. Agriculture — tourism combinations;
4. Teacher/local government employee — tourism combinations;
5. Returning to seasonal jobs (from another job located outside the area);
6. The managers of small seasonal lodges are often doing marketing and preparationwork in low seasons — if seasonal work is their only job;
7. Expanding seasons — just for a couple of hotels — by "food-art courses", mall conferences and expanding guided tours.

2. Going Away at Low Seasons

This means that employees or managers have adjusted to seasonality by leaving (temporary) the area for other purposes.

1. Working hard as self-employed during high season — taking a long "holiday" during low seasons;
2. Migrant workers — returning to this area every year;
3. Expanding personal knowledge — either by studies or by practising their trade in another environment.

3. Exporting Knowledge and Goods

This is the new adjustment to seasonality, looking more closely at what is produced, and instead of attracting new tourists to the area, local tourist products are exported — mostly food, crafts and knowledge.

1. Chefs from Fossheim hotel (a famous top class gourmet place in Norway) are working as visiting chefs at other hotels, or taking special jobs, such as being responsible for the meals of the Norwegian Winter Olympic Team;
2. Chefs and other staff are designing other menus, i.e., new meals for Scandinavian Airlines 1998;
3. Craftspeople are selling their goods in shops at other places.

Three Generations Living at a Farm — Seasonal Tourism Might Help

It is also important to look closely at seasonality from an agricultural point of view. In Norway, the agricultural policy is to keep living farms in sparsely populated areas to let those areas survive. Farming plus other occupation strategies are of great importance to fulfil such strategies.

Full time farming still exists in the Jotunheimen area , but more and more combinations with other employment is the most usual way of life. At least one of the spouses has got most additional income from other than farming. In addition, there is the problem of succession, which in many cases will force the older ones to an early retirement from the farm. An early retirement means that there will be few other occupational possibilities.

Most camping sites had their origin on a farm, and still many of the smaller ones are an inclusive part of the farm's economy. Many of those are closely managed as a part of the generation take-over system. At an age between 50 and 60 a farmer wants the oldest son or daughter to take over the farm, but will often keep control of the camping business as his generation's employment. In addition, the third generation at the farm, most often teenagers, will assist their grandparents during the Summer season.

In other countries, bed-and-breakfast or farm-stay operations will play the same roles that camping sites do in Norway. For the older generation this means freedom to do other things during the long winter season. This might free time for travelling or taking up different hobbies, or as often happens, maintenance work at the farm.

Opening Attractions in the Low Seasons — a Case of Putting Different Jobs Together

For the overall image of a destination closed attractions during the low seasons might create a bad reputation. This is especially true where attractions which are independent of the weather or other seasonal variations are not open. In addition, of course, many small producers want to get the additional income from out of season visitors. There will, however, be some management problems in opening an attraction or providing services at the tourism information offices during low or near-to-no seasons. My advice is a systematic mix of different jobs combined with a co-ordinated multipurpose service system. The Lom example is a good illustration of such possibilities.

The method of attraction used by the village of Fossbergom in the municipality of Lom is described in Flognfeldt (1997a, b, c). Most of the visitors to the Norwegian Mountain Museum, the Lom Stave Church and the Lom Rural Museum come during a high season, lasting from the end of May to the beginning of September. After this date there is no possibility of opening to the public, if every attraction is supposed to get enough income to pay guides let alone for daily maintenance.

A new tourist organisation was made ready in the Autumn of 1997. The Tourism Information Office moved to the former reception of the Mountain Museum, and agreements were made with the two other attractions to provide guides during the daytime. This means that the staff at the museums could either be working on non-tourism tasks such as preserving houses, research or documentation. The Stave Church might be open for guided tours at times they are closed today. The tourism information office will get more work , and need to employ at least one more person, which in turn will make them better able to market and inform potential tourists. The gains are obvious, both for those financing the different elements and for visiting tourists.

Alternative Production Without Many Tourists Present in the Area

An alternative way of regarding seasonality, especially in rural areas, might be to start focusing on the seasonal patterns of other production areas (Flognfeldt, 1988). These other areas should not be restricted to production in industries and agriculture, but also include different types of governmental employment such as teaching.

The main question to put forward would then be: are there periods of low season in such production areas which might coincide with high seasons in tourism? If so, one needs to plan for *a positive seasonal tourism.* In our studies school teaching is one such area, parts of agriculture production might be another.

Another alternative is to look at off-seasonal preparation of commodities for sale like handicraft and speciality food, or at further education and longer holidays. These strategies for survival might be easier for those who have already been offered a job next summer season.

For the tourism industry in this region the best might be to set up a sort of strategic plan taking all these possibilities into discussion, and try to develop a seasonal and sustainable tourism in combination with other types of work or leisure. Informally this is done, but there is still a step to take to officially accept such strategies — seasonal tourism is often regarded as inferior to all year production.

Conclusions

This paper does not conclude that seasonality is an overall blessing. Areas that are able to produce services for at least two main tourism seasons, i.e., winter and summer, will be the more prosperous ones. In many cases every possible way of widening the seasons must be examined. In most cases, however, a further examination of tourism development possibilities might show that most additional products only function until another imaginative region takes innovative steps to take over your ideas.

Before presenting an optimistic view to local authorities of how to overcome seasonality one should always try to identify as many positive seasonality elements as possible. Trying to mingle different tasks together in out of season periods could be another tool to keep an attractive place visited in more upcoming out of seasons.

Looking closer at a wider area it is hard to find evidence that imaginative additional products like those described by Baum & Hagen (1997), will be sustainable in the long run. As soon as another destination promotes better events, cheaper week-end breaks and so on, at the same quality level, or presents better educational opportunities for tourists, the market will turn to those places instead.

References

Anmarkrud, A., Flognfeldt, T., & Skaarud, B. (1997). *Reiseruteundersøkelsen i Buskerud Sommeren 1996. (The Tourism Routes Study in Buskerud County Summer of 1996).* Et oppdrag for Buskerud Fylkeskommune. Research note from Lillehammer College/Buskerud County Council: Lillehammer/Drammen.

Baum, Tom & Hagan, Laura (1997). Responses to seasonality in tourism: The experiences of perpherial destinations. In Proceedings from the Perpherial Area Tourism Conference. Bornholm, Denmark September 1997.

Butler, Richard (1994). Seasonality in tourism: Issues and problems. In A. V. Seaton *et al.*, *Tourism. The State of the Art* (pp. 332–339). Chichester: John Wiley and Sons.

Dwyer, L., & Forsyth, P. (1998). Estimating the employment impacts of tourism to a nation. *Tourism Recreation Research, 23(2).*

Flognfeldt, Thor (1988). *The Employment Paradox of Seasonal Tourism.* Paper presented at Pre-Congress Meeting of International Geographical Union, Christchurch, New Zealand 13–20 August 1988. (unpublished).

Flognfeldt, T. Jr., & Onshus, T. (1996). Reiselivsundersøkelsen i Ottadalen 1995. Rapport nr 1. Data om de tilreisendes forbruk målt i Ottadalen juni — September 1995. *(The Tourism studies in Ottadalen 1995. Working Report No. 1. The Tourism Consumption Patterns)* Lillehammer College Working Paper Nr. 25/1996.

Flognfeldt, T. (1997a). Reiselivsundersøkelsen i Ottadalen 1995. Rapport nr 2. Tilreisendes bruk av aktiviteter og opplevelser i Ottadalen juni — September 1995. *(The Tourism Studies in Ottadalen 1995. Working Report No. 2. The Tourists' Use of Activities and Attractions)* Lillehammer College Working paper nr 38/1997.

Flognfeldt, T. (1997b), Reiselivsundersøkelsen i Ottadalen 1995. Rapport nr 3. Markedsvurderinger og strategiske utviklingsmodeller *(The Tourism Studies in Ottadalen 1995. Working Report No. 3. Tourism market behaviour and some strategic development models). Lillehammer College, Working paper no 40/1997.*

Flognfeldt, T. (1997c). *Attracting Visitors to a One-Season Area. How Visitor Segments Behave along Traditional Tourism Routes in Mountain Norway and How to Adjust the Local Labour Force to those Seasonal Product.* Paper presented at TTRA Annual Conference — Norfolk, Viginia, June 15 1997 — also presented at the Conference for World Heritage Cities, Evora, Portugal September 1997.

Flognfeldt, T. (1997d). *Impacts from the Short Time Visitors to Local Communities in the Mountain areas of Southern Norway.* Paper presented at Bornholm, Denmark, September 1997. *International Journal of Tourism Research, 1(5),* 359–373.

Hartman, Rudi (1986). Tourism, seasonality and social change. *Leisure Studies, 5(1),* 25–33.

Hull, J., & Milne, S. (1998). Tourism, gender and the labour process: The case of Quebec's lower north shore. *Tourism Recreation Research 23(2).*

Müller, Hansrudi (1997). Long haul tourism 2005 — Delphi Study. In T. Flognfeldt (1997), *Tourism and Leisure Trends.* Conference report 1. TTRA-European Chapter Conference. Lillehammer College, Norway.

Chapter 8

An Analysis of the Nature, Causes and Marketing Implications of Seasonality in the Occupancy Performance of English Hotels

Douglas Jeffrey and Robin R. D. Barden

Seasonal mismatching of supply and demand and the associated over/under utilization of capacity are characteristic features of the tourist industry. Visitor demands, in terms of the number, type, timing and destination of visits can fluctuate widely over the course of the year, but the supply of tourist facilities is usually fixed, at least in the short term. The result is a range of problems in resource usage, utilization and management. The characteristics, causes and consequences of seasonality in tourism have been thoroughly explored in other papers in this volume, and in a range of previous studies (Bar-On, 1975; Witt, Brooke & Buckley, 1991; McEniff, 1992). In this paper attention will focus specifically on seasonality in the hotel industry. It will seek to identify and explain differences in the nature and intensity of seasonal fluctuations in occupancy levels within a large and representative sample of English hotels, and to extract implications from the findings for the management and marketing of hotels.

Hotel occupancy data recorded over time for a large sample of hotels provide a detailed, consistent and continuous means for measuring and monitoring seasonality in the hotel and tourist industries (Jeffrey, 1983; Jeffrey & Barden, 1999). Room and bed occupancy time series for individual hotels are a sensitive barometer of seasonal variations in demand measured against the yardstick of a fixed supply of bed spaces in the short term. Of course, seasonality is not the only constituent component of occupancy time series. Hotel occupancy series will differ in their overall occupancy levels and display differential long-term trends, as well as trends and fluctuations that are unique to particular hotels or to particular hotel market areas. If occupancy time series are to be used to measure and monitor the nature and intensity of seasonality in individual hotels, the effects of seasonality need to be separated from the other general and specific components of hotel occupancy performance. Previous applications of time series factor analysis to hotel occupancy data at the national and regional levels have demonstrated how this can be achieved (Jeffrey, 1985).

Time Series Analysis to Measure Seasonality

The method used in the analysis of occupancy time series is principal components analysis. It is used in a distinctive curve-fitting role to identify dimensions of variability

This chapter was originally published in *Tourism Economics*, Vol. 5, No. 1 (March 1999).
© 1999 IP Publishing Ltd. Reproduced by permission.

(referred to as reference curves) underlying a set of hotel occupancy time series. This special use of a familiar statistical technique has been fully discussed in other contexts (Sheth, 1969; Jeffrey & Adams, 1980) and specifically with respect to hotel occupancy data (Jeffrey, 1983). Here, attention is focused on its use in the identification of the season-ality component of hotel occupancy performance.

In contrast to more traditional uses of principal components analysis, in the study of associative relationships between variables at a point in time, the time periods (months) for which the occupancy rates are recorded are the variables, and the analysis is performed on a covariance matrix. This preserves important differences in the variance of time series between the variables (months) across the hotels (the observations). The analysis identifies dimensions of variation (referred to as reference curves) in the hotel occupancy series around the overall mean curve.

The Sample, the Study Period and the Occupancy Data

The time series analysis is performed on monthly room occupancy rates recorded in a sample of 279 hotels in England over the period January 1992 to December 1994. The locations of the 279 hotels are shown in Figures 3 and 4 below. The data were collected as part of the English Hotel Occupancy Survey (EHOS), performed for the English Tourist Board (ETIB) by BDO Hospitality Consulting. Subject to confidentiality restrictions, limited access to the data was provided. The 279 hotels are a subset of more than 900 hotels in the EHOS panel that provided continuous data over all 36 months of the study period. As the number of hotels participating in the EHOS differed from month to month, considerable manipulation of the monthly databases was necessary to produce the 279 continuous monthly room occupancy time series (Barden, 1998).

The panel of hotels in the EHOS provides a representative coverage of the English hotel industry. The reduced sample of 279 continuous contributors remains broadly representative of the population of English hotels in terms of hotel size, situation type ("large town", "small town", "seaside", "countryside" or London), tariff level ("low", "high" or "premium"), and the presence or absence of conference facilities. As Figures 3 and 4 show, all ETB regions are well represented, though an over-representation of Cumbrian hotels is apparent.

The Mean Curve

The overall mean room occupancy curve of the 279 hotels over the 36 months of the study period is plotted in Figure 1. Given the large and representative nature of the sample the mean curve approximates the national average (or industry norm) occupancy curve. A gradual rise in the curve is evident over the three-year period, as the economy moved out of recession. Average annual room occupancy rates rise from 53.4 percent in 1992, to 54.6 percent in 1993, before jumping to 57.0 percent in 1994.

Also evident in Figure 1 is the extreme seasonality of the industry as a whole, with overall occupancy rates rising each year from a January low point to a late summer peak, before declining to a winter trough again. A difference of thirty to thirty-five percentage

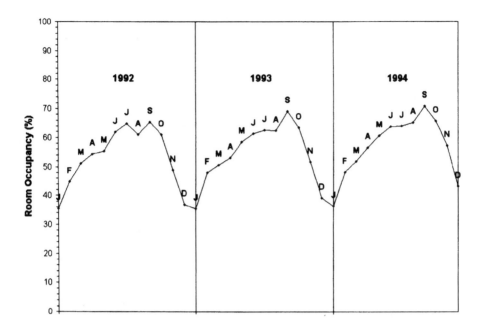

Figure 1: The Sample Mean Room Occupancy Curve.

points separates peak average room occupancy rates in September from the lowest occupancy rates in January.

The dimensions of seasonality (reference curves), picked out by the time series analysis of the 279 monthly occupancy series, are defined in relation to the overall mean curve, i.e., they are dimensions of variation around the mean. They differentiate hotels on the basis of the nature, intensity and patterns of seasonal fluctuations with respect to industry norms.

Removing Differences in Overall Occupancy Levels (RC 1) and Long-Term Trends (RC3) from the Occupancy Time Series

The time series principal components analysis identifies four reference curves, collectively accounting for 79 percent of total variance in occupancy levels around the mean. Each is defined by a set of component loadings over the 36 months of the study period. They are plotted in Figure 2 below. Two of the reference curves serve to isolate seasonality in hotel occupancy performance by removing other components of occupancy performance from the time series. RC1 (53% of total variance) approximates the mean deviation from the mean curve. It has uniformly high positive loadings throughout the study period, and when "weighted" by the component scores of the hotels, it removes the effects of differences in overall occupancy levels between the 279 hotels. RC3 (6% of total variance) defines a clear upward trend, and when "weighted" by the approximate component scores, it removes any upwards (positive score) or downwards (negative score) trend in the hotel occupancy series.

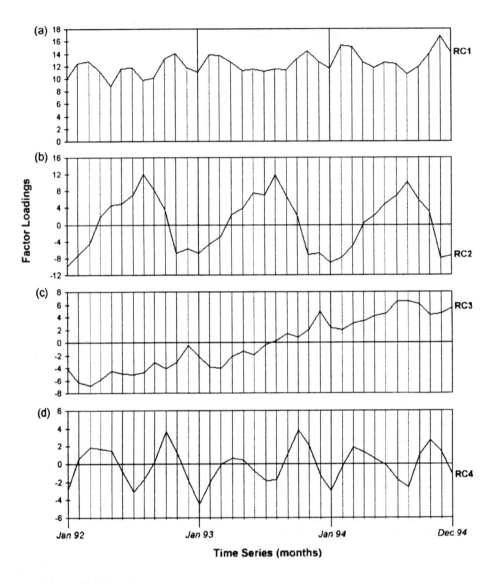

Figure 2: The Four Principal Dimensions of Hotel Occupancy Performance (reference curves).

The Two Dimensions of Seasonality (RC2 and RC4)

The two remaining reference curves in Figure 2, RC2 and RC4, identify orthogonal (independent) dimensions of variation in hotel occupancy performance that are associated with seasonality.

RC2 (15% of total variance) traces a familiar annual pattern of seasonality in tourism in northern countries (see Figure 2(b)). The curve is marked by large positive loadings from June to September, with an August peak, and large negative loadings from November to February. The curve differentiates hotels on the basis of the nature and intensity of seasonality in their monthly occupancy series. It "corrects" the national mean occupancy curve for the range of seasonality displayed by individual hotels. Those hotels with positive scores on RC2 will have more pronounced seasonal patterns, the intensity of the pattern being directly related to the size of the score. Negative scores reveal reduced seasonality, and where they drop below −1.0, the negative correlation effect of RC2 is sufficient to indicate counter-seasonal patterns.

RC4 (5% of total variance) traces a seasonal pattern with twin peaks occurring in spring and autumn, with troughs in winter and summer (see Figure 2(d)). Its effect is to "correct for" the length of season. For the majority of hotels, which have a summer season peak, a positive score on RC4 will indicate a broader extended season, and a negative score, a short and more pronounced seasonal peak. For the small minority of hotels with a slight counter seasonal pattern, a positive score will shorten and intensify that pattern, whilst a negative score will serve to broaden and flatten it.

The Regional Patterns of Seasonality

The distribution of scores on RC2 in Figure 3 reveals a clear core-periphery spatial pattern in the nature and intensity of seasonality. Seaside and remote or peripheral hotels generally have sizeable positive scores and display pronounced or extreme seasonality. Hotels in a central belt from the South East to the North West and West Yorkshire generally display negative scores, reflecting non-seasonal or counter-seasonal occupancy patterns. However, the consistency of the core-periphery is broken: by hotels in urban centres in the periphery, with negative scores and non-seasonal patterns; by hotels in more central inland tourism areas, such as the Cotswolds and the Peak District, with small positive scores and seasonal patterns; and by central London hotels, with small scores on RC2 and average seasonality. On closer inspection, Figure 3 reveals evidence of sharp differences in the size and sign of scores at the local level, a reflection of the varying degrees of success that individual hotels have in countering the effects of seasonality of demand.

Broad regional and locational patterns are also evident in the distribution of scores on RC4 in Figure 4 below. Most hotels in Cumbria have large positive scores (extended seasons), reflecting a pattern of leisure tourism characteristic of the region, where visits can be equally concentrated in spring and autumn as over the summer months. Most seaside hotels have large negative scores (short and intense seasons), but seaside hotels in the North West are able to extend their seasons, on the back of major out-of-season attractions, and their proximity to the major conurbations of the region. However, as with RC2, considerable within-region variation is apparent in the length of season, with hotels in proximate locations frequently recording sizeable scores of opposite signs. This suggests that locational constraints on seasonal extension are not restrictive, and that, with appropriate investment and marketing, most hoteliers could extend their seasons.

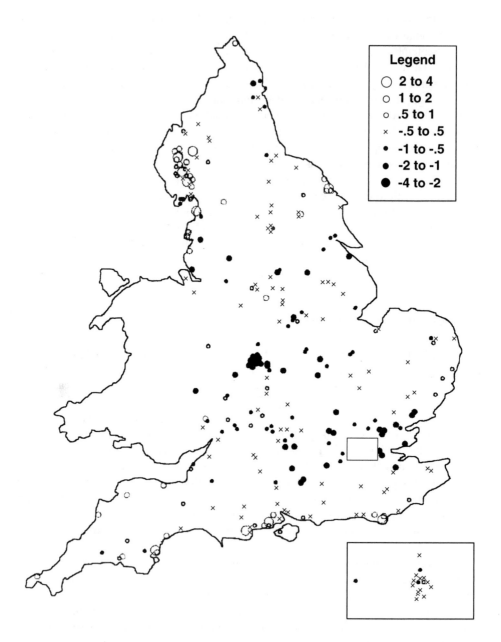

Figure 3: Regional Distribution of Scores on RC2.

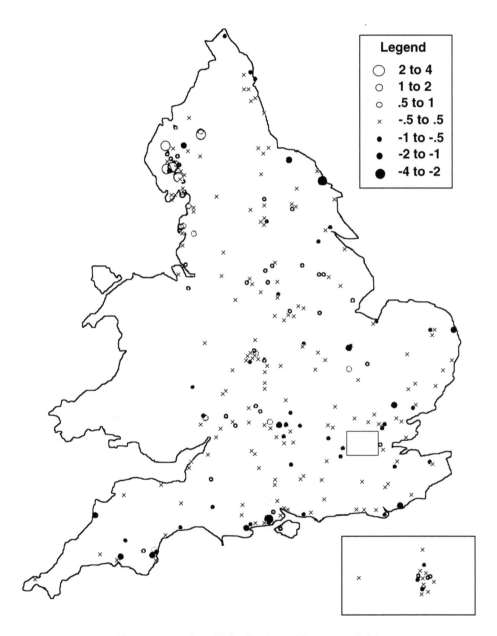

Figure 4: Regional Distribution of Scores on RC4.

The Positioning of Hotels on the Two Dimensions of Seasonality

The two reference curves make an independent and additive contribution to the analysis of seasonality of hotel occupancy performance. Each provides an independent axis of "seasonality space", within which hotels are located by their component scores. These reflect differences in the nature, intensity and length of their seasonal patterns. The distribution of the 279 hotels in this space is presented in Figure 5 below. It should be noted that hotels are positioned in relation to the origin and this approximates the national average occupancy profile or industry norm. The hotels are also differentiated by their location type and the group midpoint of each locational type is identified by a larger version of the same symbol used to identify the individual members of each group (see the legend in Figure 5 below).

The distribution of hotels in Figure 5 confirms the orthogonality of the two reference curves and the absence of a linear relationship between the nature and the intensity of seasonality (RC2) and the length of season (RC4). However, there is some evidence for a more complex non-linear relationship. The largest scores on both reference curves are recorded by the same hotels. They are a group of seaside and countryside hotels that combine large positive scores on RC2 (extreme seasonality) with either large positive scores on RC4 (extended seasons) or large negative scores on RC4 (short and intense

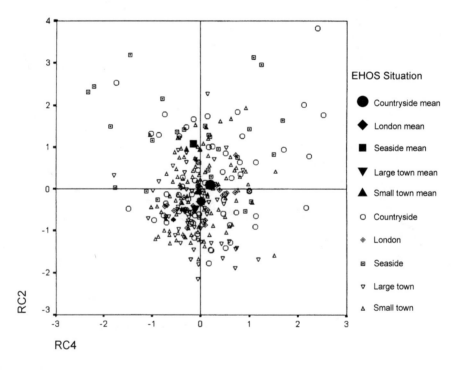

Figure 5: Distribution of Hotels on the Plane of Occupancy Performance
Space Defined by RC2 (seasonality) and RC4 (shoulder season extension).

seasons). Generally, the seaside hotels in the group combine extreme seasonality with short and intense seasons, but the countryside hotels feature both seasonal patterns.

Though the two dimensions of seasonality are orthogonal, when the sample is broken down by location type, a number of significant relationships emerge between the scores on the two dimensions (within the locational subgroups).

First, it is clear from Figure 5 and Table 1 below that some group midpoints differ significantly from the origin: large town hotels, with a group mean score on RC2 of –0.48, are less seasonal than the norm; seaside hotels, with group means of 1.08 and –0.98 on RC2 and RC4, have pronounced seasonality, and short and intense seasons; London hotels, with a mean of –0.30 on RC2, have reduced seasonality. Small town and countryside hotels have group means close to the origin. However, if these two ETB locational types are further categorised, according to market orientation, into business and leisure market hotels, (as was possible for 91 of the hotels), they display distinctly mean scores significantly different from zero (see below).

The correlation co-efficients in column three of Table 1 measure the relationships between the two dimensions of seasonality within each of the location types. The correlations are computed around the origin to preserve important differences between the group means and the overall (national) mean, as defined by the origin of "seasonality space". Though none of the relationships are close, two are significant at the 95 percent level and one at the 99 percent level. The positive co-efficients for small town and countryside hotels indicate a tendency for the more seasonal of these hotels to display extended seasons. The negative co-efficient for seaside hotels indicates a tendency for shorter and more intense seasons to be experienced in the more seasonal seaside hotels.

Explaining Seasonality in Occupancy Performance: a Questionnaire Survey and Multivariate Analysis

To further develop the explanation of seasonality in hotel occupancy, more information was sought on the characteristics of the sample hotels via a questionnaire survey. The questionnaire was directed by a detailed literature survey that sought to identify causal

Table 1: Mean Scores on RC2 and RC4 and Correlations (round the origin) between Scores on RC2 and RC4 by Location Type.

Location type	Mean scores		Correlations
	RC2	RC4	RC2:RC4
Small Town (ST)	–0.07	–0.04	0.17*
Large Town (LT)	–0.48	–0.10	–0.09
Seaside (SS)	1.08	–0.98	–0.19*
London (LOND)	–0.30	0.02	0.11
Countryside (C)	0.10	0.20	0.23**

* significant at the 95 percent level
** significant at the 99 percent level

factors involved in influencing seasonal occupancy patterns. The questionnaire supplemented information on the hotels that could be derived from other sources: hotel guides and brochures provided basic information on the characteristics of the hotels, their location and their setting; the EHOS itself also recorded information for its panel of hotels on the size, tariff level, locational type, and the presence or absence of conference facilities.

Barden (1998) presents a detailed discussion and justification of the survey procedures and questions employed, and the full list of variables derived. Here attention is focused solely on the variables that proved significant in explaining and predicting the nature and intensity of seasonality. These are listed in Table 2 overleaf. Unless it is indicated otherwise, the variables are derived from the results of the postal questionnaire survey.

Questionnaires were sent to all of the 279 hoteliers who had provided continuous data over the study period. Of these, 91 returned satisfactorily completed questionnaire forms, a response rate of 33 percent. It is on this sub-sample of 91 hotels that the subsequent analysis is based. Fortuitously, the reduced sample remains remarkably representative of the English hotel industry; with the sample hotels evenly distributed across the ETB regions and the size, situation and tariff categories employed by the EHOS (Barden, 1998).

(1) Seasonality (RC2) and Situation/Location Type

In Figure 6 below the scores of the 91 hotels on RC2 are plotted, with the hotels grouped into the ETB situation types of small town, large town, seaside, London and countryside.

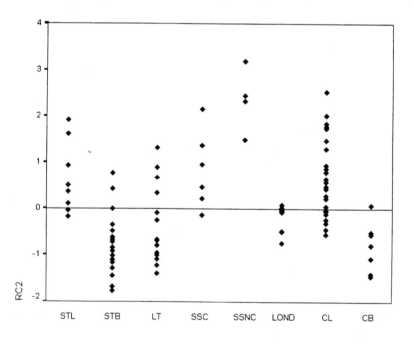

Figure 6: Scatter of Scores on RC2 (seasonality) According to Hotel Situation Type.

Table 2: Variables used in the Analysis of Seasonality and Length of Season in Hotel Occupancy Time Series.

NORTH	Nominal variable indicating a Northumbrian hotel.
CUMBRIA	,, ,, ,, a Cumbrian hotel.
EANGL	,, ,, ,, an East Anglian hotel.
ST	,, ,, ,, a hotel in a small town (population of 10,000 to 100,000).
STNC	,, ,, ,, a hotel in a non-central location in a small town.
STL	,, ,, ,, a small town hotel in a market area dominated by leisure travelers.
STB	,, ,, ,, a small town hotel in a market area dominated by business travelers.
LT	,, ,, ,, a (population greater than 100,000 excluding London).
SS	,, ,, ,, a seaside hotel.
SSC	,, ,, ,, a seaside hotel in a central location or on the seafront.
SSNC	,, ,, ,, a seaside hotel in a non-central, remote or ex-urban location.
CV	,, ,, ,, a countryside hotel in a village location.
CNV	,, ,, ,, a countryside hotel, not located in a village, but accessible to the trunk road network.
CL	Nominal variable indicating a countryside hotel in a market area dominated by leisure travelers.
CB	,, ,, ,, a countryside hotel in a market area dominated by business travelers.
LOND	,, ,, ,, a London hotel.
ACCTOUR	,, ,, ,, whether or not the hotel is located in a major tourist destination area (e.g. a National Park) or is in close proximity to notable tourist attractions (e.g. Alton Towers) (1 = Yes; 0 = No)
BOOKGRP	Proportion of total bookings from group bookings.
BOOKDIR	Proportion of total bookings from direct individual sales.
MBSHOLGP	Proportion of the hotels' guests that stay on short group/inclusive tour holidays.
MBSHOLIN	Proportion of the hotels' guests that stay on short holidays based on individual travel.
MBSHOLS	Proportion of the hotels' guests that stay on short holidays (i.e. a sum of MBSHOLGP and MBSHOLIN)
MBLONGIN	Proportion of the hotels' guests that stay on long holidays based on individual travel.
MBLHOLS	Proportion of the hotels' guests that stay on long holidays (i.e. a sum of MBLONGDRP and MBLONGIN)
MBLEISR	Proportion of the hotels' staying guests that are leisure (holiday) tourists (i.e. a sum of MBLHOLS and MBSHOLS)
MBUSTRAV	Proportion of the hotels' staying guests that are on business travellers, whether in the hotel's destination area, or in transit.
MBUSCON	Proportion of the hotels' staying guests that are on commercial business, whether at a conference, meeting or exhibition at the hotel, on business in the hotel's destination area, or in transit (i.e. a sum of MBUSTRAV and MBCONF)
MDIV	A simple measure of market orientation and market diversity. Values range from –100 (indicating 100% business and conference guests) to 100 (indicating 100% leisure guests).
ROOMS	Number of hotel bedrooms.
SIZS	Nominal variable indicating a small hotel (less than 15 bedrooms)
SIZL	,, ,, ,, a large hotel (greater than 50 bedrooms)
PRICE	Minimum published rate for a double room (rack rate).
TARL	Nominal variable indicating a "low" hotel (Provincial under £35.50, London under £53.50)
TARP	,, ,, ,, a "premium" hotel (Provincial over £67.50, London over £81.50)
CHN	,, ,, ,, a group-owned or chain operated hotel
QUALITY	The ETB quality grading in 1994: *Approved* (1), *Commended* (2), *Highly Commended* (3), or *Deluxe* (4).
ROMHIST	A measure of the romantic and historic appeal of the hotel and its setting using each hotel's brochure and the ETB's *Where To Stay* guide and hotel visits as sources of data. In deriving a value for each hotal the historic and architectural quality of the building and the aesthetic and/or historical appeal of its setting produced values ranging from 0 to a maximum "appeal" score of 5.
ROOMEXT	The number of "extra" facilities provided in the hotel's standard bedrooms (from hotel brochures and *Where To Stay* guide).
CONF	Distinguishes between hotels with no conference facilities (CONF = 0), those that can provide for up to 200 conference delegates (CONF = 1), and those hotels with the facilities to cater for more than 200 delegates (CONF = 2).
ARRPCAUG	Proportion of rooms sold at the full rack rate in August 1994.
YIELDA	Nominal variable indicating whether or not the hotelier was familiar with the term "yield management" (1 = Yes; 0 = No)
YIELDB	Nominal variable indicating whether or not the hotelier uses a yield management system in running the hotel, i.e. in handling reservations and booking enquiries (1 = Yes; 0 = No)
MKGBUDG	Proportion of hotel's revenue allocated to the marketing budget.
REDUCTS	The number of types of reductions offered by the hotel. Included in the count were child reductions, reductions for OAPs, and special off-peak reductions. Values ranged from 0 to 3.

The small town and countryside groups are further categorised into business and leisure market hotels and the seaside group into central and non-central hotels. Though there is considerable within-group variation, a link between the nature and intensity of seasonality and situation type is clearly apparent. An ANOVA confirmed between-group variance as significant at the 99.9 percent level.

Seaside hotels (SS) have the most pronounced seasonal patterns with a group mean of 1. 45***, significantly different from zero at the 99.9 percent level, and with all but one having greater than average seasonality. Most small town leisure hotels (mean = 0.59***) and countryside leisure hotels (mean = 0.72***) also display pronounced seasonality. In contrast small town business and countryside business hotels (means = −0.76*** and −0.82***) typically have non-seasonal or counter-seasonal patterns.

Within each situation type, hotels were further dichotomised by location into central or non-central/suburban and, in the case of countryside hotels, into village or non-village. Only in seaside hotels did this locational dichotomy produce significant differences in mean scores on RC2, with non-central seaside hotels (mean = 2.37***) displaying the greater seasonality than central or seafront hotels (mean = 0.84*).

(2) Correlates of Seasonality (RC2)

Table 3 highlights the significant correlations between the scores on RC2 and a range of variables, each of which can be hypothesised as being causally related to the nature and intensity of seasonality. The variables are grouped under the following headings: location and accessibility; market profile and market contact; hotel characteristics; and pricing, marketing and management.

The first column of coefficients supports the conclusions drawn earlier regarding seasonality and situation type. Additionally, significant correlations of opposite signs are

Table 3: Significant Correlations with Seasonality (RC2).

Location and accessibility		Market profile and market contact		Hotel attributes (characteristic variables)		Pricing, marketing and management related variables	
Independent Variable	Correlation Coefficient	Independent Variable	Correlation Coefficient	Independent Variable	Correlation Coefficient	Independent Variable	Correlation Coefficient
CUMBRIA**	.356	BOOKGRP**	−.368	ROOMS**	−.372	ARRPCAUG**	.332
EANGL*	−.259	BOOKDIR*	.257	SIZS**	.301	YIELDS**	−.297
ST*	−.256	MNSHOLIN**	.558	SIZL**	−.300	YIELDB**	−.286
STB**	−.402	MBSHOLS**	.524	PRICE**	−.362		
SS**	.426	MBLONGIN**	.566	TARL**	.277		
CL**	.336	MBLHOLS**	.537	TARP**	−.303		
CB*	−.258	MBLEISR**	.668	CHN**	−.294		
STNC*	−.225	MBUSTRAV**	−.513	CONF**	−.502		
SSNC**	.443	MBCONF**	−.399				
ACCTOUR**	.433	MBUSCON**	−.657				
		MDIV**	.665				

* Significant at the 95 percent level
**Significant at the 99 percent level

recorded by two regional dummy variables. They show that pronounced seasonality is characteristic in Cumbrian hotels, whilst East Anglian hotels typically display reduced seasonality. The significance of leisure-based tourism in inducing seasonality is reflected in the positive coefficient of ACCTOUR, a measure of a hotel's access to leisure tourist flows based on proximity to major tourist attractions (both natural and man-made).

The market profile variables (prefixed MB) display the strongest relationships with scores on RC2. The second column of co-efficients in Table 3 reveals:

- There is a strong positive association between orientation to the short holiday market (MBSHOLS) and the extent of seasonality, but this applies only to independently booked short holidays (MBSHOLIN), as the proportion of group-booked short holidays in a hotel's market breakdown is not correlated with RC2;
- There is a strong positive association between orientation to the long holiday market (MBLHOLS) and seasonality, but again this does not apply to group-booked holidays;
- Orientation to the conference market (MBCONF), and more especially the business, and business and conference, markets (MBUSTRAV and MBUSCON) is associated with reduced and counter seasonality;
- The highest positive correlation with seasonality is provided by an overall measure of market orientation to the leisure markets as opposed to the business and conference markets;
- High proportions of group bookings (BOOKGRP) are associated with reduced or counter-seasonality and high proportions of direct bookings (BOOKDIR) typically occur in hotels with augmented seasonality.

Significant links between seasonality and hotel characteristics are revealed in the third column of co-efficients in Table 3. Hotel size (ROOMS, SIZS, SIZL), tariff (PRICE), group ownership (CHN) and the presence of conference facilities (CONF) are all negatively correlated with seasonality.

Three significant and revealing correlations are obtained between seasonality and the pricing, marketing and management variables. The use of yield management systems (YIELDB) is associated with reduced seasonality. The significant positive correlation between RC2 and ARRPCAUG links seasonality with the management's ability to achieve full rack rates in the peak months. More interesting and revealing, however, is the positive correlation with ARRPCJAN. Traditional pricing theory would suggest a negative correlation, with the most seasonal hotels displaying the greatest price discounting in the off-season months of January. In practice the reverse is the case. The positive correlation suggests there are perhaps missed opportunities for flexible pricing to reduce seasonality amongst some of the most seasonal (usually small independent) hotels.

(3) Predicting Seasonality (RC2)

Though a large number of variables are significantly related to seasonality, there is considerable multicollinearity amongst them and a high degree of overlap in their ability to explain and predict differential seasonality. In a stepwise regression analysis, with RC2 as the dependent variable and all variables listed in Table 3 included as potential predictor variables, only five independent variables are entered in the final regression equation. The stepwise regression procedure enters one variable at a time into the regression equation. The variable entered at each step is that with the highest partial correlation with the dependent variable, given that previously selected variables are in the equation (Norusis, 1993). Only variables making a significant contribution to explained variance are entered. The results of the analysis at the final step are summarised in Table 4, with variables listed in order of entry. The five-variable predictive model produces a level of explained variance of 63 percent.

A simple measure of market orientation (MDIV) alone accounts for 44 percent of variance when entered into the equation at Step 1. Predicted scores on RC2 range from –1.2 (indicating a non-seasonal pattern) for hotels serving only business and conference markets to a score of 1.3 (indicating extreme seasonality) for hotels solely reliant on leisure markets. MDIV's regression co-efficient and its level of predictive significance remain essentially unaltered as the four other independent variables enter the equation. These serve to adjust the predicted scores on RC2 for "augmented" seasonality in seaside

Table 4: A Stepwise Regression Model of Seasonality (RC2).

Step	Variables Entered	R^2	SE	F Statistic	Standardised Regression Coefficients (by order of entry)	Significant Partial Correlations	
						Variable	Correlation
1	MDIV	0.45	0.82	70.71***	.67***	SS***	.41
						PRICE***	–.30
						MBSHOLGP***	–.29
						ACCTOUR*	.19
2	SS	0.54	0.75	50.24***	.61***	PRICE***	–.29
					.31***	MBSHOLGP***	–.28
						MBLONGIN*	.19
3	PRICE	0.58	0.72	38.64***	.57***	MBSHOLGP***	–.30
					.29***	ACCTOUR**	.23
					.20***		
4	MBSHOLGP	0.62	0.69	33.51***	.61***	ACCTOUR**	.23
					.27***		
					.20***		
					.20***		
5	ACCTOUR	0.63	0.68	28.78***	.52***		
					.26***		
					–.23***		
					–.19**		
					.16**		

*   Significant at 90 percent level.
**   Significant at 95 percent level.
*** Significant at the 99 percent level.

hotels (SS) and hotels in close proximity to major tourist attractions (ACCTOUR); and "dampened" seasonality in higher quality hotels (PRICE) and hotels which cater for the group booked (and usually out-of-season) short holiday market (MBSHOLGP).

(4) Length of Season (RC4) and Situation/Location Type

In Figure 7 below the scores on RC4 are plotted, with the 91 hotels again grouped into situation type classes, as in Figure 6 above. Again, there is considerable within-group variance, but there is also clear evidence that location and situation affect the length of season. An ANOVA confirmed between-group variance significant at the 99.9 percent level.

Extreme scores on RC4 are mainly concentrated in two situation types; seaside and countryside leisure. Most seaside hotels record substantial negative scores, indicative of short, sharply peaked and intense summer seasons. The group mean is –0.99***, significantly different from zero at the 99.9 percent level. The two hotels within the group with small positive scores are atypical of seaside hotels. One, on the Suffolk Coast, is within easy driving distance of London, and shares most of its characteristics with premium tariff countryside hotels positioned in the short holiday/executive business market. The other is a

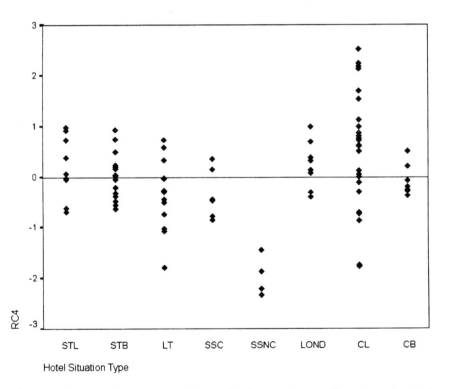

Figure 7: Scatter of Scores on RC4 (length of season) According to Hotel Situation
Type.

seafront hotel in Bridlington, with a high proportion of retired, long-stay guests, including some permanent residents. When seaside hotels are dichotomised by location, it is clear that it is those in non-central and non-seafront locations that have the largest negative scores on RC4 (category mean = −1.96***) and the shortest and most pronounced summer peak.

Most countryside hotels in predominantly leisure market areas (CL) display large or very large positive scores on RC4, indicative of broad and extended seasons. The group mean of 0.55 is significant at the 99.9 percent level, but it is not "typical". It is substantially lowered by a number of hotels with negative scores on RC4. All of these are atypical of the countryside leisure group. They are located in the countryside (and are categorized accordingly), but they are in close proximity to seaside tourist centres, and share most of their occupancy characteristics with seaside hotels.

(5) Correlations of Length of Season (RC4)

Four of the correlation co-efficients between the location variables and RC4 in Table 5 confirm the conclusions reached in the previous sections. These are reinforced by a highly significant positive correlation co-efficient for the Cumbria regional "dummy". The strong shoulder season performance of Lake District hotels was noted in discussing the regional pattern of scores on RC4 in Figure 4.

Other significant correlates of length of season are measures of the characteristics of hotels and the nature of the hotel operations: the quality (QUALITY, PRICE) of the hotel, its romantic and historic appeal (ROMHIST), the range of room facilities provided (ROOMEXT) and the relative size of the marketing budget (MKGBUDG) are all significantly positively correlated with the ability of a hotel to extend its season. These relationships would suggest that, within limits imposed by the nature of the hotel's market area, success in raising occupancy levels in the "shoulder seasons" is related to a

Table 5: Significant Correlations with Length of Season (RC4).

Location and accessibility		Hotel attributes (characteristic variables)		Pricing, marketing and management related variables	
Independent Variable	Correlation Coefficient	Independent Variable	Correlation Coefficient	Independent Variable	Correlation Coefficient
RG1**	.403	PRICE*	.227	MKGBUDG*	.242
SIT5**	.327	QUALITY**	.363		
SLB4**	−.392	ROMHIST1**	.319		
SLB6**	.364	ROMHIST2**	.316		
CLOC6**	−.468	ROOMEXT*	.221		
CLOC9**	.417				

* Significant at the 95 percent level
**Significant at the 99 percent level

combination of two factors: the appeal of the hotel, its image, setting and quality; and the commitment of hotel managements to marketing off-season accommodation products, particularly for short and additional holidays.

(6) Predicting Length of Season (RC4)

Eight variables make significant contributions to explaining variations in the length of season effect in a stepwise regression analysis. This contribution is measured by the size and sign of their standardised regression co-efficients in the final regression equation in Table 6 below. The variables are listed in order of entry into the equation. Overall, the eight-variable model explains 60 percent of total variance in the dependent variable, the scores on RC4. Multicollinearity amongst the eight independent variables is negligible, and the regression co-efficients of the variables remain essentially the same from their point of entry to the final regression equation.

The large negative coefficient for SSNC indicates the prevalence of short intense seasonal peaks in seaside hotels in non-central locations. The positive co-efficients for QUALITY, MKGBUDG and REDUCTS collectively point to higher shoulder season occupancy levels in higher quality hotels that are prepared to offer rooms at discounted room rates, particularly when supported by relatively large marketing budgets. This prognosis is more likely to apply to countryside hotels in both village locations (CV) and in accessible, free-standing, locations (CNV), and in London hotels (LOND). Conversely, hotels in Northumbria (NORTH) have lower shoulder season occupancy levels, and more pronounced summer season peaks than would be expected on the basis of their quality, size of marketing budget and degree of price flexibility.

One thread runs through the explanatory contribution of the eight variables in the model. Each can be linked to the ability of a hotel to successfully penetrate the additional/short holiday market, with its characteristic annual pattern of "twin peaks" in the shoulder season months. The locational and situational dummy variables pick out hotels which are well (or poorly) placed to penetrate this market because of the advantages (or limitations) of their location and/or situation. The remaining variables pick out features of hotels and their marketing which have proved to be attractive to additional short holiday takers. Sykes (1983). for example, found that this market segment tends to seek good quality accommodation, and high quality rooms in particular, but is also sensitive to price and attracted by the perceived "value for money" of discounted room rates.

Explaining Residual Variance in Seasonality: A Structured Interview Survey

General relationships have been specified and tested between the two dimensions of seasonality identified in the occupancy time series analysis and a range of variables measuring the locational, management and marketing characteristics of hotels. Significant relationships have been established and high levels of explained variance achieved in the predictive models. But much within-group and residual variance remains unaccounted for. Ultimately a hotel's occupancy profile is unique, a result of the unique combination of

Table 6: A Stepwise Regression Model of Length of Season (RC4).

Step	Variables Entered	R^2	SE	F Statistic	Standardised Regression Coefficients (by order of entry)	Significant Partial Correlations	
						Variable	Correlation
1	SSNC	0.22	0.81	24.94***	−.47***	CNV***	.42
						QUALITY***	.39
						MKGBUDG***	.34
2	CNV	0.36	0.74	24.40***	−.43***	QUALITY***	.34
					.37***	MKGBUDG***	.32
						CV*	.21
3	QUALITY	0.43	0.70	21.87***	−.42***	MKGBUDG***	.31
					.32***	NORTH**	−.23
					.28***	CUMBRIA**	.22
4	MKGBUDG	0.48	0.67	20.14***	−.46***	CV**	.25
					.29***	NORTH**	−.23
					.26***	LOND**	.22
					.24***		
5	CV	0.52	0.66	18.14***	−.44***	LOND**	.28
					.32***	NORTH**	−.22
					.27***		
					.24***		
					.19**		
6	LOND	0.55	0.63	17.36***	−.42***	NORTH**	−.21
					.36***	REDUCTS*	.19
					.28***		
					.27***		
					.22***		
					.20**		
7	NORTH	0.57	0.62	15.97***	−.42***	REDUCTS**	.21
					.36***		
					.30***		
					.26***		
					.21***		
					.19**		
					−.15*		
8	REDUCTS	0.59	0.61	14.95***	−.44***		
					.34***		
					.28***		
					.28***		
					.18**		
					.27***		
					−.15**		
					.17*		

* Significant at the 90 percent level.
** Significant at the 95 percent level.
*** Significant at the 99 percent level.

factors and circumstances that have produced it. To probe the causes and consequence unique variance in the seasonality of hotels, structured interviews were performed with 21 of the 91 hoteliers who had participated in the question survey, on which the multivariate statistical analyses were based. Barden (1998) presents a full account of the survey methodology and individual structured interview findings. In this paper they are used merely as a means of relating the general analyses and models of seasonality in occupancy performance to the specific characteristics and circumstances of individual hotels. In the following sections the results from the structured interviews are integrated with the facts and interpretations emerging from the earlier statistical analyses to provide further insights into seasonality in hotel occupancy performance, and to extract relevant implications for hotel management and marketing.

Marketing for Reduced Seasonality and/or Extended Seasons

It is clear that seasonality in hotel occupancy performance is mainly dependent on the type of market segments served by hotels. This means that changes in the composition of the hotel's guest profile will be clearly and directly reflected in the monthly patterns traced in the occupancy profile. On this basis, hotels should consider making the penetration of those market segments most likely to increase low season occupancies a primary marketing objective. The relevance of this objective does, however, depend greatly on the characteristics of demand for accommodation in the local market area and the feasibility of penetrating "counter seasonal" market segments. Objectives to further penetrate new market segments to raise and smooth occupancy profiles should, therefore, be based on reliable market information, and assessed via the appropriate marketing planning processes, such as those described by Middleton (1994). For some hotels seasonal closure may continue to be the most cost-effective method for dealing with pronounced seasonality. For others, market intensification strategies based on increasing penetration of existing markets, and, in the process, increasing peak season/off season occupancy differentials, might be more a feasible and appropriate option, despite the difficulties this may create for the efficient use of the hotel's resources.

However, the need to raise low season occupancy levels is a major marketing task facing most English hotels. In many, including several encountered in the structured interview survey, further increases in shoulder season and winter season occupancy levels could be gained if the inherent potential possessed by the hotel product and/or its market area is recognized and exploited.

In seeking to stimulate demand for a hotel's accommodation in the low season, the hotelier should determine which markets are most likely to respond to a marketing campaign aimed at selling the hotel's accommodation at that specific time of year. Several of the hoteliers interviewed reported some success in persuading previous guests to make repeat stays during off-peak periods. A reduction in room rate was the most commonly used incentive, but frequently an extra element was incorporated into the off-season holiday "package" to provide an added incentive. In other hotels, however, adding value to the low season accommodation product seemed to be overlooked as a promotional technique.

Adding short-term value, through the temporary provision of extra product (e.g., an extra night's accommodation free) or extra services (e.g., entertainment, themed events, the offer of "free gifts", etc.) may be a much more fruitful strategy to follow in attempting to stimulate low season demand. Additional stays may be generated, and/or extended stays may be induced, to raise occupancy levels in low season months. If repeat visits (which may involve a small discount on the room rate) are shifted to the shoulder seasons or low season then new customers may be won during the peak season (at full room rate), thereby broadening the hotel's customer base.

In one of the Lake District hotels studied, what started out as a "one-off", "themed" sales promotion has developed into an annual event at the hotel, taking place in early March. Similarly, an East Anglian hotel surveyed had developed a reputation for "wine weekends" organised through the hotel's association with a regional brewery, and these events were reflected in exceptionally high room occupancy levels in January for a seaside hotel (Barden, 1998). Such events provide an opportunity to alleviate the problems of seasonality during the hotel's low or shoulder seasons. If successful, they can create useful media and public relations opportunities, as well as near-100 percent occupancy occasions in the hotel's reservation's calendar.

Such promotions are a particularly important tool for independent hotels, hotels with less favourable locations, and hotels oriented to one segment of the market alone. Even if the small- or medium-sized hotel lacks the facilities to attract leisure guests year-round (e.g., indoor sports facilities), the hotel may be able to capitalise on the unique advantages of its location (or even unique features of the hotel) to stimulate an interest in staying at the hotel out of season. A detailed assessment of local area's touristic resources and their availability during the course of the year, precise targeting of special interest groups (micro-segments), imagination, and an innovative sales approach are the prerequisites of success in such ventures (Bond, 1996).

One of the main considerations in sales promotions is the discounting of rack rates, but the hotels should also consider the effect of the more permanent price differential between the peak season and off-season tariff on market demand. Evidence from the questionnaire and direct structured interview surveys suggest that many hotels could improve off-peak occupancy levels (and thereby reduce seasonality) if lower tariff levels are clearly defined and published for off-peak periods. Certain segments of the hotel accommodation market may be stimulated by the enhanced value-for-money signalled by such price reductions. Penetration of the short holiday group market in particular was shown to reduce seasonality in the composite model of RC2. One hotelier, at a Whitby hotel studied, pinpointed the benefits of accepting annual block-bookings of field study groups in the off-season. Another hotelier at a smaller Cumbrian hotel, aware of the potential of the short holiday group market to yield off-peak bookings, indicated his frustration at not being able to cater for the market due to limited capacity (Barden, 1998).

Of course, marketing initiatives should not be confined solely to the low periods in the hotel's occupancy profile. Hotels could also target periods with very high seasonal occupancy levels. In contrast to the pricing measures aimed at stimulating greater demand in low occupancy periods, there may be scope for many hotels to raise room rates for high occupancy periods. Slightly higher than customary "focus rates" covering a one to three month summer season, is a pricing option that smaller independent seaside hotels might find worth exploring. If higher revenues can be gained from peak season tourism markets then the possibilities for improving low season or shoulder season occupancy levels are increased. For example, the hotelier may increase marketing expenditure on low season promotions or invest further in facilities that attract non-seasonal guests. Additionally, some repeat customers may time their visit outside the peak season, and new customers may be gained in the low or shoulder season months, because of the enhanced value-for-money of off-peak season stays, if the tariff is substantially discounted.

The short break market continues to provide the best prospects for growth in the UK accommodation market (Peisley, 1996). Those hotels with lower than expected occupancy levels in the shoulder season months should seek to raise these occupancy levels, and thus increase the length of the main season, through increasing the effectiveness of their marketing effort and improving the product offered in the shoulder months specifically. Short break promotions, both those developed in house and those offered by tour operators and publicised in the hotel guides, should be the first to be considered. Other obvious markets to focus on to improve shoulder season occupancy levels, and lengthen the main season, are those based on the conference trade and on short/additional holidays taken during the week. The significance of the latter was established by the regression analysis and the lack of conference facilities was identified as a major constraint on off-season occupancy performance by a seaside chain hotel in the structured interview survey. Hotels should also consider making their relationships with tour operators and travel agents work more effectively for them in selling rooms during their low occupancy periods (Schulz, 1995).

To this point, discussion has tended to concentrate on those hotels with summer season peaks. At business market-oriented hotels the objective is more likely to be to reduce the effects of counter seasonality. Occupancy levels in the months of June, July and particularly August should form the targets for improvement for most hotels in this category. Attracting leisure guests to raise summer occupancy levels in business-oriented hotels was cited as a particular problem by some of the hoteliers interviewed (Barden, 1998). To overcome this problem, hoteliers should (a) adopt pricing and promotional tactics designed to stimulate demand for the hotel's accommodation in the summer months, and (b) develop strategies to raise the profile of the hotel as a suitable venue for summer leisure stays, conferences and functions. This may call for a particularly innovative approach to "bundling" the hotel's accommodation with other products and services within and without the hotel, and an imaginative sales approach (CBI, 1995). One other market likely to provide summer season stays is the functions market, particularly wedding parties, because of their concentration in summer. All possible connections with summer season events (such as sporting events and festivals) in the local area should also be explored and exploited as means of stimulating summer season demand for the hotel's accommodation. Heritage tourism and shopping and theatre-based tourism have provided much of the impetus for the growth of urban tourism in several English provincial cities. A recent tourism marketing program in Leeds stands out as being particularly innovative. It involves the marketing of "clubbing breaks" designed to encourage overnight weekend stays in Leeds hotels *(Yorkshire Post,* 17 September 1998). Such initiatives open up opportunities for hotels in selected urban centres to improve their occupancy performance in the summer and at weekends more generally.

What has emerged from this analysis and discussion is that marketing initiatives can moderate and modify seasonality in hotel occupancy profiles. Such marketing initiatives are likely to be most effective if they are co-ordinated and based on a detailed under-standing of the nature and extent of seasonal fluctuations in occupancy levels. The occupancy analysis needs to be performed at the individual hotel level, and marketing plans to counteract seasonality should be tailor-made to suit the particular occupancy performance patterns and precise circumstances of the individual hotels involved. This paper has provided an analytical framework within which such occupancy analyses could be performed, and has provided some policy guidelines in the search for appropriate marketing responses.

References

Barden, R. R. D. (1998). *Hotel Occupancy Performance and the Marketing of Hotels.* Unpublished PhD thesis, University of Bradford.

Bar-On, R. R. (1975). *Seasonality in Tourism: A Guide to the Analysis of Seasonality and Trends for Policy Making.* London: Economist Intelligence Unit.

Bond, H. (1996). Suburban hotels must match location with strategy. *Hotel & Motel Management, 211(1)*, 54–56.

Confederation for British Industry (CBI) (1995). *World Hosts: International Benchmarking in the Hospitality Industry.* London: CBI.

Jeffrey, D. (1983). *Trends and Fluctuations in the Demand for Hotel Accommodation: A Time Series Analysis of Hotel Occupancy Rates in England by Region and Hotel Category. 1976–1982.* London: ETB/BTA.

Jeffrey, D. (1985). Spatial and temporal patterns of demand for hotel accommodation: time series analysis in Yorkshire and Humberside, UK. *Tourism Management, 5(1)*, 8–22.

Jeffrey, D., & Adams, J. (1980). Spatial sectoral patterns of employment growth in Yorkshire and Humberside, 1963–1975. *Regional Studies, 14*, 441–453.

Jeffrey, D., & Barden, R. R. D. (2000). Monitoring hotel performance via occupancy time series analysis: The concept of occupancy performance space. *The International Journal of Tourism Research, 2(6)*, 383–403.

McEniff, J. (1992). *Seasonality of Tourism Demand in the European Community.* London: Economic Intelligence Unit.

Middleton, V. T. C. (1994). *Marketing in Travel and Tourism.* 2nd ed. Oxford: ButterworthHeinemann.

Norusis, M. J./SPSS Inc. (1993). Measuring linear association. In M. J. Norusis/SPSS Inc. *SF55 for Windows Base System Users Guide, Release 6.0.* Chicago, Ill: SPSS Inc.

Peisley, T. (1996). Travel and tourism intelligence — England. In *International Tourism Reports, No. 3.* London: Economic Intelligence Unit (EIU).

Schulz, C. (1994). Hotels and travel agents: The new partnership. *Cornell Hotel & Restaurant Administration Quarterly, 35(2)*, 44–50.

Sykes, D. H. (1983). Off-peak tourism study: An appraisal of the short and additional holiday markets. *Planning Papers No. 38.* Leeds: School of Planning and Environmental Science, Leeds Polytechnic.

Witt, S. F., Brooke, M. Z., & Buckley, P. J. (1991). *The Management of International Tourism.* London: Unwin Hyman.

Yorkshire Post (1988). 17 September.

Chapter 9

Extending the School Holiday Season: The Case of Eurocamp

Mary Klemm and Julian Rawel

Introduction

The uneven pattern of demand for holidays is one of the major problems faced by tourist businesses. Clever marketing can to some extent change people's perceptions of the best time to go on holiday, but institutional seasonality, as defined by Hartman (1986), arising from the fixed school holiday periods is the most difficult problem to overcome. Butler (1994) went as far as to say "clearly, the long school holiday in the summer remains one of the impediments, if not the largest single impediment to reducing the seasonal concentrations of tourists". Butler and others, (Clarke, 1981; Donatos & Zairis, 1991) have examined the problems and issues arising from seasonality in the destination, from what may loosely be defined as the geographical perspective. In this chapter we are concentrating on the impact of institutional seasonality on a business. Previous studies focusing on the impact of seasonality on businesses (Snepenger *et al.*, 1990; Sutcliffe & Sinclair, 1980) have shown a variety of strategies adopted by businesses from Alaska to Spain to deal with the problem. One solution to the problem of institutional seasonality is to extend the customer base to areas with different fixed holidays. This is the approach adopted by Eurocamp, originally a small British company, which by an innovative approach to extending the season for camping holidays became the leading and most innovative company in this sector.

Limitations of Seasonality

Seasonality makes it difficult for small companies to grow for a variety of reasons. There is a limit to the size of the market and also to prices which can be charged for family holidays even in high season. A successful business needs to employ full time professional staff, and to offer a career structure, inevitably more difficult where the product can only be sold for a few weeks in any year. Logistical problems arise for small companies which are successful in increasing demand because the bulk of this increase is in high season, rather than outside it (Sinclair *et al.*, 1980)

Seasonality has contributed to the view amongst investors that tourism is a risky business, for which it is more difficult to raise capital than for businesses in other sectors.

Seasonality in Tourism, pp 141–151
© 2001 by Elsevier Science Ltd.
All rights of reproduction in any form reserved
ISBN: 0-08-043674-9

Investing companies like to include tourism businesses in a portfolio with businesses that the market is perceived to be more stable. Such problems apply across the range of businesses supplying tourists, including hotels, transport providers, tourist attractions and tour operators. Despite the growth of diversified leisure and tourism businesses in the 1990s, 95 percent of tourist businesses in Europe are classed as small enterprises (Smeral, 1998). Although some businesses prefer to remain small and to benefit from the relaxation for staff provided in the off season, (Butler, 1998) many would like to grow, and the limited season provided by scholastic holidays is the main reason they cannot do so.

The Eurocamp Product — a Brief Resumé

The Eurocamp self-drive camping holiday was positioned as a lifestyle product aimed at middle class professionals with young families in the UK. Using Kotler's (1994) methodology the product attributes and benefits were as follows.

Product Attributes

Accommodation was provided in six berth tents equipped with beds, fridge, cooker, saucepans, crockery and cutlery, electric lights and wide range of garden furniture. The eight berth mobile homes had bedrooms, shower, toilet and kitchen. Bed linen was not included, but the tent or mobile home was cleaned and prepared before the customer's arrival. Eurocamp rented areas in Europe's top quality campsites where facilities included pools, restaurants, activity areas, sports facilities and very clean washing amenities. A variety of locations was chosen: on the coast; inland by rivers and beauty spots; near historic towns. Initial destinations were on the west coast of France but, gradually, these were complemented by other French areas and also Italy, Spain, Switzerland and Austria.

Eurocamp employed couriers based on campsites who spoke a local language and the language(s) of the customer. Their principal role was to welcome, inform, be on hand should any problems arise, and to organise activities for the children. Unlike other tour company representatives they were not expected to sell tours. Working with the slogan "if the children are happy then so are the parents" Eurocamp provided a range of products and services for children of different ages. These included baby packs, children's travel packs, junior tents and special children's couriers to organize activities.

Eurocamp provided a flexible travel service for UK-based customers, offering the full range of ferry, motor-rail and hotels en route to the campsite. Important extras were maps and a route planning service together with quality information on local facilities.

Product Benefits

These were both tangible and intangible. Eurocamp holidays were a premium price product, aiming to provide superior equipment, better campsites and superior service over competing companies. In fact the company was so concerned that all the tents in Eurocamp colours should look smart that in 1980 it discontinued the policy of selling the old tents in case they should be seen in a worn state on the campsites. Choice in terms of location and accommodation, start or finish dates and method of travel were seen as a benefit. Great emphasis was placed on personal service, from initial reservation to return home questionnaire.

One of the intangible benefits was the guarantee of quality and exclusivity offered by the Eurocamp brand name with its distinctive red and green logo. The name Eurocamp turned out to be a great success; it struck a chord with the pro-European attitude of many of the educated post war baby boomers who in the late 1970s were at what marketers call the full-nest stage of their lives. The name Eurocamp also capitalized on the optimism leading up to the establishment of the European Single Market in 1992 and did not require translation when the company decided to internationalize.

Eurocamp: Early Development

The company began selling camping holidays in Europe to the British in 1975. The Rent-A-Tent market, as it came to be known, was in its infancy, and the market leader was Canvas Holidays. Eurocamp was founded by a British entrepreneur who saw this growing market as an opportunity to develop a business. The company was successful and its customer base grew steadily at first and then rapidly from 4000 tourists in 1976 to 45,000 tourists in 1983. However, at this time they remained limited to the British market.

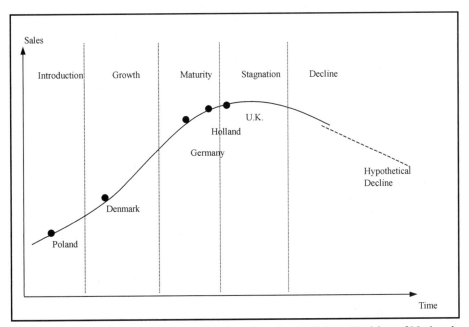

Figure 1: Product Life Cycle for Self-Drive Camping Holidays: Position of National Markets in 1998.

Search for Growth

By 1983 the company had become the market leader in self-drive camping holidays from the UK. The founder sold out to a retail company which supported the managers' desire to continue the company's growth. This promised to be difficult to achieve because camping holidays have a limited season, and Eurocamp's product was aimed at families for whom the British school holidays dictated an even shorter season. In terms of the product life-cycle it could be said that the UK market for this type of holiday was, while still growing, approaching maturity and much effort would be needed to maintain growth. Figure 1 above shows the position of the Eurocamp product in 1998 by which time it was further along this life-cycle. A SWOT analysis in 1983 would have shown the key weaknesses of Eurocamp to be its one market product and a holiday sales pattern with a short peak at the end of May and a main peak in late July and August. This short season limited the company's ability to really make its assets "sweat". For example, space was rented on campsites and tents maintained throughout the five month European season. However, occupancy was often weak outside the school holiday periods with the result that space had to be sold at discounted rates.

The Decision to Internationalize

The company managers believed that if the company wished to continue growing it was faced with a number of important choices. These were as follows:

- increase market share through acquisition;
- widen the appeal of the holidays through product development (for example, the intro-duction of mobile homes);
- development of new UK markets (for example, selling through travel agents as well as direct);
- diversification into other types of holiday;
- introduce the Eurocamp product to a non-UK customer base.

Being prudent managers, they followed the first three options to improve profitability by increasing numbers of customers and market share within existing seasonal constraints. Existing tour operators such as Inn-Tent, Carefree Camping and Sunsites were acquired. The proportion of mobile homes was increased to cater for customers who wanted a more en-suite experience and Eurocamp started to sell holidays through high street travel agencies. The fourth option was rejected because it would dilute Eurocamp's brand image and expertise in the Rent-A-Tent market.

Being entrepreneurially driven, management decided to pursue the fifth option, the one which was the most risky, but potentially the most valuable. Within UK tour operating this course of development was, at the time, almost completely untried. By taking the product to non-UK customers, the company endeavoured to escape the constraints of the tradi-tional UK peak seasons. Indeed, two classical reasons frequently cited for companies going international, levelling out seasonal fluctuations and compensating for low levels of domestic demand, applied directly to Eurocamp (Johanson & Finn-Weidersheim-Paul, 1975).

The company knew that the summer, or more importantly the school holiday periods of European tourists, were different from those in the UK and that ability to adapt to these markets/seasons would enable a significant extension of the high season. Of course, this was not an option without risk. Rent-A-Tent holidays were an untried product for mainland Europe, even though demand for traditional camping and caravanning was high. But Eurocamp had confidence in its product, reputation and brand. Therefore the goal of solving the problem of seasonality was felt to be worth the risk involved.

Market Development

Phase 1: The Netherlands

Eurocamp started to develop the Netherlands market in 1982 following research that indicated market potential. The Dutch were keen campers; they had been also showing interest in Eurocamp on the campsites and most important their main holiday season was in July rather than in August. However, there were several ways in which the company had to adapt its product and systems for the new market. In the Netherlands camping was seen as a poor man's holiday, so in order to position Eurocamp for a more affluent customer and get the correct marketing mix, local expertise was needed.

A senior advertising executive, a vice president of J.Walter Thompson Amsterdam, was recruited as Eurocamp's first European agent to lead a marketing campaign, funded by Eurocamp, focusing on the image of quality time, freedom and enjoyment for parents and children of professional families. The product was adapted, for example, by providing larger beds and coffee filters as the Dutch are taller and prefer ground coffee. The marketing approach differed from that of the UK in terms of focus and distribution. Eurocamp UK was a direct sell brand, but research indicated that in Holland it would be more effective to use the travel agency sector as well. Eurocamp's agent chose two chains of Dutch travel agencies, Holland International (the then Dutch equivalent of Thomas Cook) and ANWB (the Dutch Automobile Association), whose market positioning and exclusivity of distribution provided the best match for Eurocamp. A 50/50 agent/direct-sell split of bookings was projected for the first year. At the end of the 1984 season, 1,500 bookings (parties, not individuals) or 13.5 percent of the Eurocamp total bookings for that year were recorded.

The Dutch market saw steady growth. The theme approach was developed, direct sell techniques improved and a third distribution partner, RABO Bank, which was very strong in small rural towns and villages, was recruited. By 1992, bookings had grown to over 18,000 or 26 percent of Eurocamp's total market. That represented a peak and, by the late 1990's, the proportion of Eurocamp's bookings from the Netherlands had settled at around 25 percent.

A great advantage for Eurocamp was that this new market enabled the company to fill its capacity in July. The Dutch high season dovetailed conveniently in front of the British high season (see Figure 2).

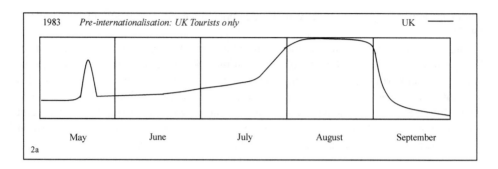

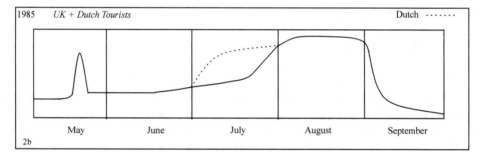

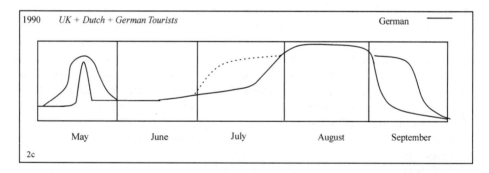

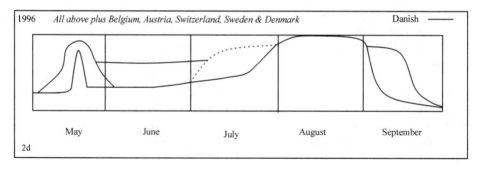

Figure 2: Eurocamp Seasonal Booking Pattern: An Indicative Sketch.

Phase 2: Germany

As the Dutch market grew, so did the competitive environment. Eurocamp's UK management decided that the time was right to look at other markets. Germany seemed the obvious next step. Serious approaches had been made by a number of German companies wishing to start a Eurocamp tour operation. German campers and caravanners were to be seen in large numbers on many of Eurocamp's camp-sites, especially the more southerly and westerly ones.

Initial research found two potential joint partners, both with Eurocamp's proven successful formula of marketing and entrepreneurial skills. One was the Managing Director of the Dusseldorf office of a Swedish advertising agency, the other was the Marketing Manager of Seiko in Germany. Detailed qualitative and quantitative research was undertaken and a market potential established. Despite Germany spreading its holiday periods across the regions, a strong holiday taking pattern in early May and in July was established, thus helping to complement the UK pattern (see Figure 2c).

Much of the Dutch model was replicated. The agency agreement was similar, as was the family slogan. The marketing was aimed at the higher income earners aged 25 to 45 with children. The product positioning was unique within Germany, especially as the type of customers Eurocamp was aiming at were not people who would normally take camping holidays. The slogan "if the children are happy, the parents have time to relax" reflected the marketing approach. Marketing was primarily direct sell and, due to the size of the country, focused on two key regions, Rheinland Westphalia and Bavaria.

An encouraging first year saw 1530 bookings which was about the same as Holland in its first year. This equated to 4.5 percent of the total Eurocamp market as opposed to 13.5 percent in the first Dutch year reflecting on how Eurocamp as a whole had grown. Whilst the core positioning remained in place in subsequent years, the scope offered by Germany's huge population ensured that new markets could be developed by simply promoting the Eurocamp brand within new regions.

A major innovation within the Eurocamp marketing portfolio was, however, the introduction of a dynamic sales promotion strategy. Eurocamp identified the then growing IKEA chain as a perfect partner in terms of lifestyle positioning. A partnership, whereby Eurocamp became IKEA's selected tour operator, was developed. Full page advertisements were taken out in the IKEA catalogue and brochure distribution and bookings outlets were set up within many of IKEA's German stores — a very different type of agency sales promotion.

Bookings grew dramatically in the early 1990s, with 2015 bookings in 1989 rising to 14,378 in 1992. By 1997 Germany accounted for 22 percent of Eurocamp's business (see Figure 3).

Phase 3: Belgium, Austria and Switzerland, Sweden and Denmark

These markets represented smaller, but significant contributions to Eurocamp's internationalization strategy. As the Dutch and Germany markets grew, the individual agents realized the possibilities of expanding out of one nation state into countries with a similar culture and language. For Holland, the Flemish speaking Belgian market was culturally a good fit, but far too small to warrant a stand-alone marketing operation. A promotional strategy through VTB, the Flemish motoring association, was launched, but using a customized Dutch brochure. The promotional strategy aimed to create a pull from potential customers, directing them towards VTB retail outlets. The Belgian market grew to comprize around 15 percent of Dutch bookings.

In the German speaking market, Austria and Switzerland had a good cultural and linguistic fit. Initial promotion was through IKEA stores, but a separate sales office was eventually set up in Switzerland to focus on developing an important September market. Figure 2 (d) shows how this was important in further extending Eurocamp's summer season into the autumn. The two new Austrian and Swiss markets eventually accounted for around about 15 percent of the total German business.

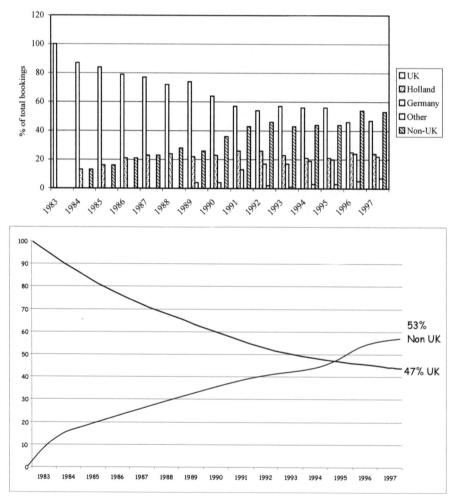

Figure 3: International Bookings Growth.

Other markets were also tested. In 1992, Eurocamp developed a sales operation in Sweden, hoping to capitalize on its important June high season. However, difficulties in the Swedish economy and the long travelling time from Sweden to Eurocamp camp-sites meant that success was unlikely to be sustainable and the operation was discontinued in 1994. A Danish sales operation was started in 1994 through an existing Danish tour operator, Larsen Rjeisen. Again, early summer high season business was important and the much closer proximity to mainland Europe has ensured quite some success.

The Seasonal Booking Pattern

By 1998, over 50 percent of Eurocamp's business came from its European sales operations. Success in these markets reduced Eurocamp's vulnerability to the downturn in the UK's domestic market which occurred in the early 1990s. This alone justified the original decision to go international. The principal long-term gain for Eurocamp was an increase in business during the traditional "shoulder" periods which showed a trough in UK bookings. Eurocamp's headquarters in the UK tightly controlled the availability of accommodation so that its European agents marketed and sold what was most advantageous to the Euro-camp group as a whole.

Figure 2 shows, in simple diagrammatic form, how the high season was progressively expanded and those classical peaks and troughs levelled out. By the mid-1990s the high season had increased from around six weeks to nearer twelve. Figure 3 shows how international bookings grew between 1983 and 1997 to give Eurocamp a more balanced portfolio. In the late 1990s the potential of East European markets such as Poland were being investigated.

An Integrated Internationalization Strategy

Eurocamp is an example of a small tour operator's approach to institutional seasonality, where the institutional limitations are the fixed school holidays. Success appears to have been simple to achieve, but in practice great attention needed to be paid to the need to adapt to the different cultural norms and marketing practices of different countries. Seasonal opportunities provided the catalyst. Good practice ensured success.

Specifically, the reasons for this success were as follows:

- *Focusing on international markets, despite domestic success.* Eurocamp was continually searching for new opportunities. Despite success in the UK market, Eurocamp allocated planning time away from purely domestic matters to develop an external orientation;
- *Taking care in selecting international distributors.* Eurocamp spent quite some time researching and searching for the appropriate agents and developing the right agent formula, which varied with each new market;

- *Distributors were treated as equals.* Agents were recruited for their expertise and given almost complete autonomy. This was critical to the success of Eurocamp in each market;
- *Customizing the marketing approach.* Eurocamp customized its marketing to each individual market, relying on its agents to develop the correct approach. The company adopted a flexible approach to both the target market and the marketing channel;
- *Customizing the product.* The product was tailored, within reason, to the needs of consumers in each market. For example, on site representatives were recruited who spoke Dutch and German as well as English. Travel documentation was specifically produced for each market;
- *Starting in a synergistic market.* Eurocamp's internationalization process began in a country (The Netherlands) where cultural norms and behaviour — sometimes termed the psychic distance — were close to the UK. It then moved on to countries such as Germany where the psychic distance was greater. Where necessary, it was also prepared to withdraw;
- *A distinctive and contemporary name.* Eurocamp's name was important for success in European markets. It met a number of classical criteria for successful branding that could be applied nationally as well as internationally. The name Eurocamp was easy to pronounce, recognize and remember and had the advantage of being both linguistically acceptable and culturally distinctive in all markets.

Conclusions

The conclusion of this study is that successful internationalization can enable tourism companies to extend their season — if not to break out of the straightjacket imposed by fixed school holidays, at least to expand it enough for the company to grow. Since 1983 Eurocamp was able to more than double in size, to raise capital on the stock market, to employ more professional staff and logistical support and take over competitors. With its more international customer base the company has insulated itself to some degree from shocks to the British economy and by finding new markets has overcome the problem of saturation in the British market.

However, successful internationalism is not an aim to be taken lightly. To date, Eurocamp is possibly the only UK tour operator to have successfully, in a big way, transferred its brand and product to the market in mainland Europe. Thomson and Airtours, especially the latter, have successful European tour operations but these have been developed by acquisition rather than by organic growth. The new parent companies have provided financial muscle and strategic expertise but neither Airtours nor Thomson have become European brand names and their European subsidiaries have continued to sell their traditional products using local names and distribution systems.

Eurocamp recognized a domestic problem and found a gap in the market to solve it. Perhaps the 1980s and early 1990s, before the advent of the vertically integrated multinational giants, was the perfect time for Eurocamp to develop internationally and to carve out a positive niche. But, without that real attention to international detail, success might well have not been achieved.

References

Butler, R. W. (1994). Seasonality in tourism: Issues and problems. In A .V Seaton (ed.) *Tourism: State of the Art*. Chichester: Wiley.

Butler R. W. (1998). Seasonality in tourism: Issues and implications. *The Tourist Review. International Association of Scientific Experts in Tourism 3*.

Donatos, G., & Zairis, P. (1990). Seasonality of foreign tourism on the island of Crete. *Annals of Tourism Research, 17(4)*.

Hartman, R. (1986). Tourism, seasonality and social change. *Leisure Studies, 5(1)*.

Johanson, J., & Finn-Weidersheim-Paul. (1975). The internationalisation of the firm: Four Swedish cases. *Journal of Management Studies*.

Smeral, Egon (1998). The impact of globalization on small and medium enterprises: new challenges for tourism policies in the European countries. *Tourism Management, 19(4)*.

Snepenger, D., Houser, B., & Snepenger, M. (1990). Seasonality of demand. *Annals of Tourism Research, 17(4)*.

Sutcliffe, C. M. S., & Sinclair, T. (1980). The measurement of seasonality within the tourist industry: An application to tourist arrivals in Spain. *Applied Economics 12(4)*.

Chapter 10

Managing Seasonality in Peripheral Tourism Regions: The Case of Northland, New Zealand

Jane Commons and Stephen Page

Problems ?

Introduction

Seasonality is inextricably linked to tourism, since tourism flows to destinations and regions are conditioned by a complex array of factors that influence and impact upon visitor behaviour. One of the distinguishing features of tourism flows compared with migration flows, which are more permanent, is the transitory and seasonal nature of such movements. Tourist flows are significantly affected by the availability of leisure time, particularly holiday entitlements and especially the growth of the leisure society. In addition, a number of researchers have highlighted the formative influence of the "cycle of the seasons" (Bar-On, 1975; Patmore, 1983; Collier, 1994; Laws, 1995) as exemplified by Collier (1994) where "weather probably [is] the critical factor in the choice of holiday time and/or destination". This point is further debated by Patmore (1983) as "one of the most unyielding of constraints is that imposed by climate, most obviously where outdoor activities are concerned. The rhythms of the seasons affect both the hours of daylight available and the extent to which temperatures are conducive to participant comfort outdoors". In this respect, the combination of climate and institutionalized seasonality (i.e., holidays and events at specific times of the year such as Christmas and Easter) impact on the demand for tourism.

The consequences of seasonality for the tourism industry are manifold; it not only causes major problems for the suppliers of tourism services and products, but has significant ramifications for other stakeholders such as residents, tourism employees (Ball, 1988) residents and tourists themselves. The implications for suppliers are summarised by Cooper *et al.* (1993) where "it is not possible merely to stockpile the product — a hotel room which is unsold on a particular night, an unsold seat on a flight, or an unsold theatre ticket all have an economic value of zero". For the tourism industry, managing the peaks and troughs associated with seasonality (Soesilo & Mings, 1987; Bull, 1995; Allcock, 1994) are not solely confined to coastal tourism and winter sports resorts as capital city tourism also experiences such problems (Searle, 1989) as even urban tourism destinations face problems of seasonality (Page, 1995–1999). However, seasonality is particularly pronounced in destinations located in peripheral regions (Page, 1993; Blomgren & Sorensen, 1998) where an economic dependence upon tourism is evident. The problems of seasonality also have a knock-on

Seasonality in Tourism, pp 153–172
© 2001 by Elsevier Science Ltd.
All rights of reproduction in any form reserved
ISBN: 0-08-043674-9

effect for the tourism industry where management strategies have to be developed to address seasonal variations in income, leading to cost-spreading (Anon, 1996), ways to overcome inefficient use of fixed facilities (McEniff, 1992; Allcock, 1994), the demand for labour and the impact on "workers employed ... for part of the year [who] may have no opportunities for employment during the rest of the year" (Witt *et al.,* 1991). The seasonal nature of tourism employment (Saleem, 1992) can inhibit training and career prospects for employees (Witt *et al.,* 1991), especially in rural areas (Page & Getz, 1997). In addition, seasonal demand patterns in tourism may pose significant problems for residents and the local environment, where inflationary pressures on goods and the transport system (Craik, 1991) may impose negative externalities on the local economy.

   Although it is possible to highlight the negative effects of seasonality for the tourism industry, this does not imply that the industry is powerless to address the effects. Current management responses to seasonality are normally focused on three areas: employment, facilities and costs. Witt *et al.* (1991) argue that "there are four principal strategies for managing seasonality: changing the product mix, market diversification, differential pricing and encouragement/facilitation by the state of the staggering of holidays". Despite industry strategies to address seasonality, Bonn *et al.* (1992) do highlight that it is perhaps the most pervasive problem confronting ... managers of the tourism businesses' and it is still the case that the understanding of the factors affecting seasonality are poorly understood (Bar-On, 1975). Therefore this chapter examines the problem of seasonality in one region of New Zealand, Northland, to illustrate the extent to which it is the principal concern for decision-makers, planners and tourism businesses. The chapter commences with a discussion of the regional context of the study, emphasising patterns, trends and issues affecting tourism development in Northland. This is followed by an analysis of tourist behaviour among Northland's main domestic tourism market — Auckland residents. Implications for the tourism industry to address the problems of seasonality in relation to the domestic tourism market are then discussed.

The Northland Region of New Zealand

Within New Zealand, tourism has been expanding at a constant rate during the 1980s and 1990s (Page & Meyer, 1996; Page & Thorn, 1997), with 1,541,136 international arrivals for the year ended June 1997 which generated NZ$3.5 billion for the national economy. This is complemented by an estimated domestic tourism market of 10.3 million trips a year which generates NZ$2.5 billion which is steadily declining at the expense of outbound travel. There has been a growing literature evolving on the development, impact, management and marketing of tourism in New Zealand (Tourism Policy Group, 1995), although there has been a comparative neglect of tourism in those regions which are not on the main tourist routes. For those regions off the main tourism circuits (e.g., Northland), there has been a lack of research focused on the development, patterns and flows, organisation and management of tourism in these regions (Page & Thorn, 1997; Tourism Policy Group, 1995). In the Northland region, no major academic piece of tourism research has been published despite the region's proximity to one of the principal gateways to New Zealand — Auckland until the study by Page *et al.* (1999).

The region comprises a largely agricultural hinterland with a number of key towns and the administrative centre — Whangarei (Figure 1). The total population for the region in 1995 was 136,800 with 54,400 located in the Far North District, 64,900 in Whangarei District and 17,450 in the Kaipara District. In the north, a number of tourist resort areas (Paihia, Russell, Kerikeri, Kaikohe and Kaitaia) account for the main concentrations of population and services. Employment in the region is predominantly derived from

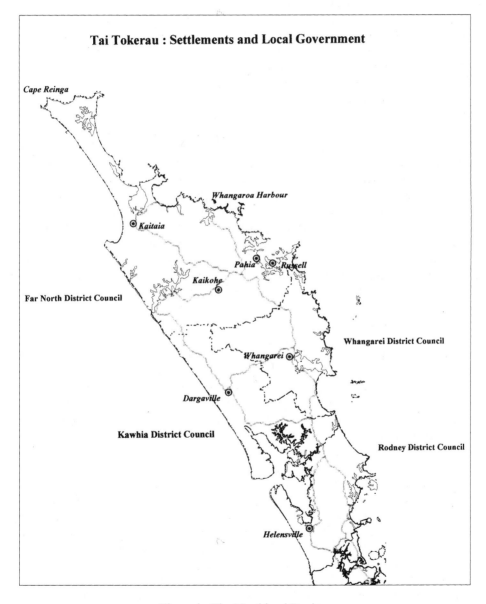

Figure 1: The Northland Region.

community and personal services, wholesale trade, retail trade, restaurants and hotels and manufacturing. In the case of Northland, the expansion of Marsden Point oil refinery in Whangarei in the 1980s accounted for the region's outperformance of other regions. The regional economic development benefits of the oil refinery construction project and impact on business was a function of a fast growing population and the development of small businesses to cater for local demand. However, since the 1980s, population growth rates have slowed in Northland's urban areas.

Within Northland, tourism and small business development, in the main, is not viewed as being dependent upon local population demand. It may supplement tourism markets as a source of demand but is a business phenomenon which is externally conditioned outside the Northland region and directly influenced by international and national economic conditions. In the absence of substantial government assistance to tourism business development and given the dependence upon the seasonal domestic market, one would not expect a dramatic growth in tourism business activity because much of the nation's tourism development has been focused on the core tourism areas. However, one would expect a degree of new firm formation in peripheral regions such as Northland due to the perceived expansion of growth opportunities in tourism as a result of some spillover effects from tourism development in core areas and a limited degree of spatial dispersal of tourists in the 1990s. Even so, with the exception of the Bay of Islands, no sub-regions within Northland would meet the criteria as a tourism growth pole supported by regional policy or local economic development initiatives. A number of other indirect effects such as the tar sealing of State Highway 12 on the region's west coast to develop a tourist circuit and scenic route (the Kauri Coast) in the late 1980s and early 1990s, may have improved accessibility to a predominantly remote rural area and stimulated a number of seasonal tourism business opportunities. But to all intents and purposes, the economic characteristics of Northland as a tourism region is one which is peripheral to the main areas of tourist activity and development.

The existing sources of data for international visitors to the region are the estimates generated from the International Visitor Survey (IVS) (New Zealand Tourism Board, 1996a) and the Domestic Tourism Study (New Zealand Tourism and Publicity Department, 1991) which is currently being updated. This was also supplemented in the 1970s and early 1980s by a regional visitor survey periodically undertaken by the Northland United Council (now the Northland Regional Council) (Thorn, 1992). However, what is clear is that "there is a lack of reliable data on visitors in Northland" (New Zealand Tourism Board, 1996b, p. 58) and this remains a major impediment to tourism research on the region. The most detailed data source is the Murray North *Far North Sub-Regional Tourism District Study* (Murray North, 1990) which only covers one-third of the region. Its analysis of tourism in Northland observed that it was dominated by domestic tourism, seasonally concentrated in January, with 696,000 visits by domestic visitors in 1988/89, the sixth most frequently visited region in New Zealand. The number of person nights spent in the region have declined from 1,108,000 visits in 1985/86 to 694,000 in 1988/89 although the length of stay for domestic visitors increased slightly over the same period from 3.8 to 4.2 days. Table 1 summarizes the data for 1987/88 and illustrates the dependence on the geographical coterminous market of Auckland, the source of 50 percent of trips and shows a further 30 percent of trips are from within the Northland region itself. Northland is dependent on the variable

Table 1: The Northland Domestic Tourism Market 1987/1988.[1]

Purpose of visit Leisure	VFR	Business	Sport	Other
48%	31%	8%	3%	10%

(1) Region of origin

Auckland	52%
Northland	28%
Bay of Plenty	6%
South Island	4%
Taranaki	2%
Wellington	1%

(2) Locations visited

	% of visits	Mean length of stays (d)
Whangarei	19%	4.2
		1.7
		3.9
		4.0
		3.6
Dargaville	4%	
Bay of Islands	19%	
Kerikeri	5%	
Rural/Small Towns	53%	

Average length of stay in Northland 4.1 days

(3) Accommodation used (person nights)

Licensed Hotel Motel	7%
Motel	7%
Friends/relatives	49%
Camping ground	15%
Holiday home/bach	16%
Other	6%

(4) Transport used

Air	2.7%
Bus/coach	8.5%
Private car	84%
Other	4.8%
	100%

Source: Murray North (1990).
[1]Domestic (15 years and older); 831,101 visits; 3,060,130 visitor nights.

and highly seasonal visiting friends and relatives (VFR) market, which is extremely price sensitive and adversely affected by poor weather conditions (e.g., in 1988/89 and 1966/97 two cyclones caused visitors to curtail holidays). The private car is the principal source of transport used by visitors visiting the region (Table 2).

Table 2: Segmentation of Northland's Rural and Small Town Visitor Market 1987/88.

(1) Overseas (15yr and over)			
446022	Visitors		
49043	Visitor nights		
(2) Purpose of visit			
Holiday	VFR	Business	Other
43%	29%	10%	18%
(3) Origin of business			
Northland		33%	
Auckland		54%	
Rest of North Island		10%	
South Island		3%	
Length of stay (nights)		3.6	
(4) Accommodation (person nights)			
Licensed Hotel/Motel/Motor Inn		4%	
Motel		4%	
Friends and relatives		51%	
Holiday home, bach		20%	
Camping ground/cabin		13%	
Other		8%	
(5) Transport used			
Air Travel		3%	
Bus/Coach		11%	
Campervan		1%	
Rental car/van		2%	
Private/Company car		82%	
Other		2%	
(6) Seasonality			
April–June		20%	
July–September		15%	
October–December		25%	
January–March		40%	

Source: Murray North (1990).

In terms of international visitors, the data is comparatively more recent and is derived from the International Visitor Survey for 1995/96 (New Zealand Tourism Board, 1996a). The number of international visitors to Northland has increased from 140,294 visits in 1987/88 to 202,471 in 1995/96 and 204,000 in 1997/98. This region was only visited by 15 percent of tourists during their stay (Page & Hall, 1999). Thus, the region's significance as a destination for international visitors is ranked comparatively low despite its proximity to Auckland and it appeals predominantly to the Australian, North American and European markets. The high spending Asian markets (e.g., South Korea and Japan) appear to have made few inroads into the region due to the organized inclusive tours they take being focused on Auckland, Waitomo, Rotorua and Taupo (Hall & Page, 1999).

The New Zealand Tourism Board's (1996b*) Tourism in Northland: A Draft Strategy for Sustainable Growth and Development* outlined the future direction the region's tourism industry should develop to the year 2001. It estimated that visitor spending in the region totalled NZ$300 million and supports 6000 full time jobs. While international visitors only comprise 20 percent of the total visitor mix, the New Zealand Tourism Board (1996b) forecast an increase in visitor expenditure to NZ$475 million in the year 2005. This equates to a NZ$20 million increase each year to the year 2001 and expects to support 10,000 people in employment, increasing at a rate of 500 jobs a year although research by Page *et al.* (1999) highlighted how inflated these estimates were. In terms of the regional tourism economy, the strategy identifies six sub-regions for tourism.

- *The Far North*, including a 90 mile beach and Cape Reinga dependent upon group tours which are transit oriented, visiting from the base in the Bay of Islands for a day trip. The growth of the free independent traveller (especially backpackers) characterize the region. This business is complemented by domestic holidaymakers in the summer season (January to February) and many of these visitors are distributed throughout coastal locations in the region;
- *The Bay of Islands,* focused on the Paihia area is a favoured location for international visitors given the heavy concentration of motel accommodation. Estimates show that even in the summer period, international visitors outnumber domestic visitors by three to two. The New Zealand Tourism Board (1996b) estimated that 80 percent of international visitors were independent travellers from the main source markets and the majority of the region's tourism operators (including the Regional Tourism Organisation — Destination Northland) is located there. The inclusion of yacht-based visitors over the summer period also contributes to the visitor mix;
- *Hokianga,* located on the rural west coast attracts largely independent travellers and much of the existing accommodation is based on baches (holiday homes)., camp grounds and few serviced accommodation units. Relatively little is known about tourism patterns, flows and visitor characteristics in this area but visitor numbers are thought to be small due to limitations associated with infrastructure and transportation;
- *The Kauri Coast,* also located along the West Coast and dominated by State Highway 12 is an alternative transit route for visitors seeking to take a circuit route through Northland after travelling through the area on State Highway 1. Its main attraction is the distribution of Kauri forest focused on the Waipoua Forest managed by the Department of Conservation and a number of camp sites and scenic lakes (e.g., Waipoua Forest and Kai Iwi

Lakes). With the exception of commercial travellers and independent travellers, limited numbers of visitors visit the area although research data on the area is non-existent;

- *Whangarei,* the region's administrative and service centre contains the main airport with feeder services to Auckland and a range of accommodation which services domestic holidaymakers in the main. The Town Council has invested NZ$6 million in the Town Basin development to accommodate yachts and to stimulate a visitor zone of services (cafes, restaurants and attractions) in an urban context;
- *The Mangawhai Coast,* within Kaipara district largely caters for domestic tourists focused on motor camps and beaches.

Although seasonality has not attracted a great deal of attention in previous research, a recent study by Page *et al.* (1999) which examined tourism business development, did highlight the issue of seasonality from a number of perspectives. First, employers were asked to estimate the number of full and part time people employed during the year. It indicated that between the quietest and busiest times of year, employment changed by 65 percent and Page *et al.* (1999) identified the spatial dimensions of employment in the region. Second, businesses were asked to record the quietest and busiest months. The principal months of business were: December through to April with May to October the quietest months, a feature triangulated by face to face interviews with Visitor Information staff in the region. As a result, most businesses were only operating at full capacity for four to six months of the year, with excess capacity during the shoulder season. What is interesting is that this seasonality is not necessarily a function of the region's weather.

Figure 2 shows that even in the main winter season, the region's image of the "winterless North" is well deserved because it is up to 6.9 degrees warmer than other parts of New Zealand.

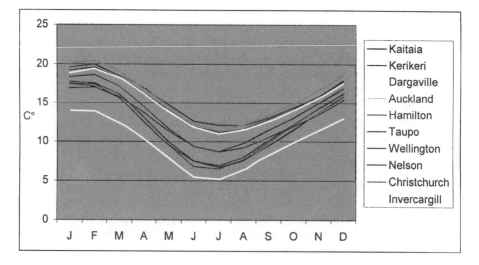

Figure 2: The Northland Climate.

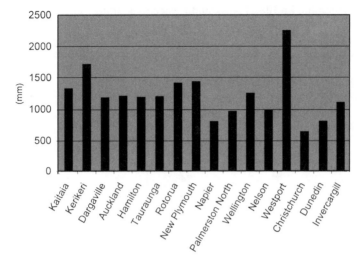

Figure 3: Rainfall in Northland.

However, in the case of rainfall (see Figure 3) its high annual rainfall may be a contributing factor to the seasonal distribution of visitor activity apparent in the region. Therefore, to examine the factors affecting domestic visitors to Northland, attention now turns to the survey of Auckland residents with a view to understanding the factors influencing their visitor behaviour and pattern of visitation to Northland.

Survey of Auckland Residents Visitation Patterns to Northland

Following the survey by Page *et al.* (1999) which identified the issue of seasonality from a supply side perspective, and business experiences the regional tourism organisation, Destination Northland provided funding to examine the dimensions of seasonality. Although there is not space within this chapter to examine the scope of the resulting study (See Commons 1999 for more detail), one dimension of the demand side of tourism was examined: the travel habits of Auckland residents who comprise the main domestic tourism market. A postal survey of Auckland residents was undertaken in December 1998, with 1498 respondents aged 18 years or older randomly identified from the nine electoral rolls of Auckland. A postal survey method was chosen as a cost effective and efficient survey instrument to reach a large geographically diverse sample population in a city of one million residents. Of the initial 1498 questionnaires distributed with reply-paid envelopes, 516 were returned. A further 85 questionnaires were then posted out to replace those which were returned due to a respondent having moved and 32 of these were usable. This provided a sample of 548 residents and a 34.62 percent response rate which is reasonable for postal surveys (see Page *et al.*, 1999 for a discussion). The questionnaire comprised mainly closed questions and a range of Likert scales which examined attitudes towards Northland as a tourist destination. Of the 548 Auckland residents who responded to the survey, 312 (57%) had travelled to Northland during the last year and were able to

Table 3: Demographic Profile of Auckland Residents Visiting Northland.

Characteristic	Number	% Northland sample
Sex		
Male	135	43.27
Female	177	56.73
Age (years)		
Under 25	34	10.90
26–35	61	19.55
36–45	75	24.04
46–55	74	23.72
56–65	29	9.29
Over	38	12.18
Annual income (NZ$)		
Under 20,000	67	21.47
20,001–30,000	43	13.78
30,001–40,000	61	19.55
40,001–50,000	32	10.26
50,001–60,000	25	8.01
Over 60,000	63	20.19

Source: Commons (1999).

complete the Northland section of the questionnaire. Therefore, that sub-sample is the basis of the analysis and discussion of seasonality presented here.

The demographic profile of respondents in Table 3 which indicates that no one particular age group dominated the sample, with a higher representation in the 36–55 age group.

To assess the extent to which this profile is representative of the visitor population, Table 4 provides an interesting comparison with a visitor survey of domestic and international visitors undertaken in 1997–98 based on nearly 800 face to face interviews at major destinations (Forer & Page, 1998a). Although the two surveys under consideration are not

Table 4 : Demographic Profile of Visitors from Northland Survey 1997–98.

Age range	%	Annual Income (NZ)	%
Under 20 yrs	6.84	Under $20,000	21.3
20–29	34.45	$20–29,999	17.5
30–39	19.71	$30–39,999	21.8
40–49	14.75	$40–49,999	14.8
50–59	12.47	$50–59,999	9.8
Over 60 yrs	11.80	Over $60,000	14.8

Source: Page and Forer (1998: 331,333).

strictly comparable, it is evident that similar age groups of visitors visited the area (despite different methods of grouping age). Likewise, comparable results were recorded for the income of visitors to Northland in both surveys indicating a degree of similarity in the results from both studies.

In terms of the reasons why Auckland residents travel to Northland, 50 percent stated it was normally for a holiday, being the market typically associated with seasonal demand, although ownership of holiday homes (baches) may in fact conceal a degree of all-year round travel which is not dependent upon the availability of accommodation. A further 25 percent responded that visiting friends and relatives (VFR) was another reason for travel to Northland which remains a major source of domestic travel in New Zealand (Pearce, 1995). Forer & Page (1998a) observe that such travel is "variable and highly seasonal ... [and] ... extremely price sensitive and adversely affected by poor weather conditions". Business travel accounted for only twelve percent of the stated reasons for travel to Northland while eight percent reported that they visited for a special event, which was somewhat low given the growth in this form of tourism promotion in New Zealand (Ryan *et al.*, 1996). A further five percent of respondents travelled to the region for sports-related activities.

Kruskall — Wallis tests were used to identify significant differences between the sex of the sample. The p-value of 0.001 for business travel for males and a p-value of 0.023 for VFR travel for women indicates the major distinction between sex and reason for visiting the region. Similar tests were also performed by age group with a p-value of 0.013 for business travel for those aged 46 to 55 years of age and a p-value of 0.038 for those aged under 25 years of age more likely to visit Northland to attend a special event. What this indicates is that Northland's current promotion of special events in the region has failed to target the higher spending visitors (i.e., those earning NZ$60,000 or above). A factor analysis was then conducted to examine the reasons for travelling to Northland to determine the correlated responses in the data to generate a more compressed set of variables that may explain the motivations grouping the visitors into a number of groups.

Table 5 indicates that three factors accounted for 71.8 percent of the sample. Factor 1 identified a visitor group which primarily travel to Northland for a holiday and not for business. Factor 2 indicates that special events and sporting events are significant enough to consider visiting a destination in its own right. Lastly, Factor 3 indicates that visiting friends and relatives is a major element in visitors' motivation to travel to the region.

Table 5 : Factors Present in the Reasons for Travelling to Northland.

		Opinion	% of Sample
Factor 1	travels for does not travel for	– holidays – work	25.5
Factor 2	travels for	– special events – sporting events	23.5
Factor 3	Travels for	– visiting friends and relatives	22.8

Source: Commons (1999)

Respondents were asked how many times they had visited Northland in the last year to try to gauge the level of repeat visitation to Northland. The majority of respondents (75%) had visited Northland one to three times and 15 percent four to six times in the last year. It might have been expected that respondents would have visited Northland more often than that given Auckland's proximity to the region, the development of holiday homes (baches) and the recent growth of short-break domestic holidays. Respondents were asked whether they visited Northland every year and 54 percent said they did. From this result the North-land region seems to have a reasonably high level of repeat visitation from Auckland, no doubt partly due to the ease of reaching the region from Auckland with a private vehicle. The respondents that did visit Northland every year were then asked if they visited the region at the same time every year. Only 31 percent said that they did. The high percentage of respondents that do not visit Northland at the same time every year suggests that the majority of respondents are not bound by "traditional" visitation patterns but rather may be open to change in the timing of their visits. These respondents may be able to be encour-aged to move their visitation to the shoulder or low seasons.

The survey then asked respondents during which months they visited Northland. The results appear in Figure 4. The responses formed an expected pattern of visitation for the Northland region given its image as a summer destination. The rise in visitation in June and July is pertinent. This rise during the rugby season (July–September) may represent the respondents who nominated "sports" as their reason for travelling to Northland. It may also be that there is already a proportion of travellers who recognise Northland as a year-round destination and value the lack of crowds of visitors at this time.

It is interesting to compare the timing of respondents' Northland travel with the timing of respondents' general domestic travel in New Zealand to assess the extent of seasonality. The pattern of general domestic travel is shown in Figure 5.

The comparison of Figures 5 and 6 shows that Northland experiences a longer summer season of Auckland visitors than the rest of the country. Northland's domestic visitation levels do not exhibit the steady decrease towards winter that can be seen in the general

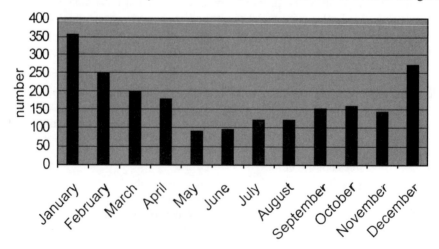

Figure 4: Months During Which Respondents Visited Northland.

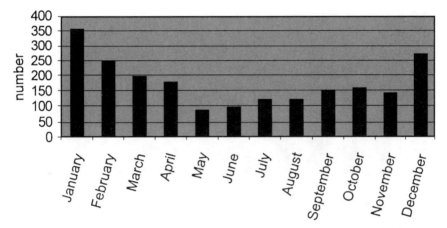

Figure 5: Timing of Respondents' Domestic Travel in New Zealand.

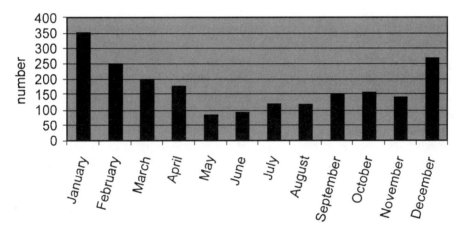

Figure 6: Timing of Respondents' Travel to Northland.

pattern of domestic travel among Aucklanders. Northland's visitation can also be seen to decrease over winter to a greater degree than Aucklanders' domestic travel to the rest of New Zealand. The second comparison which can be made is with the months nominated by Northland's tourism-based businesses as being their busiest (see Figure 7). Figure 7 shows a much busier mid-to-late summer period over February and March than is represented in by the domestic visitation in Figure 6. This suggests that this mid-to late summer period is in part inflated by international visitors. The winter season is shown by businesses as being quieter than the visitation levels in Figure 6.

There is also a drop in domestic travel to Northland in November which is not represented by the businesses in Figure 7, highlighting the compensating factor — international visitors. The third comparison one can make is with the total guest nights spent in Northland as recorded by the Commercial Accommodation Monitor. This survey is only of

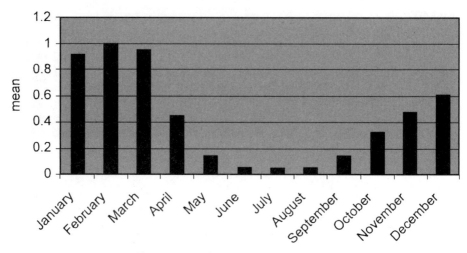

Figure 7: Businesses' Busiest Months.

commercial accommodation so that occupied by the VFR market is not represented. Although Page & Hall (1999) question this data source and its reliability as a statistical measure of visitation and seasonality, it remains the main measure of tourism supply.

The distribution of the total guest nights for Northland is shown in Figure 8 above. The figure shows a similar pattern to the one of Auckland residents domestic travel shown in Figure 6. It may also highlight the use of accommodation by domestic and international visitors that is very seasonal.

Respondents were asked how many nights they usually spent in Northland per visit. Respondents were found to have a mean length of stay there in the upper end of the "one to three" range (55%) which approximated to three nights. This is significant considering

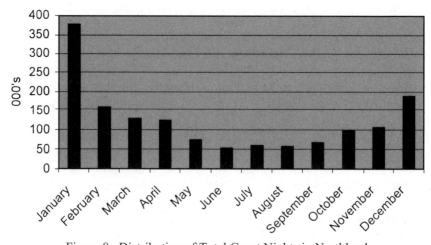

Figure 8: Distribution of Total Guest Nights in Northland.

that Page & Forer (1998) found the average length of stay to be 0.2 nights but then went on to argue that the average length of stay "for holidays under 31days is 4.12 nights". North (1990) also found the mean length of stay to be 4.1 days. Clearly Northland is currently a short-break domestic location for Auckland residents with the exception of the summer holiday period in late December–January. The Commercial Accommodation Monitor of June 1999 found that the average length of stay in Northland in June 1999 was two nights (down from 2.3 nights in June 1998). Although this survey does not take into account accommodation used by the "visiting friends and relatives" market, the significant increase of the commercial average from two nights to three or four nights of other research surveys indicates how important this private accommodation sector and holiday accommodation (baches) are within the region. The four to six' night grouping (27%) is also substantial but stays in Northland of seven nights or more (10%) are clearly not usual amongst Auckland residents. This is not unexpected as Auckland's proximity to Northland means that Aucklanders can make several short trips throughout the year, more convenient than one extended stay. This result also reflects the opportunities for travelling presented throughout the year. For those restricted by work and schooling, short breaks such as a weekend or a public holiday long weekend, can be undertaken several times over a year while an extended travel period can usually only be taken once.

Respondents were asked whether their length of stay in Northland had ever been affected by the weather. Some 77 percent of respondents had not, which suggests that either most respondents travel during the normally fine weather of summer or are prepared for changeable weather if travelling at other times. Disruption of Northland travel plans by the weather has been a contentious topic of late, as parts of the region experienced major flooding in 1998. As a result, it might have been expected that the proportion of respondents who had had their plans disrupted might have been higher, either through actual experience or through changing their plans because of media coverage. However, these events do not appear to have adversely affected visitor behaviour whilst visiting Northland.

In terms of accommodation usage, motel usage was the most popular form of leisure travel accommodation (Hall & Page, 1999) which is evident in the Northland region for 27 percent of respondents. This is closely followed by 23 percent staying in VFR accommodation and 16 percent in holiday homes or baches. Caravans and campsites are popular among 13 percent of the sample, especially in the summer season with only eight percent staying in hotels. The remaining 13 percent of respondents stayed in a diverse range of accommodation types (e.g., boats, bed and breakfast establishments, luxury lodges, backpacker hostels, work-related accommodation, timeshares and rental homes). A much more even distribution of visitation in Northland resulted than might have been expected.

Forer & Page (1998) presented a pattern of visitation in the Northland region which shows a very high concentration of visitation from Orewa through to the Bay of Islands. It also shows the secondary route up through Cape Reinga and the other touring routes used. This pattern is based on domestic visitors comprising only 47.44 percent of the Forer and Page (1998) sample. When this pattern is broken down to show the domestic component it can be seen how different international and domestic travel patterns in the region are. This pattern 'appears to suggest that international visitors are more likely to explore the central and eastern roads while New Zealanders head into a number of off-beat areas more

Table 6: Opinions of Auckland Residents Towards Northland (ranked in descending order of agreement).

Statement	Mean
I would recommend Northland to friends and family	1.7087
Northland has interesting historical attractions	1.8581
Northland has a wide range of outdoor activities	1.8878
Northland is a very popular New Zealand destination	2.1364
Northland is a great destination for families	2.1689
Northland is a great destination at any time of year	2.2175
Northland offers value for money as a destination	2.5497
Northland has a wide range of indoor activities	3.4708
Northland is only worth visiting in the summer	3.5049
Northland's towns and attractions are too crowded	3.5309

Source: Commons (1999).

associated with small bays and quality, unexplored beaches' (Forer & Page, 1998). These results support the finding of this study that the pattern of visitation of Auckland residents tends to be widely spread over the region and not greatly dominated by the main centres of Whangarei and the Bay of Islands. This indicates that domestic visitors may be more important than international for the generation of tourism-related income for the region.

The last question in the survey of Auckland residents was a list of ten opinions of Northland with which respondents could agree or disagree by answering questions on a five point Likert scale. The statements attempted to elicit views on a wide variety of topics and the mean response for each is shown in Table 6.

The highest mean response was for the statement "I would recommend Northland to friends and family" which is very positive from Northland's point of view. This indicates that whatever the ranking of the other statements, the overarching view is that respondents would recommend Northland as a destination. This is especially important given the wide recognition of how significant positive word-of-mouth is for a destination as a form of promotion. It is also positive for the region that "Northland has interesting historical attractions" (mean 1.85) since the New Zealand Tourism Board argued that one initiative to increase low season visitation is "further development and increased promotion of historic, cultural and natural heritage tourism" (New Zealand Tourism Board, 1996). Another interesting feature, given Northland's marked tourism seasonality, is the statement "Northland is a great destination at any time of year" which was ranked sixth with the relatively high mean of 2.2175. Linked to this is that the statement "Northland is only worth visiting in the summer" ranked in ninth place. Given the region's population distribution, the statement "Northland's towns and attractions are too crowded" ranked last with the low mean of 3.5309. It is also notable how low on the list 'Northland offers value for money as a destination' ranks. This is consistent with other findings by Commons (1999) that the perception of poor value for money at a destination, could be a deterrent to low income travellers. As well as deterring travel in the high season, this perception may also deter travel in the low season for these income groups.

Implications

From the survey, it is apparent that the use of Factor Analysis, Kruskal-Wallis tests and cross-tabulations of the data, establishes that two main groups of Aucklanders visit Northland:

• Those aged 18–25 years of age, largely seeking a holiday or to visit friends and relatives, staying in, and visiting the urban east coast and inland destinations (e.g., Whangarei, Paihia, Russell and Kerikeri). This group exhibit the greatest degree of seasonality in their patterns of visitation, staying in caravans, camping grounds and with friends and relatives for one to six nights on average;
• Those aged over 55 years of age who are all-year round visitors and pursue holidays and VFR-related activities, visiting similar areas to the other main group, with a preference for the smaller towns and motels, staying on average for four to six nights and have a high use of Visitor Information Centres.

Between 47 and 56 percent of each group visited Northland each year, illustrating the strong awareness of the region and the dominance of personal, family and work-related determinants of travel to the region. Weather is not a major constraint on travel patterns and therefore not a significant explanatory variable in patterns of seasonality in Northland. The timing of travel is very much a function of age, and to a lesser degree the sex of the respondents with only 31 percent of the sample stating that they visit the area at the same time every year. In other words, there is scope for promotional work to influence the dominant pattern of short-break holiday traffic to the region from the Auckland metropolitan area. This is supported by the very favourable image respondents had of the area, since they are willing to recommend it to other people as a holiday destination. The most interesting implications arise from a comparison of the visitors' willingness to travel domestically if specific inducements are offered. For example, Commons (1999) found that among the 548 Auckland respondents who replied to the initial survey, they identified discounted accommodation and transportation as the two principal drivers of additional discretionary spending on domestic tourism. This was followed by the staging of a special event which did not necessarily have to be weather contingent. However, Commons (1999) compared these responses with those of a sample of Northland tourism business owners on ways to address seasonality in visitor arrivals. Although staging special events was prominent in the responses, businesses did not favour discounting mechanisms for the low season. This highlights a key mismatch in the perception of the demands of the customer, and the extent to which the tourism industry is willing to accommodate them with discounts. It also exposes a major gap which the regional tourism organisation — Destination Northland — will need to work on.

This study of tourism and seasonality has also identified the limited value of mass marketing campaigns to promote the region to Auckland residents. In particular, it high-lights the need for more carefully targeted marketing at two levels. First, at the target groups, via newspaper articles and television advertising. Secondly the need for more comprehensive visitor information that is circulated to Northland residents who host friends and relatives. The Northland residents are arguably the most important ambassa-dors of the region's tourism product and resources.

Conclusions

This study indicates that 'the impact of seasonal demand variation is one of the dominant policy and operational concerns of tourism interests in both the public and private sectors' (Baum, 1999). Northland is no exception to this, with its marginalized or peripheral loca-tion in the wider scheme of tourist visitation in New Zealand a major concern for policymakers (Page & Hall, 1999). Although this chapter has predominantly focused on the demand aspects of seasonality in one major domestic market, it does confirm similar findings from other studies — that understanding the formative influences on seasonality in particular locations is a complex process. It is not simply a case of modelling visitor patterns and correlating demand with single explanatory variables such as climate or local-ized weather patterns. Northland's principal domestic tourism market is within a two to three hours drive of the Auckland metropolitan area and it is less climatically contingent. This leads one to search for a more complex array of variables or specific tourist behav-iours that condition the prevailing pattern of demand. In the case of Northland it is certainly the case that seasonality "is at the same time one of [the tourism industry's] most widely recognized and least well researched features" (Allcock, 1994). Yet even in this specific regional context it is apparent that "given that seasonality is largely institutional-ised or directly affects major characteristics of the product (to do with climate), many bounds on demand are not variable by price or marketing inducements" (Bull, 1995) alone. But such inevitability in seasonality fails to recognize the action which the tourism industry and private sector can take to address the issue.

One of the first requirements for the tourism industry is to recognize the principal factors which may lead to additional travel in the low season (price reductions, promotions and special events) and the power of harnessing the tourist as an effective and sophisti-cated consumer. Moving from a seasonal destination to an all-year round visitor region is not a simple task, but the perceptions of peripherality, the region's resource base and opportunities for an extended visit need to be portrayed to the domestic market in the competitive environment for domestic tourism in New Zealand (Page & Hall, 1999). Throughout the chapter, it has been assumed that addressing seasonality is a problem and a key goal of the tourism industry. Yet there is evidence in Northland that a proportion of tourism operators seek a period of recuperation outside the main tourist season because they operate their business for lifestyle reasons. Therefore, for some operators, an all-year round operation is not the pattern of supply they wish to offer. In this context, Destination Northland will need to focus on the all-year round destinations along the east coast and build special events and activities around these areas in the low season to ensure effective efficiencies and synergies from a concentrated pattern of tourist activity. In the medium to long term, Northland has the potential to develop a less accentuated pattern of seasonal demand for a core region of tourist activity focused on the urban destinations. This could be supplemented by a summer season pattern of a more dispersed pattern of activity which incorporates a rural hinterland and seasonal tourism attraction system. This rational approach to tourism development and planning would provide a catalyst for urban tourism development based on existing resorts and towns and aid in the establishment of a regular event destination image.

Acknowledgements

This chapter is derived from research undertaken by Jane Commons in 1998–99 as part of a funded research project which comprised her Master's Thesis. The authors would like to acknowledge the financial assistance provided by the Chief Executive of Destination Northland, Brian Roberts. Additional financial assistance was provided by Massey University's Graduate Research Fund in 1999.

References

Allcock, J. (1994). Seasonality. In S. Witt. & L. Moutinho (eds). *Tourism Marketing and Management Handbook* (2nd ed.). Hemel Hempstead: Prentice Hall International.

Anon (1996). *Advanced Leisure and Tourism.* Oxford: Oxford University Press.

Ball, R. M. (1998). Seasonality: a problem for workers in the tourism labour market. *Service Industries Journal, 8(4)*, 501–513.

Bar-On, R. (1975). *Seasonality in Tourism: A Guide to the Analysis of Seasonality and Trends for Policy Making.* London: Economist Intelligence Unit Limited.

Baum, T. (1999). Themes and issues in comparative destination research: Cases from the north Atlantic. *Tourism Management, 20(3),* 627–633.

Blomgren and Sorensen (1998).

Bonn, M., Furr, H., & Uysal, M. (1992). Seasonal variation of coastal resort visitors: Hilton Head Island. *Journal of Travel Research, 31(1),* 50–56.

Bull, A. (1995). *The Economics of Travel and Tourism* (2nd ed.). Melbourne: Longman Australia Pty Ltd.

Butler, R. (1994). Seasonality in tourism: Issues and problems. In A. V. Seaton, *et al.* (eds) *Tourism: The State of the Art* (pp. 332–339). Chichester: John Wiley and Sons.

Collier, A. (1994). *Principles of Tourism: A New Zealand Perspective* (3rd ed.). Auckland: Longman Paul.

Commons, J. (1999). *An Exploration of Tourism, Seasonality and Market Development in Northland, New Zealand.* A thesis presented in part as fulfilment for the degree of Masters in Business Studies, Massey University, Albany, New Zealand.

Cooper, C., Fletcher, J., Gilbert, D., & Wanhill, S. (1993). *Tourism: Principles and Practice.* London: Pitman Publishing.

Craik, J. (1991). *Resorting to Tourism: Cultural Policies for Tourist Development in Australia.* Sydney: Allen & Unwin Pty Ltd.

Forer, P., & Page, S. J. (1998). Tourism in Tai Tokerau: General patterns and Maori perspectives. In *The James Henare Maori Research Centre, Sustainable Maori Tourism in Tai Tokerau: The South Hokianga and Kaikohe Regions* (pp. 289–358). Auckland: Auckland University.

Hall, C. M., & Page, S. J. (1999). *The Geography of Tourism and Recreation: Environment, Place and Space*. London: Routledge.

Jeffrey, D., & Barden, R. (1999). An analysis of the nature, causes and marketing implications of seasonality in the occupancy performance of English hotels. *Tourism Economics, 5(1)*, 69–91.

Kennedy, E. (1999). Seasonality in Irish tourism 1973–1995. *Tourism Economics, 5(1)*, 24–48.

Laws, E. (1995). *Tourist Destination Management: Issues, Analysis & Policies*. London. Routledge.

Lundtorp, S., Rassing, C., & Wanhill, S. (1999). The off-season is 'no season': The case of the Danish island of Bornholm. *Tourism Economics, 5(1)*, 49–68.

McEniff, J. (1992). Seasonality of tourism demand in the European Community. *Travel & Tourism Analyst, 3*, 67–88.

Metservice. (1999). *New Zealand Meteorological Service: Summary of Climate Observation, 1969–1998*. Website (http://www.metservice.co.nz/knowledge/data_climate_summaries.asp (September 13 1999).

Murray North (in association with Boffa Miskell) (1990). *Far North Sub-regional Tourism Development Study*. Auckland: Murray North.

New Zealand Tourism Board (1996). *Tourism in Northland: A Draft Strategy for Sustainable Growth and Development*. Wellington: New Zealand Tourism Board.

New Zealand Tourism Board (1996b). *International Visitor Survey*. Wellington: New Zealand Tourism Board.

Page, S. J. (1994). Perspectives on tourism and peripherality: A review of tourism in the Republic of Ireland. In C. Cooper & A. Lockwood (eds) *Progress in Tourism, Recreation and Hospitality Management, 5* (pp. 26–53). London: Belhaven Press.

Page, S. J. (1995). *Urban Tourism*. London: Routledge.

Page, S. J. (1999). Auckland. *Travel and Tourism Intelligence City Reports, 2*, 1–18.

Page, S. J., Forer, P., & Lawton, G. (1999). Small business development and tourism: *Terra Incognita?" Tourism Management, 20(4)*, 435–460.

Page, S. J., & Getz, D. (eds) (1997). *The Business of Rural Tourism: International Perspectives*. London: International Thompson Business Publishing.

Page, S. J., & Hall, C. M. (1999). New Zealand. *International Country Report* (pp. 71–99).

Page, S. J., & Meyer, D. (1996). Tourist accidents: An exploratory analysis. *Annals of Tourism Research, 23*, 666–690.

Page, S. J., & Thorn, K. (1997). Towards sustainable tourism planning in New Zealand: Public sector planning responses. *Journal of Sustainable Tourism, 5*, 59–77.

Patmore, J. A. (1983). *Recreation and Resources*. Oxford: Basil Blackwell.

Pearce, D. (1989). *Tourist Development*, 2nd ed. Harlow: Longman.

Pearce, D. (1995). *Tourism Today: A Geographical Analysis*, 2nd ed. Harlow: Longman.

Ryan, C., Smee, A., Murphy, S., & Getz, D. (1998). New Zealand events: A temporal and regional analysis. *Festival Management and Event Tourism, 5*, 71–83.

Saleem, N. (1992). Seasonality in tourism: A curse or God-sent strategy. Tourism in Europe: the 1992 conference, Durham (July). Centre for Travel and Tourism, Houghton Le Spring, UK.

Sørensen (1999). Modelling the seasonality of hotel nights in Denmark by country and nationality. *Tourism Economics, 5(1)*, 9–24.

Thorn, K. (1992). *A Review of Northland Visitor Surveys*. Auckland: Murray North.

Tourism Policy Group (1995). *Tourism Research Bibliography 1985–mid-1994*. Wellington: Ministry of Commerce.

Chapter 11

Seasonal Visitation at Fort Edmonton Park: An Empirical Analysis Using a Leisure Constraints Framework

T. D. Hinch, G. Hickey and E. L. Jackson

Introduction

Hinch and Jackson (2000) have argued that leisure constraints theory has value as a frame-work for understanding tourism seasonality. That paper reviewed the literature on seasonality in tourism and the evolution of leisure constraints research as part of its argument that leisure constraints theory holds much potential for gaining insight into the causes of seasonal variation in tourism. The logical follow-up to that argument is to test it through empirical analysis. This chapter uses a leisure constraints framework in an attempt to do just that. Empirical data were collected regarding the perceptions of visitors to Fort Edmonton Park — an historic park in Edmonton, Canada, in terms of their seasonal preferences related to visiting the attraction. The study is exploratory in nature and, while it provides important insights into the seasonal constraints from the visitors' perspective, it is not claimed to be definitive. It does, however, contribute to our understanding of the way that leisure constraints theory can be used to understand seasonality in tourism.

The chapter opens with a brief overview of the relevant concepts in the tourism season-ality literature and in the constraints literature (for detailed reviews refer to Hinch and Jackson, 2000). A description of Fort Edmonton Park follows, inclusive of an overview of current seasonal visitation patterns. An outline of the research methods used in the study is then presented. The study findings are then detailed and discussed in the context of two alternative leisure constraint models, the first of which is labelled the hierarchical model of leisure constraints (Jackson, Crawford & Godbey, 1993) while the second is labelled the non-hierarchical model (Henderson & Bialeschki, 1993). The chapter ends with a discus-sion of the insights gained by using a constraints framework, along with recommendations for continued empirical investigation in this area.

Key Concepts and Theoretical Frameworks

Tourism activity is characterized by seasonal patterns. In Canada, tourism activity peaks in July and August, bottoms out in January, and is generally in transition between these extremes for the balance of the year (Stanley & Moore, 1997). While the patterns vary

Seasonality in Tourism, pp 173–186
© 2001 by Elsevier Science Ltd.
All rights of reproduction in any form reserved
ISBN: 0-08-043674-9

substantially throughout the world and among different types of travellers, the existence of seasonal variation is almost universal. The implications of these variations are substantial, with the prevailing industry view being that the low periods represent the underutlization of capacity while the peak periods create problems of congestion and overuse (McEnnif, 1992). Considerable industry effort has been directed towards modifying these patterns but there has been much less effort on the part of academics to understand the fundamental causes of seasonality. There has, however, been some interesting debate and speculation about two basic groups of factors, one of which has been labelled as "natural" while the other has been termed "institutional" (Bar-On, 1975; Hartman, 1986). Natural factors refer to those factors associated with regular temporal variations in natural phenomena, particularly those associated with cyclical climatic changes throughout the year related to temperature, precipitation, wind, and daylight (Allcock, 1989; Butler, 1994). The second grouping of factors is referred to as institutional, in that the factors in this group reflect the social norms and practices of society (Hinch & Hickey, 1997). These factors are typically based on religious, school and industrial holidays. Notwithstanding the recognition of these types of factors, there has been little published research on their relative importance in influencing patterns of seasonality. One of the implications of this lack of understanding is that strategies to influence seasonal patterns have only enjoyed limited success.

In contrast to the atheoretical characteristic of much of the research in the realm of tourism seasonality, leisure constraints research has a strong theoretical foundation. Leisure constraints research seeks to understand factors that impede leisure participation and otherwise compromise the realisation of leisure-related goals (Jackson & Scott, 1999). By asking the question, "What is it that stops people travelling at certain times of the year?" tourism seasonality research can be positioned within this theoretical framework. Two alternative leisure constraint frameworks will be considered for the purpose of this paper. The first is a hierarchical model that postulates a series of constraints that must be negotiated sequentially before leisure participation (Jackson *et al.*, 1993), while the second takes an alternative view by suggesting that constraints are dynamic and integrated (Henderson & Bialeschki, 1993). These alternative frameworks will be discussed in more detail within the context of the findings of the study.

Fort Edmonton Park

Fort Edmonton Park is located on a 65-hectare site on the south bank of the North Saskatchewan River in Edmonton, Alberta. The Park, which is owned and operated by the City of Edmonton, is considered to be a major attraction in the provincial capital of approximately 850,000 people. Fort Edmonton can be described as a living history interpretative centre which is purported to be Canada's largest historical park (Hinch, 1998). The Park features a number of restored buildings along with other built facilities, and interactive programs that depict the living and working conditions of the fur trade and pioneer periods of Edmonton's history. Extensive interpretative programming occurs mostly in the peak summer months and is employed as a way to animate the site and to breathe life into the history of Edmonton. The guiding mission of the Park is to provide "diverse opportunities for people to learn, grow and enjoy themselves through the conservation, animation, and experience of Edmonton's history" (Fort Edmonton Park, 1996).

A typical visit to the Park starts with a train ride that takes the visitor to a replica of the fur-trading fort that operated in the Edmonton area in 1846. This fort is intended to serve as the starting point for a patron's visit followed by a "walk through time" along three streets featuring restored buildings from the 1885, 1905 and 1920 periods (Hinch, 1998). Given the physical nature of this "walk through time," patrons are exposed to the natural elements as they move throughout the site.

The province of Alberta experiences relatively extreme temperature fluctuations from season to season. The average temperature for each season is: 4.2 C in Spring, 17.1 C in Summer, 5.1 C in Fall, and −16 C in Winter. Precipitation averages 425 millimetres, of which 150 millimetres falls as snow. Alberta is known as "sunny Alberta" because it receives over 2500 hours of sunshine per year (Edmonton Infopage, 1997).

A visit to Fort Edmonton in any other season besides summer would mean potentially subjecting oneself to cold temperatures, including those that are well below freezing. Furthermore, the buildings and facilities offer visitors a rather rustic refuge from the cold weather and climate, as many of the buildings contain no modern heating or insulation. All historical buildings and facilities were moved to Fort Edmonton Park from other areas of Edmonton and preserved as representative samples of the era from 1885 to 1920. To safeguard the authenticity of the buildings and retain the facilities as they existed when they were first built, the decision was made to not install modern heating or insulation (Fort Edmonton Park, 1996).

Fort Edmonton Park represents a good example of a major urban tourist attraction characteriszd by a high degree of seasonal variation in visitation. Two of the Park's chief weaknesses as identified by staff included the variability of the weather and the low profile of the Park during the off-season (Fort Edmonton Park, 1996). Figure 1 illustrates the extreme seasonal variation in visitation to Fort Edmonton Park. Visitation patterns for Fort Edmonton Park feature a peak in the summer followed by a dramatic decline in visitors during the rest of the year. The Park is typically closed to the general public during late fall, winter, and early spring due to decreased visitation. It does, however, open for special events, guided tours, and private functions.

Visitation to Fort Edmonton Park is measured in three distinct categories. General admission includes people who visit during regular hours of operation. This category made up 71.7 percent of overall visitation to the park in 1996. As Figure 1 indicates, in January 1996 the number of people visiting Fort Edmonton categorized as general admission was negligible. General admission to the park remained relatively low until the month of May when 16,020 people visited. Over 85 percent of total general admission to Fort Edmonton Park during 1996 took place during the months of May to August. The months of June, July and August were by far the busiest ones, with general admission reaching a peak of 43,247 visitors for the month of August. General admission declined dramatically during late summer and early fall with 8873 visitors in September, 4760 in October, 148 in November, and 573 in December.

A second category of attendance to the park involves structured programs. Included in this category are people visiting the park as part of a school program or guided tour.

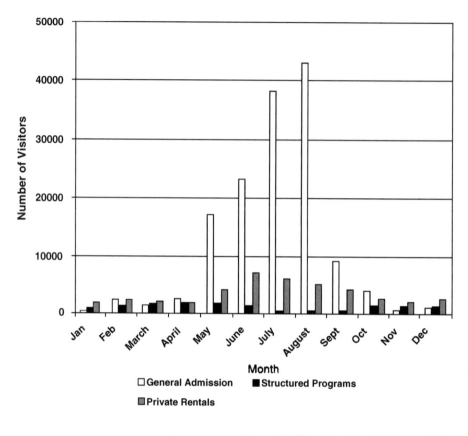

Source: B. Monaghan, Fort Edmonton Park
(personal communication June 1997)

Figure 1:   1996 Monthly Visitation to Fort Edmonton Park.

Structured programs accounted for only 5.7 percent of total visitation to Fort Edmonton during 1996. Despite the relatively low numbers, it is interesting to note that more people took part in structured programs during the spring and fall shoulder seasons rather than in the peak season of summer. The second lowest level of visitors taking part in structured programs occurred in July, which created a modest yet distinct reversal to the aggregate seasonality pattern.

A third category of attendance to the park consists of participants in functions associated with private rentals. Weddings, parties, and meetings dominate these functions. Visitation via private rentals accounted for 22.5 percent of overall visitation during 1996. The peak month of visitation for private rentals was June, with 7600 people. Despite this summer peak, visitation through private rentals during the months of May (4406 visitors), September (4637 visitors), October (3274 visitors), and December (3753 visitors) revealed a much more even distribution of visitation than that of general admissions.

While visitation associated with structured programs and private rentals helps to offset the seasonal pattern of general admission visitors, at an aggregate level the Park is still characteriszd by an extremely peaked visitation during summer. This study adopts two leisure constraints models to provide insight into the perspectives of general admission visitors to Fort Edmonton Park in regards to their seasonal preferences in terms of visiting the Park.

Methods

Study methods included a quantitative as well as a qualitative dimension. The quantitative dimension involved an exit survey of 118 general admission Park visitors. The purpose of this survey was to identify how natural and institutional variables are related to seasonal visitation from the perspective of these patrons. A series of closed-ended Likert-type questions were included as part of the larger 1997 Fort Edmonton Park Visitor Satisfaction Survey. This survey was conducted during the months of June through October. Each questionnaire was administered orally by Park staff to patrons as they exited the park. The respondents represent a convenience sample. Given the relatively small size of this data set, the reported analysis will be restricted to descriptive statistics concerning seasonality and the constraints framework.

The qualitative dimension of the study was intended to develop a more in-depth understanding of visitors' perceptions and feelings toward seasonal visitation and to attain a better understanding of the relationship among natural and institutional variables as constraints to seasonal visitation. Ten patrons who were visiting Fort Edmonton Park during August of 1997 were interviewed while they were in the Park. The respondents consisted of seven female visitors and three males, with five of the respondents coming from outside the city and an equal number coming from within Edmonton. Examples of the type of questions asked included: "What time of the year would you consider it best to visit the Park?", "Why do you prefer that time of the year?" and "What do you perceive as the benefits and drawbacks of visiting during any other season besides summer?" Each interview lasted between ten and 20 minutes and all interviews were taped and then transcribed.

Natural and Institutional Factors within a Hierarchical Constraints Framework

Jackson, Crawford & Godbey's (1993) hierarchical model of leisure constraints integrates many of the broadly accepted as well as the emerging understandings in this area (see Figure 2 below). One of the key characteristics of this model is the order in which constraints are assumed to be encountered and negotiated. In the context of seasonality, leisure preferences are the starting point. A major consideration at this stage is the centrality of seasonal factors in terms of motivations for travel. Natural seasonal factors such as climatic conditions may be the primary attraction for a potential tourist, e.g., Canadian "snow birds" travelling south during the winter or conversely, international tourists travelling to Canadian ski resorts during the same season. Alternatively, natural season-ality features may be of secondary importance to a visitor. Temperature, precipitation and other natural factors may represent environmental conditions that enhance or detract from a travel experience but which do not serve as the central attraction. In the former instance, natural factors assume a strong role as intrapersonal constraints (i.e., they are directly related to the central motivations of the traveller) while in the latter case, they may actually function as structural constraints (i.e., they may come into operation once preference to travel to a destination has been established).

Once seasonal travel preferences have been established, the next level of constraints in the model exists at an interpersonal level. Anyone who prefers to travel with others will have to find travelling companions with similar seasonal travel preferences. Assuming that the intrapersonal and interpersonal constraints have been met, the last form of seasonal constraints that faces a potential traveller is structural in nature. Seasonal factors that have been described in the literature as institutional would seem to be much more prominent in this instance. Seasonal cycles in personal income, school and work commitments, travel industry operations, and even attraction schedules like the timing of sporting or cultural events present an assortment of constraints to travel at different times of the year. While some of these constraints are uniform for a broad spectrum of potential travellers (e.g., the scheduling of school holidays in a given region), these constraints may theoretically be negotiated in a number of different ways at an individual level (e.g., temporarily removing a child from school or organizing a school trip as part of the curriculum). Not just the pres-ence but also the ability to successfully negotiate these constraints has a direct bearing on the seasonal travel patterns of an individual.

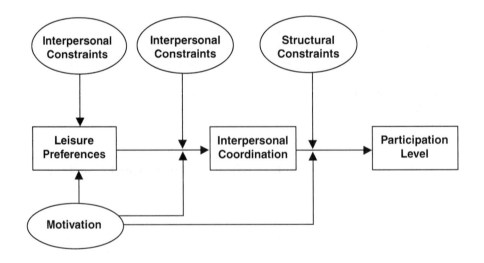

Based on jackson, *et al.,* 1993

Figure 2: Hierarchical Model of Leisure constraints.

The relevance of this framework to developing insight into seasonal visitation to Fort Edmonton Park is closely tied to being able to identify and classify factors or constraints as intrapersonal, interpersonal and structural. The hierarchical and sequential premise of this framework can then be used to illuminate the process that an individual must negotiate through to move from leisure preferences to participation at a site like Fort Edmonton Park. By understanding this process, Park managers are in a better position to develop useful strategies to help potential visitors negotiate through the constraint process thereby influencing the aggregate patterns of seasonality.

One of the primary objectives of the study was to understand the relative influence of natural and institutional factors in the decision of general admission patrons to visit Fort Edmonton Park during different times of the year. To this end, respondents were asked "How strongly do the following factors influence your decisions to visit or not visit Fort Edmonton Park?" Three natural factors (precipitation, temperature, and sunlight/cloud cover) and three institutional factors (school commitments, long weekends/public holidays, and work commitments) were presented and respondents were required to rate each of them on a ten-point Likert-scale (a score of one meant that the factor was not a strong influence at all on their decision to visit while a score of ten signified that the factor had a very strong influence on their decision to visit or not visit the park).

The aforementioned factors were selected for investigation based on previous studies of tourism seasonality, in which the natural variables of precipitation (rain, snow, etc.), temperature, and sunlight and cloud cover were stated to be important along with the institutional variables of school commitments, work commitments, and long weekends and public holidays (Allcock, 1989; Butler, 1994). The relative importance of each specific factor can be assessed in several ways. With regards to mean scores for each particular factor, work commitments had the highest mean score with 7.86 out of the maximum score of ten (see Figure 3 below). The second highest mean score was 7.5 for precipitation, the

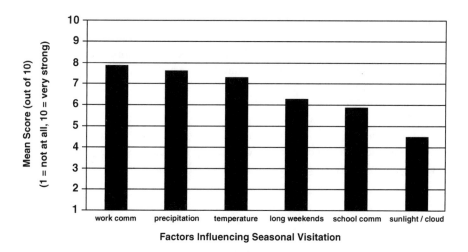

Figure 3: Mean Score for the Importance of Selected Natural and Institutional Factors on Seasonal Visitation to Fort Edmonton Park.

third highest was 7.08 for temperature, followed by 6.07 for long weekends/public holidays, 5.45 for school commitments, and 4.62 for sunlight/cloud cover. This analysis suggests that variables in both institutional and natural groupings rate as relatively strong influences on respondents' decisions to visit or not visit Fort Edmonton Park.

If the assumption that natural factors are more likely to be intrapersonal constraints and institutional factors are more likely to be structural constraints is accurate then there are some interesting implications that arise from the indicated strength of these factors in influencing behaviour. The influence of individual natural and institutional factors is clearly not uniform. Natural factors ranked 1, 4 and 5 while institutional factors ranked 2, 3 and 6. The fact that a factor may be classified as an intrapersonal or institutional constraint does not necessarily correlate with the relative importance of that factor in influencing seasonal visitation. It does, however, suggest that if the institutional factors are best positioned as structural constraints then strategies that would help potential visitors to negotiate through constraints related to work commitments are likely to have more influence on changing seasonal visitation patterns than are strategies related to modifying long weekend and school commitments. Similarly, if natural factors are more closely tied to intrapersonal constraints, then the fundamental preferences of potential visitors are more sensitive to precipitation and temperature than to variations in sunlight and cloud cover. Different types of strategies are needed to influence seasonal visitation related to these constraints because they are closely tied to potential visitor motivations. It is not a simple matter of negotiating through these constraints but rather one of influencing fundamental leisure preferences and perhaps ensuring that perceptions match reality in terms of seasonal patterns of precipitation and temperature at Fort Edmonton Park.

The relative importance of natural and institutional variables in an aggregate sense and the way they influence the respondents' decisions to visit or not visit Fort Edmonton Park during each season were asked through two additional questions. The first of which was: "Assuming that the park is open year round, how important would factors like weather conditions be in your future decisions to visit or not visit Fort Edmonton Park during the following seasons?" Respondents then assigned a value on a ten-point Likert scale signifying the relative importance of natural factors on their decision to visit the park during each of four seasons (a value of one meant that it was not at all important and a value of ten meant it was very important). A parallel question was then asked about institutional factors. It asked, "Assuming that the park is open year round, how important would factors like school and work commitments be in your future decisions to visit or not visit Fort Edmonton Park during the following seasons?"

An analysis of the mean scores for each season in terms of the natural factors revealed that summer had the lowest score (6.44), followed by fall (6.89), spring (7.19), and winter (8.14) (Table 1). Winter emerged as the season in which factors like weather conditions

Table 1: Mean Score of the Importance of Natural and Institutional Factors by Season.

Factor / Season	Summer	Fall	Winter	Spring
Natural	6.44	6.89	8.14	7.19
Institutional	6.73	7.15	7.31	7.44

were considered most important in the decision to visit the Park, with a mean score of 8.14 indicating an average overall rating just less than "very important." Summer had the lowest mean score with natural factors considered not as important as they were in other seasons. This finding can be interpreted as meaning that anticipated variation in these natural factors in the summer was generally in a more acceptable range for the respondents than variation at other times of the year. It is interesting to note, however, that despite having the lowest mean score, a value of 6.44 indicates that natural factors were still considered to be "somewhat important" when considering visiting the park during the summer season.

The season in which institutional variables were the least important for the decision to visit the park was also the summer, with a mean score of 6.73. This was slightly higher than the mean score for summer when measuring the importance of natural variables by season. Summer was followed by fall with a mean score of 7.15, winter at 7.31, and spring at 7.44. The biggest spread between the indicated importance of natural and institutional factors exists during the winter season. Given the assumption that natural factors tend to act as intrapersonal constraints and institutional factors tend to act as structural constraints, then one of the implications of this difference is that low visitation during the winter reflects low motivation related to climatic conditions rather than structural constraints related to work, school and holidays. Rather than developing strategies to help potential visitors negotiate structural constraints, strategies that address basic motivations would likely be more influential in terms of altering winter visitation patterns. During all of the other seasons, structural constraints associated with institutional factors were indicated as being more important than intrapersonal constraints related to natural factors. Strategies that help potential visitors to negotiate through these constraints would seem to hold more promise for increased visitation than strategies aimed at modifying preferences related to natural factors.

A total factor score was calculated for both questions by summing the scores for each season and dividing the total by four. While this procedure suffers from the limitation of obscuring the importance of the variables by different seasons, it offers the opportunity to compare the relative importance of an aggregate measure of natural and institutional groupings on the decision to visit Fort Edmonton. The total mean score for natural variables was 7.17, indicating an average overall evaluation of the importance of natural variables as being "somewhat important" in respondents' decisions to visit the park. The total mean score for institutional variables was 7.16, indicating an average overall evaluation of the importance of institutional variables as being "somewhat important." This analysis suggests that, in aggregate, both natural and institutional variables were considered to be effectively identical with regards to their importance when respondents consider visiting Fort Edmonton Park.

Natural and Institutional Factors Within a Non-hierarchical Model of Leisure Constraints

In contrast to the hierarchical model of leisure constraints, Henderson and Bialeschki (1993) took a qualitative approach and concluded: "constraints are not sequential and hierarchical, but dynamic and integrated." While this conclusion is still under debate, their model (see Figure 4 below) presents a useful constraints framework with which to explore seasonality using qualitative methods. This fit was illustrated particularly well with the data collected in the more qualitative component of the study that featured open-ended interviews with ten Park patrons. Henderson and Bialeschki's (1993) model reflects four themes of leisure constraints based upon women's experiences. With slight modifications, these themes also emerge from the Fort Edmonton Park seasonality data.

Theme 1 — Intervening and antecedent constraints, while distinct, are not mutually exclusive and interact with one another to influence preferences, negotiation, and participation in visits to the Park throughout the year.

Antecedent constraints encompass Jackson *et al.*'s (1993) category of intrapersonal and interpersonal constraints while intervening constraints roughly parallel the category of structural constraints. The Park data suggest that natural factors dominate the antecedent constraints while institutional factors dominate intervening constraints. However, neither set of factors is mutually exclusive, as reflected in the comments of one individual who mentioned both types of constraints as influencing her seasonal visitation:

> "Usually the only time I get to do stuff like this is during the summer and that's because I'd rather the weather in the summer ... but also because it's the only time that I can get to actually do these things."

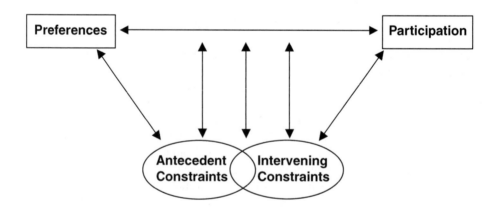

Based on Henderson & Bialeschki, 1993

Figure 4: Non-hierarchical Model of Leisure Constraints.

Theme 2 — Constraints (particularly antecedent, but also intervening) influence leisure preferences for seasonal visitation.

Antecedent constraints, such as the classic natural factor of weather, are particularly influential on the preference to visit the Park at specific times of the year. Given the outdoor setting of the Park, a common refrain is that climatic conditions in the summer are preferable to those during the other seasons. A typical comment is:

> "Summer is my favourite time to come down here just because on a summer day you can really get the most out of your visit. You can walk around in comfort and take your time, go for an ice cream, visit all of the buildings, and enjoy sunshine."

Theme 3 — Constraints (particularly intervening, but also antecedent) impact throughout the negotiation process as patrons make decisions about participation at different times of the year.

If an individual does have a preference to visit the Park during the off-season, it is often possible to negotiate through constraints, especially those that are intervening in nature. When asked if her school commitments prevented her from visiting the park during the school year, one individual responded:

> "I don't think that school commitments would really get in the way for me. I just finished up at the U of A [University of Alberta] and I'm now going to Grant MacEwan [a local community college] and I'm able to manage my time effectively during the year. I usually have time during the weekends, so if I wanted to do something or go visit somewhere during the winter, I'm sure that I would have time to do so on my weekends."

The willingness to negotiate through this constraint is in part a function of the individual's personal priorities. One of the other interviewees responded to the same question with the comment that:

> "Being a student, most of my year is spent studying and concentrating on school. I'm trying to get into medical school so I've been really concentrating on getting good marks. So for most of the year, I don't have time to travel or get to see places like this because of school and the time that I have to put into it. When the summer comes, it's like a release valve from all the pressures of school. It gives me a chance to get away and to travel and relax I guess."

A variation of this constraint faces a parent with children in school. Parents may, in fact, feel that this constraint is even stronger than their own work and school commitments They may feel a particularly responsible to ensure that their children meet their formal educational requirements in terms of school attendance.

The desire to negotiate intervening constraints is, to a large extent, a function of the strength of the preference to participate at a given time of the year. In the case of the individual who expressed a very weak interest in the Park it is not surprising that the typical constraints found in the off-season were viewed as being insurmountable.

Theme 4 — An interactive link between preferences and participation was evident in the negotiation process.

People's actual experience while visiting the Park at different times of the year tended to influence preferences as in the case of the individual who had previously visited in the autumn.

> "I was here two years ago in October and I think I enjoyed it more than coming in the summer ... Why? It wasn't as hot and there weren't as many kids. It also wasn't as overcrowded. You could poke around a little more and ask questions without all of the traffic. It was a little cooler, which is how I prefer it."

The impact of experience on preference could also work the other way as in the case of the individual who had visited the Park at Christmas and experienced unbearable cold. This patron stated, "I didn't really enjoy it that much ... I'm not sure if I would do it again."

Conclusions

As suggested at the beginning of the chapter, this study was exploratory in nature. It follows up on the authors' previous argument that there is merit in adopting leisure constraints frameworks to develop a better understanding of tourism seasonality. More specifically, it did this by way of an empirical examination of seasonality at Fort Edmonton Park. This was done using two leisure constraints models — hierarchical and non-hierarchical.

The hierarchical model of leisure constraints was used to gain insight into data collected through a survey of general admission patrons to Fort Edmonton Park. Key findings included the fact that the influence of individual natural and institutional factors was not uniform between or within these groups. Under the assumption that natural factors were closely related to intrapersonal constraints while institutional factors were more closely associated with structural constraints, a variety of management implications emerged. The essence of these implications was that the positioning of institutional factors within the structural component of the model means that these factors can be managed to facilitate negotiation through constraints. Strategies aimed at these factors can be used to encourage potential patrons to more successfully pursue their leisure preferences to visit the Park at different times of the year. For example, Park management could develop strategies that help potential visitors to negotiate constraints related to work commitments (e.g., extend or shift the hours of operation of the Park to better correspond with the non-work time of selected target markets). A different type of strategy would be needed in terms of natural factors in that they fall within the intrapersonal constraint category of the hierarchical model. These constraints come first in the hierarchy and are manifest in an individual's leisure preferences. In the case of seasonal visitation to Fort Edmonton Park, temperature and precipitation were recognised as major constraints. If Park managers would like to influence patterns of seasonal visitation at this stage of the leisure constraint process, they would have to alter the fundamental preferences of potential visitors. While promotional campaigns may help in this regard, an effective strategy to alter these preferences would likely need to take the form of a prolonged educational process. More immediate success would probably be found in targeting those segments of the market that are already predisposed to visit at selected times of the year.

The non-hierarchical model of leisure constraints as proposed by Henderson and Bialeschki (1993) provided additional insight into seasonality at Fort Edmonton Park. Using this framework, data collected through qualitative methods were analysed and greater understanding of the relationship between natural and institutional seasonality factors was gained. It was found that natural factors tend to be more prominent as antecedent constraints than as intervening constraints. Perhaps because of this, they were also found to be a strong influence on preferences for seasonal visitation. From an applied perspective, these conclusions suggest that market for Fort Edmonton could be segmented by seasonal preference. Specific management strategies could then be developed to help those that are so inclined to negotiate the intervening constraints (mainly institutional in nature) that act as barriers to their visits to the Park during low seasons.

Both of these leisure constraint models provided important insight into seasonality within the empirical context of this study. These insights were, however, limited by a small sample size and by the relatively superficial understanding of the relationship between seasonality factors as described in the seasonality literature and intrapersonal/antecedent and structural/intervening constraint groupings as described in the leisure constraints literature. Perhaps the most critical weakness lies in the assumption that natural factors can be classified as intrapersonal or antecedent constraints while institutional factors are best classified as structural or intervening constraints. Verification as to the accuracy of this assumption is needed. Other more sophisticated types of analysis such as factor and cluster analysis should also be applied in the context of larger data sets. Continued work in this area will advance our understanding of tourism seasonality. It will contribute to a much stronger theoretical base and, as a direct consequence, it will contribute to a higher rate of success in terms of attempts to manage seasonal patterns in tourism.

References

Allcock, J. B. (1989). Seasonality. In S. F. Witt & L. Moutinho (eds), *Tourism Marketing and Management Handbook* (pp. 387–392). Englewood Cliffs, NJ: Prentice Hall.

Bar-On, R. R. V. (1975). *Seasonality in Tourism: A Guide to the Analysis of Seasonality and Trends for Policy Making.* London, England: Economic Intelligence Unit.

Butler, R. W. (1994). Seasonality in tourism: Issues and problems. In A. V. Seaton (ed.), *Tourism: The State of the Art* (pp. 332–339). Chichester, England: John Wiley & Sons.

Edmonton Infopage (1997). Edmonton climate (texinfo ed. 2.1.) [On-line]. Available http://bbdsedson.com/edmonton/climate.htm

Fort Edmonton Park (1996). *Fort Edmonton Park 1997–1999 Business Plan*. Edmonton Parks and Recreation, Edmonton, Alberta.

Hartmann, R. (1986). Tourism, seasonality and social change. *Leisure Studies, 5(1)*, 25–33.

Henderson, K. A. & Bialeschki, M. D. (1993). Exploring an expanded model of women's leisure constraints. *Journal of Applied Recreation Research, 18*(4), 229–252.

Hinch, T. D. (1998). Sustainable urban tourist attractions: the case of Fort Edmonton Park. In C. M. Hall & A. A. Lew (eds) *Sustainable Tourism: A Geographical Perspective* (pp. 185–198). Essex, United Kingdom: Addison Wesley Longman Limited.

Hinch, T. D., & Hickey, G. P. (1996). Tourism attractions and seasonality: Spatial relationships in Alberta. In K. Mackay & K. R. Boyd (eds). *Tourism for all Seasons: Using Research to Meet the Challenge of Seasonality* (pp. 69–76). Winnipeg, Manitoba: University of Manitoba.

Hinch, T. D. & Jackson, E. L. (2000). Leisure constraints research: Its value as a framework for understanding tourism seasonability. *Current Issues in Tourism, 3(2)*, 87–106.

Jackson, E. L., Crawford, D. W., & Godbey, G. (1993). Negotiation of leisure constraints. *Leisure Sciences, 15(1)*, 1–11.

Jackson, E. L., & Scott, D. (1999). Constraints to leisure. In E. L. Jackson & T. L. Burton (eds). *Leisure Studies at the Millennium* (pp. 299–321). State College, Pa: Venture Publishing, Inc.

McEnnif, J. (1992). Seasonality of tourism demand in the European Community. *Travel and Tourism Analyst, 3*, 67–88.

Stanley, D., & Moore, S. (1997). Counting the leaves: The dimensions of seasonality in Canadian tourism. In K. Mackay & K. R. Boyd (eds). *Tourism for all Seasons: Using Research to Meet the Challenge of Seasonality* (pp. 13–18). Winnipeg, Manitoba: University of Manitoba.

Author Index

Subject Index

CHESTER COLLEGE LIBRARY